THE *Untold Story* OF SITA
AN EMPOWERING TALE FOR OUR TIME

DENA MERRIAM

sitaram PRESS

The profits from this book will be donated to the Global Peace Initiative of Women (GPIW.org) to empower women everywhere in their quest to make this a more peaceful world.

FIRST EDITION

ISBN - 978-0-578-46534-0

Cover art: painting by Manish Kumar of Vintage Arts, Udaipur, India
Interior Layout and Cover Design by WEGOTYOUCOVEREDBOOKDESIGN.COM
Editing by PARVATIMARKUS.COM

To Mata Sita and Shri Ram
at whose feet I eternally reside
and to their devotees everywhere
who bring their love into the world.

TABLE OF CONTENTS

PREFACE

It is somewhere between dark and daylight—at the hour when the mind is stillest, when dreams submerge into the ocean of mind but before the mind becomes aware of the outer world, before the stars retreat and the sun sends the harbingers of its ascent, before the birds begin to stir but after the night creatures have gone to rest—it is at that time that the inner world lights up our vision and we can see things we normally do not see and hear what our human ears cannot usually hear.

It was during such a time that the inner world opened to me and I saw a great light, unlike anything the human eye can perceive. This light shone over a most beautiful world, where there were many couples enjoying each other's presence, reveling in love and tenderness. A great love pervaded the whole scene and my heart filled to overflowing with joy. The love others were experiencing was also my love. I thought, this is the love that Shri Ram and *Mata* (Mother) Sita brought to earth. It was to awaken this love that they came, this love that belong to all as it flows freely through everyone and everything.

At first there was just love, and then I saw the light assume a beautiful greenish color and became aware of the formless presence of Shri Ram, pervading all. As I wondered at the intensity and immensity of the love I felt, I heard the words: "This is the love Shri Ram brought to earth. He awakened a new quality of love." I understood that he and Mata Sita came to unlock the love that is encoded in all creation, so humanity could advance in its evolution and fulfil its potential. The voice I heard from deep within was neither masculine nor feminine. It was a voice I recognized, as I had heard it before during such states of absorption.

I dwelt in this ecstatic awareness for some time. Gradually my eyes opened and I became conscious of the outer world; the light faded away, as did the scene before me. My consciousness withdrew from the inner world and opened to the outer one.

For all of my adult life I have been a devotee of Shri Ram and Mata Sita, but it was not until I started writing this book that I came to feel a personal relationship with them. They became very real living guides for me. I found myself basking in their presence, seeing them behind closed eyes, listening and reflecting deeply on the words I was hearing and recording, talking to them, and trying to understand with my intellect what was being revealed in my heart. Sita's story carries the memory of a world lush with divine forces that appeared in various forms through rivers and forests, winds and solar rays. Often my mind would be doubtful and question where these stories were coming from. Were they my memories or someone else's? Was my mind creating narratives through its imaginative powers? But my heart would respond, "Hush and listen, for Mata Sita is speaking to you."

Many ages ago in ancient India, Shri Ram came to establish the foundation for a society based on universal principles of righteous action, in harmony with the universal laws, known as *dharma*. What is at the heart of this dharma? Love.

Love is what keeps the universal laws in motion. Love is what holds the magnetic and gravitational fields together. It is the force of love that is the cause and mover of all manifestation, which will eventually transform back into the unmanifest ultimate reality. It is this love that Shri Ram and Mata Sita displayed for each other, for all the people of their kingdom, for the creatures of the forest, for all forest life, for Mother Earth herself and even for the stars that dwell at such a distance. Together they exemplified a complete and perfectly balanced human love. They demonstrated the possibility for humanity to realize on earth the rarified quality of higher, divine love, which is based not on emotion or self-interest, not on desire or possessiveness, but on the well-being of the whole.

Only by awakening the true essence of dharma, the love that is imprinted in our nature, will we be able to realize the higher possibilities that await human life.

In 2015 and 2016 I went on two pilgrimages, which are described in the Commentary section of this book. It was after those pilgrimages that during many, many months as I sat in my daily meditation, memories began to stir and images arise, conversations heard. I was engulfed in these visions of the past and could not but record them as precious messages were conveyed.

The experience of writing these stories has left an indelible impression on me, for this process has brought me into the living presence of Mata Sita and Shri Ram. My greatest hope and aspiration in sharing these stories is that it will do the same for you.

Jai Shri Ram, Jai Sita Ram. Jai Ma.

Dena Merriam

A NOTE FOR READERS

The story of Shri Ram and Mata Sita is told in the Hindu epic, the Ramayana (see Appendix I: Short Ramayana Summary p. 358). The classic version of the tale is the Valmiki rendition. Scholars now consider the last "book" (*kanda*) of Valmiki's Ramayana as coming at a later date and being penned by a different author. This is important because it is in that kanda, which takes place after Ram is crowned king of Ayodhya, that Sita is brought low by the patriarchal assumption that she is nothing more than the wife of Ram, who was kidnapped against her will by the demon king Ravana and rescued by Ram, the hero. It is here that her purity is questioned, her reputation sullied, and she is forced to retreat to a forest hermitage where she bears her twin sons and raises them before she asks Mother Earth to open and receive her once again.

The Untold Story of Sita approaches Sita not as an appendage of Ram, but as his divine equal in every way. While Ram is an incarnation of Lord Vishnu, known as Narayan, Sita is an incarnation of Lord Vishnu's female counterpart, Mahalakshmi, called Narayani. In the celestial realms they are known as Narayana and Narayani, while on earth they are known as Ram and Sita. Nothing—the exile, the kidnapping, the separation from Ram, her supposed trial by fire and her time away from the kingdom at a hermitage—happens without her consent and her knowledge of the underlying reasons behind each action.

I also rescue the female rishis of this ancient age from obscurity, and show them as the equals of their husbands. In other words, Anasuya is not only the wife of Rishi Atria, she is herself a wise sage and is called Rishi Anasuya. It is time that female empowerment extends up to the realm of the sages and gods (as well as to all us females here on earth) and we acknowledge the spiritual attainments and contributions of woman as equal to that of their male counterparts.

Part One

MITHILA, VIDEHA KINGDOM, BHARATA (INDIA)

CHILDHOOD IN MITHILA

I was born in the ancient kingdom of Videha, also known as Mithila, into a poor *Brahmin* (priestly caste) family. Misfortune had come to my family several generations earlier, and we had been taken in as servants by the Janak family. My father served in the household of *Maharaja* (king) Hrasavaroma Janak and later under the renowned Seeradhwaja Janak. His father and grandfather had also served in the household, and so by the time my father came along, our family had gained a well-respected place in the palace and was greatly valued by the other attendants and servants. My father's body and mind were wholly devoted to the Maharaja and his family, and this was the understanding of our role in life that was conveyed to me from early childhood.

There was no task too lowly for my father if it in any way would serve the needs of the Maharaja. I don't remember my mother; she died when I was young, and so my family consisted of my father and me. Although a number of the servants took turns caring for me when I was young, most often I accompanied my father when he performed his various chores, as he was loathe to let me out of his sight.

When I was a child, the responsibility for the kingdom's governance passed from father to son. When Seeradhwaja Janak became the ruler, he was revered by all the people, even beyond the normal feelings of devotion and obedience to a Maharaja. It is an understatement to say that my father had the highest regard for the new Maharaja. For those of us in the household, Janak *Baba* (father), as we called him, was more like a father to all of us, young and old alike, even at his young age. In the kingdom, he was considered not only the Maharaja but a *rishi*, a great sage. Few Maharajas could match his stature. My father was not alone in believing this.

I was told by my father from an early age that the Maharaja did not distinguish between people's stations in life because he saw the interior of a person, not the outer form; he saw into a person's heart. This was a well-known fact. and it was a quality that elevated him in the people's minds even more. There was a mutual love relationship between the Maharaja and the people, and thus the kingdom enjoyed an unusual sense of harmony and peace. Opposition to him was unheard of, and there was no questioning his deeds, which were always for the good of the people.

The palace where I grew up and served was beautiful but had little display of excessive wealth or grandeur. Simplicity and beauty existed side by side. The palace was decorated with the artistry of the people—painted vases and other pottery, murals and finely woven cloths. The *Maharani* (queen) Sunaina had a keen sense of beauty, and she helped to create a refined and elevated atmosphere, not only in the palace but also in all of Mithila.

The Maharaja and Maharani had no children. It was said that this was because of the ascetic nature of Janak Baba. Much of his time was spent visiting the rishis and sages or hosting them at the palace, or in meditative seclusion. They came from far and wide to visit the one they called the Rishi Maharaja, and the blessings these visits brought created much activity and joy in the kingdom. All of the people benefited from the wisdom of the Maharaja as he would help solve the problem of any person, and thus he became our nearest and dearest Baba.

It was a happy environment for most people, except my father, who had a dour and brooding temperament despite the blessing he received from being near to the Maharaja. To say my father was strict would be too mild a description. A perfectionist when it came to performing his duties for the Maharaja, he often would redo the tasks of the other servants and attendants because he said those tasks could be done better. But he always did so humbly, too humbly I often thought. "One can always do better," was a refrain I often heard him repeat, and I would silently protest, "Is it always possible to do better?"

My father never failed to remind me that our family survived the many misfortunes that had visited us through the kindness of the Janak family. "We owe our lives to them," he repeatedly told me. "Without their kindness, I don't know what would have happened to us."

As I grew older, I began to inquire of my father what those misfortunes were and why they had come to us, but he never answered. He only gazed out into space with a blank stare and shook his head. Once he replied, "It is not for you to know," and so I left it at that, not satisfied but too timid to press him. I didn't accept that he would never let me go far from him, that I could never accompany the other children on the rare occasion of an outing to the forest. This brought me many tears and much protest, but he was adamant. Worst of all, I could never go down to the river, as bathing in the river was off limits to me. I seemed to be the only one who had this restriction, but my father was insistent, and no amount of pleading could move him.

During the day, up until the age of about eight or nine when I received my own chores to perform, I would accompany my father as he oversaw the various activities needed to keep the household functioning smoothly. In the evening before my father retired, he would seek the blessings of Janak Baba. Sometimes I would be allowed to tag along, standing shyly by the doorway as my father rested his forehead on the feet of the great sage. I remember gazing at the two of them: the stately figure of Janak Baba, with his tall frame, his dark hair pulled back and a flowing beard, spotted with grey even at a young age. He seemed to bear an elder's wisdom from young adulthood. His figure was slender as he did not take in much food; the features of his face were finely chiseled, with a straight nose and full lips that were overshadowed by his beard. His face was kindly and calm. My father had a very different appearance. Although he was also tall, he always stooped, with bent shoulders, so as to appear of shorter statue that his Maharaja. He was exceptionally thin, as he ate even less than Janak Baba, and his face always wore a stern expression, which only softened when in the presence of his maharaja. When I had the occasion to accompany my father on this nighttime ritual, I would always hear the Maharaja say in a gentle voice, "Rest well, Dushyanta. May you have a peaceful sleep."

No matter the hour, my father would perform this ritual as he knew that the Maharaja slept little and would receive him. My father would be unable to sleep without this blessing. Once I asked him why, and he replied that if he died in the night he wanted to make sure he had received Janak Baba's blessing. This response brought me no comfort. What would become of me if my father died in the night?

Sometimes Janak Baba would leave the palace for weeks on end, visiting one of the sages in the kingdom or retreating into solitude for his own meditations. My father would be anxious at those times and often he would sit up through the night waiting for Janak Baba's return, as if his life depended on his arrival.

I mistook my father's sternness for lack of caring, and so the seed of feeling unloved began to germinate in me. As I grew older, the timidity that I felt in his presence as a child transformed into resentment. Perhaps it was the lack of any motherly qualities in his nature, or perhaps it was the absorption in his work of service, but he seemed to take no notice of the emotional peaks and valleys that accompany a child's development. My feelings seemed inconsequential, and so I learned to keep them to myself.

The first explosion between my father and me happened when I was about twelve years old. One of the servants had come to borrow something from my father. Aditi was a kindly middle-aged servant who had a liking for me. More than the other servants she expressed an almost motherly affection for me as a child. When she would perceive an expression of loneliness on my face, she would press me against her well-padded chest and whisper words of encouragement. When she came this day and saw me tidying up the room that I shared with my father, she mentioned to him casually that I would someday make a good wife.

He replied sharply, "Meenakshi will never marry." She appeared shocked by his tone but didn't want to question him and so quietly left the room.

"*Pitaji* (papa)!" I exclaimed. "Why did you say that?

"Because it is true," he replied in a stern and determined voice.

"Am I so unattractive that nobody will marry me?" I asked in a hurt tone. I did not think myself ugly, but I also did not think myself beautiful. In fact, I had never thought much about my outer appearance. But I was coming of age, growing into womanhood, and for the first time I became conscious of my appearance, questioning whether I was indeed unattractive. I was of middle stature, neither tall nor short, on the thin side, with a somewhat darkish complexion, but not unusually so. My hair was too thin and did not make a luscious braid as it twisted down my back, but how could that matter? The only unattractive thing about me was a mole on my lower right cheek, but again I didn't see how that mattered. We were taught in Mithila to focus on inner not outer beauty, on our character, so how could my appearance affect my ability to marry?

My father's face softened just a bit. "Your appearance is fine, Meenakshi. It has nothing to do with that. I am determined that you should not marry because if you do, some great misfortune will befall you, as has befallen me."

"Why do you keep saying that?" I began to cry. "For my whole life I have heard you talk about misfortune. What misfortune, Pitaji? Why can't we be happy like everyone else? Why are we less fortunate than they? Why, Pitaji? Why?" The tears were flowing profusely. Never had I shown such emotion to my father, but the thought that he was blocking what might be my only route to happiness was too much to bear.

My father didn't answer. He stared straight ahead into the air. Finally he said, "There are things we cannot change, child. Neither you nor I can change what has been done in the past. Even Janak Baba cannot change it. But he has taught me patience and sacrifice and forbearance. This is what I wish for you. You must learn to accept what has been given to you in life. If you perform your duties diligently, you will find contentment, as I have. "

His words did not satisfy me, and my tears increased. Rather than taking me in his arms and soothing me, my father replied, "You must accept what I have told you and not think of marrying in this life. It is for your own good, to spare you much misfortune." With those words he left the room, and I sank into despair. After that, greater distance crept between us, and fewer words were spoken.

Despite my own troubles with my father, I could see that he was a model servant, respected by the others in the household. And I did try to follow his behavior, speaking modestly and respectfully to all, no matter their position in the household, never contradicting, never placing demands, putting my own needs, desires, and feelings aside for the good of the household. It was a difficult but valuable training. Whenever my father saw me seeking something for myself or expressing dissatisfaction, one look from him would squash whatever was arising in my mind or heart.

Gratitude was a quality much valued in the household, and this was set by Janak Baba and his wife, Sunaina Ma. They never failed to express gratitude to their servants and attendants and did their best to make life easier for us. It was our understanding that each person fulfilled an essential function in the household that was as important as any other role. No work was demeaning, and no one was treated as being worth more or less than the others, but as a young girl I did not fully understand this concept and had a feeling that my father, after his long and hard service, was more deserving than the others. Whenever any indication of this feeling emerged, my father was quick to respond.

One day he said to me, "Meenakshi, you must find contentment in what has been given to you in life. We are very fortunate to be able to serve Janak Baba. I have such gratitude for this, and I pray that you do as well."

I nodded. "I know, Pitaji. You have taught me this. I will find happiness in serving."

"I do not speak of happiness, Meenakshi, only contentment. It is contentment that I wish for you."

Again I nodded. I could not say that I shared his feelings for Janak Baba, although I very much wanted to. Janak Baba was too distant a figure for me. I had great respect and reverence for him, but felt very shy in his presence and so never came in close proximity, never looked directly at him, never spoke to him. When I observed him from a distance, I could sense the joy that bubbled out of him, and I could see the love that everyone held for him. His smile, his laugh, lit up the whole palace. Why could Pitaji not have this joy? Why couldn't I?

As I grew older, I began to appreciate the respect the other servants showed my father and to feel a bit of pride in my father's honored position in the household. He supervised the other servants and made sure the household functioned smoothly, with no chore left undone. If any servants took sick or for some reason could not perform their functions, my father would immediately take over. No task was too menial or lowly for him. This bothered me as I thought he often took on chores that were beneath his station, but for the most part I kept quiet.

One day when I was about 15, I came upon my father scrubbing the floor of the entry to the palace. Despite his age, he was on his hands and knees, oblivious to all else. His health was not the best. I could hear his heavy breathing and grew alarmed. "Pitaji, what are you doing on your hands and knees?" I whispered as I bent down beside him. "This is not right." He turned his gaze to me and didn't respond. When I questioned him again in a more urgent tone, he ordered me to go to our room and wait for him there.

I hurried back to the small room we inhabited behind the palace, my chest heaving, disturbed by his tone, knowing I had stirred his displeasure. Instinctively I knew he would be angry about my questioning him. On the way I met Aditi. She caught me by the arm and, when she saw the expression on my face, asked what was wrong.

"Pitaji is on his hands and knees washing the floor to the entry," I blurted out. "I see in his face the strain it is causing him, but he won't listen to me. Is there no one else to scrub the floor?"

She shook her head slowly in disapproval. "The woman responsible for this chore left the household this morning, and we are all busy preparing for the Maharaja's guests who are soon to arrive. But he should not have done this. He could have asked any one of us. Don't bother about it, Meenakshi. Don't question your father now. He is so determined that the palace look its very best for the guests."

When my father returned to our room later that day, I could see by the flushed look on his face and the heaving of his breath that he was not well. But I did not say anything. I looked away, pretending to be busy. When he spoke to me I answered in monosyllables.

"Look at me when I speak to you, Meenakshi." His tone was harsh.

I turned to face him, my eyes brimming with tears.

"What is this resistance I sense in you?"

I didn't answer. When he persisted I blurted out, "Pitaji, what will the others think to see you on the floor like that?" But as soon as the words were out of my mouth I regretted them. If I ever wanted to withdraw words spoken, this was the moment.

"What others think . . . is this your concern? Is this what I have taught you? Is there any task to be ashamed of when we are preparing the palace for Janak Baba's guests?" His voice betrayed his disapproval of me. "I am surprised at you, my child."

I should have known to stop there but I didn't. "But Pitaji," I protested. "I can see the strain it is causing you. Surely one of the younger servants . . . ."

He cut me off. "Yes, there is a young servant, and I will see that she takes up the task." Little did I know that this young servant was to be me. "What has gotten into you, Meenakshi?"

I didn't answer. I knew that I was wrong, yet I couldn't help but feel that Pitaji had humiliated both himself and me. Finally I said is a small voice, "We are Brahmins, are we not, Pitaji?"

This statement did not have a good effect on my father. He raised his hand as if to strike me; I looked up at him in fear. He had never done that before. Then he paused and lowered his hand, regaining his self-control. I could not bear to see the look of pain on his face, so I burst into tears and ran from the room. For the rest of the day I sat outside, hidden behind a leafy tree. As dark was approaching, I saw him come to me. Instead of scolding as I assumed he would, he lowered himself quietly beside me and spoke in a gentle voice.

"I want you to understand something, Meenakshi. Look at our Maharaja, who is our model in every detail of life. Have you not heard how he goes from village to village helping the people plough their fields? Do you realize what hard work it is to use one of these new ploughs? I would not have the strength to do this, yet he does it again and again. He does not stand and instruct them. He teaches by doing. I have seen him sweat and toil in the fields, showing the farmers how to turn the soil. Is that a task fit for a Maharaja? In this way he is teaching us there is no work too humble. There is no greater or lesser among us. Our Maharaja does not see himself to be any different from the poorest in his kingdom. I have heard him say this many times. It is only that his duties are different. And our duty is to do whatever is required in this household to ease his burden and the burden of the others here so that he can govern and guide us, free of cares. If that means performing what you call the lowest of tasks, I am happy to do it. And I hope you also will be. This is the path to contentment."

"I understand what you are saying, Pitaji, and I will keep trying. I am sorry that I am not a model servant. But I will keep trying, I promise you." I looked at him sadly, glad that he was no longer angry with me, but frustrated with myself that I couldn't be as he was.

"I cannot change your attitude. I can only point you in the right direction, my child. You yourself are the only one who can change the way you feel, and I pray for your well-being that you will be able to do so."

My heart was heavy the whole of that day and the next, and the next, despite the festivities that accompanied the arrival of the Maharaja's guests. But it grew heavier a few days later when the guests had gone, and my father came to tell me that the servant responsible for scrubbing the floors and other laborious tasks was too ill to return. He looked at me hopefully as if he wanted me to offer to take up the task, but I refrained from saying anything.

Then the words came out of his mouth. "Meenakshi, I am asking you to take up the tasks that this servant had been assigned." I looked at him in shock, but nodded my assent. Was he punishing me? Was my questioning of him such an egregious act? Was he trying to humiliate me? For weeks my tears mingled with the water that I splashed on the floors. My father would come to inspect my work and would inevitably find fault with it and make me repeat the whole process. The other servants looked upon me with sympathy, which made me feel even worse. I couldn't forgive him for delegating to me the lowest of responsibilities. After a few months, Aditi came to my defense, but to no avail.

"When she learns there is no distinction between any of the tasks, we will reassign her," Pitaji replied.

"But her body is not strong, and I am afraid this will damage her health," she insisted.

He shook his head. "It is not to punish her, Aditi, but to help her learn. It is for her own good. She must not be so concerned with appearances."

Pitaji would not relieve me of these duties, so I resigned myself to serving as the lowliest among the servants, and the distance between my father and me grew even greater. Rarely did we speak now. On occasion I would find him looking at me as if he wanted to approach me, to say something that would mend the broken trust between us, but then I wondered whether it was just my imagination, a vain hope that he really did care. I did not have the courage to approach him, and so we remained as far apart as planets that only pass each other in the darkness of empty space, barely exchanging a greeting.

Two years passed, and despite Aditi's many attempts to intervene, nothing changed. I began to wonder if I was destined to spend my life in this manner. Finally, one day I summoned up the courage to speak with him in what I thought was a reasoned manner. "Pitaji, I thought by now I would be able to work under Aditi in the kitchen. I would really like that."

"Are you unhappy with your responsibilities, Meenakshi?"

I didn't answer, and he continued coolly, "If they are too much for you, then perhaps I should relieve you of your duties and take them upon myself."

"No, Pitaji, I didn't mean that," I hurried to assure him. My reasoned manner was quickly departing, giving way to hurt and emotion. Why did he not understand me? Why did he make it so difficult for me? And so I blurted out, "Why are you punishing me, Pitaji? What have I done that is so wrong? Have you no feeling for me? I made one mistake, I admit, in questioning you, but I have made up for that, have I not?"

"Punishing you?" he inquired in the same cool tone. "I am trying to teach you how to serve, as I have had to learn over the years.

No task is too minor, too unimportant, Meenakshi. For want of a small task, the whole palace would fall into chaos. Do you not yet understand this? You can serve this palace and this kingdom just as well by scrubbing the floors as you can by tending to the personal needs of the Maharaja. What matters is the spirit in which you perform your responsibilities, not what those responsibilities are. I have tried to teach you time and again that there is no distinction between the types of work one does. When you truly know this, everything will change. Then I will feel that I have fulfilled my responsibility in raising you to be a proper servant, a servant whose only thoughts are for the welfare of the one you serve."

My hurt feelings blinded me to what he was saying. All I knew was that he treated me differently than he treated the others. To the others he was kind and caring. If they had difficulty finishing their work, he would come to their assistance. But with me, it was different. They adored him because of his kind nature, but this nature was not one he showed to me.

"You don't treat me like you treat the others. You treat me as if . . . . as if you don't care at all about me . . . as if I don't matter to you at all. And it has always been this way," I cried as I ran from the room.

"Meenakshi!" he called after me. I knew that I had hurt him, but I couldn't contain myself. I couldn't stop the words from gushing from my mouth. To speak rudely to one's elder, let alone one's father, was a serious offense, but I could not contain the feelings that were long held back. "Come back." He continued to call after me, but I didn't turn around.

I hid myself in the forest that day, relinquishing all of my tasks. Let him punish me, I thought, I don't care anymore. In my mind I repeated again and again the conversation between us, convincing myself that I was right, that he didn't care for me, that I was a burden on him, for which he would never forgive me.

I must have fallen asleep in the forest. I awoke many hours later to the sound of my name being called by a woman's voice. I thought surely Pitaji must have sent Aditi to fetch me, but I wouldn't let her find me. I had intended to stay in the forest through the night as I didn't want to see my father so soon. Perhaps I wanted to frighten him, for him to think that something had happened to me, to see if he had any feelings, any love at all for me. I rose to penetrate further into the woods, but Aditi caught sight of me and came running. When I saw the expression on her face, I stopped. Something was wrong. Finally she caught up with me.

"Meenakshi, we have been looking for you all day. Something terrible has happened. You must come quickly."

My body stiffened when I heard these words, as if I knew what she was about to say. "Is it Pitaji?" I asked in a frightened voice, not wanting to hear the answer.

She nodded and drew me into her arms. I heard her sob, but I was frozen, not daring to ask what had happened. After a few minutes she whispered, "Your father had an accident, my dear." I didn't respond. "He sent one of the servants up to the roof to repair a leak. But he questioned whether the repair was done properly and so he went to check on it himself. As he was climbing to the roof, he slipped and had a bad fall." She fell quiet. I was too stunned to respond. "Oh, Meenakshi." She held me tight in her embrace. "This should not have happened."

"Is he all right?" I finally managed to ask.

She shook her head and whispered, "I am afraid not, dear."

"He is not dead, is he?" I asked as the horror of the news was beginning to hit me. She nodded. Suddenly the full force of what she was saying came over me, and I screamed, "Nay!" as loud as I could. "It can't be." My voice was as sharp as a crack of thunder, sending violent waves through my body. I couldn't contain them. It was as if I had been struck by lightning. My whole body shook. Aditi drew back, startled. Then she gathered me again in her arms and let me spill all the tears that I had. We stayed like this for quite some time. Then she slowly led me to where the body of my father lay as the other servants prepared for the cremation.

"Pitaji, I am so sorry, so sorry for everything. Why did you leave me?" I inquired of the empty form which no longer contained my father. "You have left me all alone now," I whispered in a choked voice.

I was numb for the next few days. Aditi stayed with me, but finally I had to settle into the new reality. For no reason, I began to have fears that I would be sent away, but Aditi assured me that this would never be the case. Janak Baba had loved my father, she said, and there would always be a place for me in the household.

"You will work under me now, in the kitchen," Aditi told me, about a week after the incident. But I had other thoughts. After I began to recover from the shock of my father's death, the heavy weight of guilt set in. I considered myself responsible. If I had not spoken so harshly to him, if I had not run off, if I had returned when he called me back, perhaps he would still be alive. Perhaps he had been upset at my behavior when he tried to climb to the roof and thus lost his footing. I was at least partially to blame for his death, and I could not accept being rewarded now for what I had done.

I shook my head. "No, Aditi, I want to continue as before with the duties my father had assigned to me."

"But Meenakshi, it is not necessary. You no longer have to . . . ."

"I am pleading with you. It is the only way I can keep close to my father. This is what he had wanted for me, and it will help me feel that he is still with me. It is what I want." I did not speak to her of my sense of guilt as I was too ashamed to tell anyone of the incident. I would keep that hidden in my heart, and only I would know of my terrible deed. Aditi did her best to change my mind, but I insisted and finally she nodded her consent.

I was determined to fulfill my father's hopes for me. I would become the best of servants. I would perform the lowliest of the tasks until I saw no difference between them and the more desired duties. This is what I told myself as I tried to push away the deeper reason for my decision. I tried not to think about the fact that I was really seeking to punish myself for what I considered to be my misdeeds, for questioning my father, for disturbing his peace of mind. And so I resumed my duties, but things were not as they were before. His death had such a deep impact on me that it brought about an internal change.

Every night as I retired from the day's work, I would hear my father's words, as if he were just returning from seeking Janak Baba's blessing. For the first time now I recognized the deep peace that he would bring as he returned from the Maharaja's room. I no longer felt the distance, the sense of rejection. I felt that I too benefited from that blessing.

One day I asked Aditi whether the Maharaja had seen my father before he died. Had he given him a blessing as he lay there dying? I knew what that would have meant to my father. With Janak Baba's blessing, he would have left this world in peace, regardless of any dispute with me.

"Yes, my dear." She reassured me. "The blessing was there. He was very saddened by the news of the accident and came immediately to see your father before he passed. We left them alone, and so I don't know what was said. But I have no doubt that he asked the Maharaja to ensure your future." She was silent for a few minutes and then added, "Even though he was harsh on you, Meenakshi, your father had great love for you. Never doubt that."

"I doubted it for many years," I replied with tears in my eyes. "It took his death to convince me otherwise."

"Your father's thoughts were always for your future, for your well-being, that you be taken care of and spared the worst of the misfortune . . ." She didn't finish the sentence and I didn't press her.

"My father always told me he would give his life for Janak Baba, and he did, Aditi. He did give his life for him. I know he was content to die while serving, while fulfilling a task he thought important. It is what he wanted—only to serve his Janak Baba, our Janak Baba," I said quietly and then added. "It was what he wanted for me, as well.

Aditi, I am trying to have that attitude, the feeling that my father had," I confessed.

"Don't blame yourself, Meenakshi. Be patient. It will come to you as you grow older. We all strive for that, but your father had perfected it. He truly had no thought of himself. It was as if he were an extension, a limb of the Maharaja, with no separate identity."

"You are right," I murmured. "He had no separate identity. I used to begrudge him that, Aditi, but I didn't understand him. I argued with him, but what I would give now to have him back," I said mournfully.

"You have to follow your own path, my dear. Your father's way may not be your way. Are you ready now to help me in the kitchen?"

I shook my head. "I will find peace in performing the duties my father had given me."

"I will not ask again, but you make sure to let me know when you are ready."

I nodded, knowing it would be a long time, if ever, before I could free myself of my guilt.

The years passed. I hardly had any interaction with the other servants. I would rise before them, eat alone, and retire as soon as my work was done. Even on festival days I kept to myself. I became remote from everyone, even Aditi, who as she began to age became less active in the household. When she tried to check in on me, I would feign a smile and tell her how close I felt to my father now that I was fulfilling his wishes for me. She would simply shake her head.

Often when I grew tired and felt worn down by the manual labor, I would repeat to myself my father's words: "There is no lower or higher work. It is the attitude with which one performs one's duties, not the duties themselves that matter." I must perfect the work my father had given me, I told myself again and again. When I have perfected it, well, I will see what happens then. Indeed, the whole focus of my life had become the perfection of my work, no matter what it was. But I didn't feel the contentment I saw in my father's face after a day's work. My mind was focused on the work, not on the one I was serving. In fact I could not say who I was serving, or what. I was simply trying to appease my guilt over my father's death.

A certain numbness came over me, and I came to recognize that I was performing my duties in a perfunctory manner. It was the best I could do, and I fully expected to spend the rest of my life in this way. However, one morning when I woke up, something had shifted in me. I awoke with a sense of lightheartedness that I had not known before. I had risen before the others as was my custom and went to start the day's work. As I knelt to begin washing the floors, I suddenly stopped and began to chuckle to myself. I realized that I didn't mind these duties at all. I realized that I could be assigned any task and it wouldn't make a difference to me. Scrubbing the floors or selecting the clothes for Sunaina Ma, it didn't matter. At that moment I caught a glimpse, just a glimpse of how my father thought, of his bearing, of his dignity. I realized that no chore or assignment could ever demean him because of his innate dignity, because of who he knew he was. His dignity came from inside, not from the outer world, not from how others perceived him.

"Oh Pitaji," I murmured. "If only I could have realized this sooner. If only I could be like you. I have been trying, but help me please. Help me become like you." I put all my heart into those words, which were truer to my feelings that anything I had ever expressed.

Not long after that, early one morning after I had finished washing one of the hallways, I saw some of the women servants going down to the river to bathe. When they saw my work was completed, they greeted me and then continued down the hall. Unexpectedly one of them turned and asked if I wanted to join them. I had never done so before, as my father had instilled in me a fear of the river. I started to shake my head no and then stopped myself. Something in me nodded assent. "Let me just grab some of my clothes to wash," I replied. I hurried back to my room. They waited until I returned, then we all went to the river.

Only I understood what it meant for me to go down to the river with the others. Since my father's death I had abided by all his restrictions, but now I felt free. I awoke to the fact that I was now in charge of my own life and could make my own decisions. I would start with the river.

I entered the waters hesitantly, one small step at a time, somewhat nervous at this first intimate meeting. The others rushed into the river and submerged themselves. The water was cool and inviting, and it felt wonderful against my skin. I ventured in up to my thighs but could go no further, as I felt the tug of the tide and realized I needed to be cautious. The others were done with their bathing before I could gather my clothes for washing.

"We will wait for you, Meenakshi," they said, but I encouraged them to go back as they would be needed in the palace.

"No need to wait. I won't be long," I replied. "I will just wash these few things." They hesitated, but when I urged them to return, they consented.

I quickly washed the few items I had brought with me. By accident I let go of one of my scarves, which got caught in a wave and began to drift away from me. I reached out to retrieve it, but it drifted further from my reach. I entered deeper and then deeper into the river, until I was out way beyond my comfort level. The scarf still escaped my grasp. I didn't understand the power of the river. I realized I had to give up the attempt to retrieve the cloth and try to regain my footing and make my way back to the shore, but it was too late. The current was too strong; it gathered me in its arms, drawing me further from the shore. I began to panic as the waves pulled my head under the water. I fought for air as I struggled against the current. Realizing that I was helpless against the running tides, the thought came into my mind to let go and allow myself to be consumed by the river.

Just as the thought of death came over me and I began to cease from struggling, just as I was about to give in, to release my life and stop fighting for breath, I felt the currents reverse and begin to draw me closer to the shore. My legs touched bottom and, as I lifted my head above water, I saw Janak Baba standing at the river's edge, his eyes fixed on me. He was drawing me in. I could feel the power emanating from his body. As if in response to his command, the river brought me closer to the shore until it threw me against the river bank. With trembling limbs I climbed onto the rock-strewn shoreline, my whole body shaking.

I sank onto the earth in front of Janak Baba, gasping for breath. He reached for me and lifted me to my feet. Holding my arm to prevent me from collapsing, he took off his shawl and wrapped it around me. At his touch my trembling ceased. I lifted my eyes and, for the first time in my life, I was able to look directly at him and see the greatness of the man who stood before me. In his eyes I saw such kindness and warmth, and a love I had never experienced from my father. At that moment, my heart opened and I wept.

THE ARRIVAL OF SITA

For many years there had been a dearth of rain in the kingdom, and the Maharaja had been doing intense *tapasya* (spiritual disciplines) to understand the causes of this drought and to mediate the effects of the changing climate. It was said that forces coming from other parts of the earth were causing these disruptions. But Janak Baba had always taught that benefit can come from difficult times, and so the drought led to new ways of cultivating food. One day when Janak Baba was meditating by the river, the *devi* (goddess) of the river arose and spoke to him.

"Use my waters to nurture the crops," she said. At first Janak Baba didn't understand, but then she guided him on how to dig ditches so her waters could flow into the fields. This helped for some time, but after more years with little rain, the flow of her waters also grew weak. When the people had to do without food, the Maharaja joined them and underwent extensive fasting during these years. Janak Baba did not despair; he saw this as an opportunity to build alliances with other kingdoms. We had been a self-sufficient kingdom, supplying all the needs of our people, but now we could no longer feed our population. Our Maharaja had never needed to seek assistance, but gradually he began to say there would be benefit in trade, and so new relationships were formed.

It was Maharaja Dasaratha of the nearby Kosala Kingdom who approached Janak Baba, offering grains to alleviate the shortages.

Theirs was a larger and much more powerful kingdom, and Janak Baba was at first hesitant to receive this gift without offering something in return. It was said that Maharaja Dasaratha recognized his hesitation to receive without giving and wanting to respect this, Dasaratha asked for the works of Videha artisans in exchange. Janak Baba readily accepted, knowing that they were sowing seeds of a future alliance. There was huge gratitude in the kingdom. Janak Baba told his ministers that someday we would repay Ayodhya in full for this generosity. The assistance given by Ayodhya saw the people of Videha through difficult times, and gratitude was embedded in our hearts.

Janak Baba and Sunaina Ma were advancing in years and had no heirs, but there was no concern in the kingdom about this, because we knew that our Maharaja would take care of all the necessary responsibilities. One day rumors spread that the Maharaja was bringing together the sages of the kingdom for a very special *puja* (devotional ritual) to ask for a child, a daughter. Everyone wondered, "Why a daughter?" Maharajas everywhere longed for a son to continue their reign, but we were different. We all knew that our Janak Baba was not like the other Maharajas. His vision extended far beyond our kingdom.

Around that time a certain sage from far away came to visit the palace, and he asked the Maharaja if it were true that he was offering pujas so that a daughter would be born to him and his wife. Janak Baba could see the look of shock on his face, so he smiled and asked, "Why does this surprise you?"

"Maharaja, is it true that you have no son?" Janak Baba nodded, his smile broadening. "Are you not concerned about succession?" he inquired. "Someone to reign when you are gone?"

"Kingdoms come and go. I am concerned with the welfare of the earth," he responded. "I have observed increasing disturbances in the rhythms of nature and believe that only the supreme *Shakti* (the Divine Feminine) herself can again bring balance and harmony to the natural world. Without regaining this balance, I fear there will be much more suffering. Her presence is needed now, and I will invoke her again and again in the hope that she will respond and pour her love over all the living creatures on this earth by appearing in physical form." And so the meditations and pujas continued.

One day some months later, the Maharaja set out early in the morning before the first hint of dawn. Sunaina Ma was there to see him off. He had told her that he intended to travel to the driest part of the kingdom, the region most in need of relief, where he would meditate. He waited for her to join him. When he saw that the Maharani was not stepping into the chariot beside him, he asked, "Sunaina, will you not come to receive your daughter?"

She looked at him in amazement. There was nothing on earth that she wanted more than a child, but she honored and respected the austerities of her husband and so had resigned herself to being childless. He indicated that yes, for sure, their daughter would arrive, and so she stepped into the chariot beside him.

When they came to the barren fields—fields that had not yielded crops for many years— they stepped down from the chariot and the Maharaja went into deep meditation. The Maharani began to pray, reciting the mantras her husband had taught her to invoke the supreme Devi. The hours passed, dawn flowed into midday as the sun made its way across the sky. The sun made its descent and soon night set in, bringing a silence and stillness as they continued their meditation and invocations.

It was just before dawn when Sunaina Ma's eyes flew open. She had heard the first cry of a child! She roused Janak Baba from his meditation, her eyes glowing with joy. "I heard a cry," she exclaimed in excitement, "a most melodious cry. It was more like a song calling out to the world." During his meditation, Janak Baba had seen the beautiful Mahadevi, the Great Goddess, who acknowledged that she was responding to his call.

When Janak Baba beheld the small desert creatures that had

gathered around, he looked at them with gratitude in his heart. "She is coming for you as well," he said, "not only for us humans." He took the plow that he had crafted especially for this moment and walking to the center of the field, he dug it into the earth. With that motion he took a vow that his daughter would belong to the earth and all of her creatures. She would not belong to him, Sunaina, or any man. She belonged to all. He had not called her forth to extend his kingdom, to perpetrate his reign, or to gain greater power or wealth, but to help and heal the natural world that was growing increasingly imbalanced. After his plow hit the earth and a small depression was created in the dry soil, she manifested in that very spot. It would not be long before word spread that the daughter of Vasundhara Devi, Mother Earth herself, had been born. Within minutes the rains began, at first in small droplets and then in a downpour to water the thirsty land. Janak Baba lifted up the infant, held her against his chest, and gave thanks.

It was around this time that Janak Baba sent for me, just a few months after I nearly lost my life in the river.

"Janak Baba has come to see me about you," Aditi told me one evening.

"About me?" I asked in surprise. She nodded.

"He asked me to tell you that your tapasya is now over."

"My tapasya?" I looked at her in confusion. I knew in a general sense what tapasya was — the long difficult meditation practice that the sages engaged in to bring certain beneficial results for themselves and for the world. Our Maharaja engaged in tapasya for the sake of the kingdom, but I, a poor servant, had no notion of these matters. I had not engaged in any meditation practice. I knew nothing of this.

She nodded again. "You have undergone much hardship, Meenakshi, since your father's death and even I can see how this has benefited you. He asked that you now be assigned to serve the Maharani. It will be for a brief period and then you will be given another assignment."

"I don't understand," I murmured. "You know that I am perfectly content as I am. I haven't sought anything more." In truth, I was fearful of moving into a position with more direct access to the Maharaja and Maharani. I was far more comfortable serving out of sight than within the purview of the whole household.

"Do you not trust his wisdom, my dear?" When I didn't answer, she continued. "Do you remember after your father had the accident, you asked me whether Janak Baba had come to bless him?" I nodded. "I was not in the room, but one of the other servants was. He recently told me of those last moments. He relayed to me that as your father lay dying, the Maharaja expressed gratitude for his many years of service and said he would fulfil any last request. I want you to know his dying wish. Your father folded his hands and with all of the life left in him beseeched Janak Baba to look after you, to guard you from any misfortune and, if he saw fit, to find appropriate service for you beyond what you were performing. "The Maharaja nodded and made that commitment. 'She is a good servant and a good daughter, and perhaps I have been too harsh on her,' your father said. 'She was the blessing that came to me in the midst of all my misfortunes, and I owe that to your care for my family for so many generations.'"

"Why did nobody tell me this sooner?" I asked, my eyes tearing. "If I had known . . . ."

"What would you have done differently?" Aditi asked.

"I don't know," I murmured.

"Forget the past, Meenakshi. Think of your future. Janak Baba has called for you, and you cannot refuse him."

So that is why he saved me from the river that day, I thought. I was deeply moved to think he would remember that commitment to my father of so many years ago. But that was the nature of our Baba. His word was ironclad. Never would he retreat from a commitment, and his patience was unlimited. His tapasya had a taught him to know the right time for every action.

Aditi continued. "I never doubted that when Janak Baba felt the time was right he would intervene. He would call you at the appropriate moment. Now is that time, Meenakshi. I am less active in the household, and someone like you is very much needed, someone who carries the dedication that has been passed down through the generations from your great- great-grandfather and on to your father and now to you. You have this responsibility."

I nodded my consent. "Please convey to Janak Baba how grateful I am, not just for his consideration of me, but for fulfilling the last wishes of my father. That means a great deal to me, and I will do my utmost to follow in his footsteps."

After Aditi left, I could not help but wonder if my recent change of heart had something to do with the turn of events. Did Janak Baba know the shift that had taken place in my attitude over the last few months? And was it Janak Baba's blessings that had changed me, that had turned my resistance and self-pity into a sense of gratitude, that made me eager for the opportunity to perform the least desirable tasks, that enabled me to finally see the dignity of my father's life and the truth of what he had been trying to teach me throughout my childhood?

Dignity was a quality much valued in our kingdom. Although our lives in the kingdom of Videha were simple, our needs and wants few, we saw this simplicity as a form of dignity because of the respect we accorded all of the natural world and all of the people in our kingdom. Nobody took too much, lest others go without, and this we would not tolerate. Every child who lost a parent was cared for. Every aged person was honored. There was little breaking of the trust between people. Everyone was accorded the same respect and honor and care. Janak Baba understood that for a society to be in harmony, everyone had to be looked after without exception. I suspect that is why my family was taken in after misfortune befell us.

Everyone in our society understood the rhythms of nature and lived in accordance with the natural cycles. To us, its laws were sacred and the key to our prosperity, and our prosperity lay not only in the abundant resources of nature but also in the wisdom that flowed from our Maharaja, which guided every aspect of our lives. From him we had learned that as long as we upheld the natural laws, our needs would be provided for one way or another. He taught that it was because of this that Maharaja Dasaratha had come to our aid when we most needed it. Difficult times were there to teach us certain lessons, he said, but we had to remain true to our principles and beliefs.

There was no thought to take more from nature than was needed, for we were also conscious of the needs of the animal and plant kingdoms. In earlier days most of our food had come from the abundant forests and valleys, which had been overflowing with so many varieties of fruits, nuts, roots, and wild grains. But as we grew in numbers and encroached upon the forests, these foods diminished, and so the Janak family led us in the cultivation of crops. But we had not forgotten how the forests once served all of the needs of our ancestors, and so a deep gratitude remained embedded in our minds and spirits. Gratitude, respect, and love for all life—this was the essence of dignity our Janak Baba taught us.

Our gratitude was also for the earth, for her soil, which provided more and more of our food. We honored her, respected her and were grateful, and this feeling became even stronger when we learned that the earth goddess had given us a daughter. She had given the people of Videha one who could not only protect our kingdom but also help restore balance to the whole of the natural world.

The long withholding of rains had alerted us to the fact that even if we abided by the laws of the natural world and gave our gratitude, there were others on earth who might behave differently, and all would suffer from their ill acts. Thus we became more and more aware that there were forces at play that we could not comprehend, but we trusted that our wise Maharaja knew how to counter these forces and was busy doing so. When we saw the rains return after his years of tapasya and pujas, after his extreme patience and persistence, we were more convinced than ever that the powers of our Maharaja extended far beyond the material realm. So when he brought home his daughter, we viewed her as he did: a gift from the gods, indeed, as the great Shakti herself.

While the village people said she was born of the earth, there was whispering throughout the household that she was a self-manifesting one, the great Devi of whom the sages spoke. She took physical form through her own will. Janak Baba did not dissuade this talk, but he allowed the villagers to proclaim that she was the daughter of Vasundhara Devi, the earth goddess. And so she was named Sita, which means "furrow" of the earth.

SITA'S EDUCATION

Sita's presence transformed the household. Everything now revolved around her. Janak Baba and Sunaina Ma would spend hours sitting in her presence, watching her sleep, taking turns holding her. I had never seen our Baba like this, and we were all surprised that anything in the material world could so transfix him—our Baba who had transcended all attachments. But they were not the only ones who were mesmerized by her; this was a condition that came of all of us in the household. If something was needed for the infant, all the servants would rush to bring it. I would have a hard time leaving the room where she lay, such was the attraction to her. I would find myself gazing upon her and for the first time in my life a palpable love entered my heart. I felt for this child as I had never felt for anyone. There were no words to describe that feeling.

"Mata," I whispered one day when I found myself alone with her, "it is through you that I have come to know joy. You have brought light into my life and I will serve you faithfully to the best of my ability for the rest of my days."

From the beginning, the servants and others called her "Mata." It just came naturally. Although outwardly we were the ones caring for her, we sensed that inwardly she was caring for us; in the truest sense she was our Mata. Sunaina Ma laughed at first when she heard us calling her Mata, but then her laughter subsided and she said, "You are all correct. Although she is the mother of the world, I must see her as my child. That is the nature of *maya* (illusion)."

For several months after Sita's arrival, Janak Baba did not leave the palace except to visit the immediate localities. His habitual travel to distant sages paused, for a while at least. But as Sita approached the first year of her birth, he accepted an invitation to visit a certain sage. He came to say goodbye to Sita. I was there with Sunaina Ma. As he explained to Sita where he was going, Sunaina Ma looked at me with a smile, amused that Janak Baba would speak to the infant as if she were fully grown. But as he rose to take his leave, Sita held out her arms to him and their eyes locked. For a moment he didn't say anything or move, but then, as if in response to her, he said, "Okay, I will take you along."

Sunaina Ma began to protest, but Janak Baba simply put his fingers to her lips. "She has asked to come and I cannot refuse her."

"You cannot care for her alone."

"I am perfectly able to, and I am sure the hermitage will be happy to receive her."

"If you insist on taking her, then bring Meenakshi and Usha with you." Usha was a younger servant and had great devotion to the household. She often assisted me in my work.

Janak Baba looked at me. "Yes, Meenakshi, you may come, and go tell Usha as well."

I had never traveled away from the palace, and I had never visited a sage's hermitage; this would be a totally new experience for me. It took us all day to reach the hermitage, but this was due to the many stops we made. The Maharaja used such trips as an occasion to visit the villages and speak with the people, who always insisted on offering him a meal, and he could not refuse them. This was the first time for them to meet *Rajakumari* (princess) Sita. As word spread that the Maharaja was passing through, accompanied by his daughter, people came from many villages to greet them. I was amazed at how open and receptive Janak Baba was to the crowds that gathered. He did not seem to mind in the least the many attempts to touch and hold her, and Sita was all smiles and giggles.

When we finally arrived at the hermitage, the sage seemed not at all surprised that we had baby Sita with us.

"I was expecting you," he said to her. "And I am glad you have come for your first lessons."

The sage took Janak Baba into his hut while I went to the hut assigned to Sita, Usha, and me. It had been a long journey, and I was sure that Sita would be ready for bed as she had stayed awake throughout the whole journey. Usha and I quickly prepared the bedding for her and then Usha laid her down and reclined beside her. I began to sing quietly. When I looked over she was fast asleep, but I kept humming until I also began to nod off. Sometime later I awoke with a start. I was slumped over the bed where Sita was sleeping, or had been. I saw that the bed was now empty, except for Usha, who was fast asleep.

"Mata!" I called out several times. She was not in the hut. My cry woke Usha and the two us went outside in a state of near panic. It was late in the night. Sita could not have gone far, I reasoned. I searched the whole courtyard, but she was nowhere to be found. A faint light illumined the hut where Janak Baba and the sage had been sitting. I would have to go alert them. Hesitant to disturb them but not knowing what else to do, I told Usha to keep searching while I approached the hut. The door was slightly ajar, and I saw Janak Baba and the sage and a few others sitting deep in meditation. What was I to do? As I stood there, trembling in fear, Janak Baba slowly opened his eyes and motioned to a corner of the room. There I found the sleeping Sita. He said, in not more than a whisper, "She walked in not long ago. She walked in." In his whispering voice I could hear his amazement, as baby Sita had not taken her first step as of yet.

Surely I had misheard him. "Walked?" I asked.

He nodded. "Leave her here and go back to bed, Meenakshi. Everything is fine."

From that night on, Sita walked everywhere. She was so pleased with her new capability that she would not sit still. She would take off before I realized it, and I had a hard time keeping up with her. She had her eye on the hermitage gate; whenever it opened she hastened toward it. The forests lay beyond and, at a certain moment, I realized that this was where she wanted to go.

The day before we were scheduled to depart, Sita managed to escape my watchful eye and slip out the open gate. I rushed after her, but Janak Baba stopped me. "Let her explore," he said. "Clearly she needs to go there. She has been looking in that direction these last few days."

"Maharaja, shouldn't I follow?"

He nodded. "But at a distance. Give her the room she needs."

I called Usha and the two of us followed her. She seemed to know exactly where she was going. Without any hesitation, she went into the forest, where she lifted into her arms a small animal that had been wounded and was hiding behind a tree. Then she turned around and, with the animal in hand, returned to the hermitage with Usha and me some yards behind. She handed the animal to her father, who had been waiting for our return, and began to cry. Janak Baba understood immediately.

"We will help this little animal," he said gently to her. She shook her head, the tears still flowing. A number of the hermitage residents, hearing a commotion, came out to see what was wrong. They made a little bed for the animal and bandaged its broken leg, but the animal died in the night. Sita was quiet after that. She was no longer interested in the gate or in leaving the hermitage. She stayed by her father's side, and soon it was time to depart.

We had been gone but a week, but when Sunaina Ma saw us, she said it seemed a year had passed because Sita had grown so and was now walking. And the experience with the little animal seemed to have affected her. She left as an infant, but returned a child.

Sita now accompanied Janak Baba on many of his visits to the sages. He always took a few of the servants, but I didn't often have the opportunity to accompany them. The servants returned with stories of Sita's interaction with the hermitage students or with the animals in the nearby forests, and we all took great pleasure in their accounts as they made us feel as if we had been there ourselves. On such occasions we would gather round in the kitchen after the day's work was done and the servant who had gone on the journey would share a story of Mata Sita. We would laugh with delight, as we all had come to feel as if she were our own.

Some years later, Janak Baba announced that he was going back to see the sage that he had visited with Sita on her first journey from the palace. She was eager to go. I didn't expect to be asked to accompany them and so was surprised when Sunaina Ma asked me to go along.

Soon after we arrived, Sita asked her father to go to the forest where she had found the wounded animal.

"You remember that?" He was surprised.

She nodded. "I saw the wounded animal while I was sleeping. That was how I knew where to go."

"Of course you may go into the forest. You are free here to go wherever you wish."

I accompanied her as she went deeper and deeper into the forest. She seemed to be looking for something. Finally I said to her, "Mata, I think we should turn back before we get lost."

"How can we get lost?" she smiled. "I have to find something before we return."

"What is it you are looking for?"

"I don't know its name, but I will know it when I see it. I feel it calling me."

"Mata, is this some game?"

She shook her head. "Not at all. It is a very serious matter. Please, have patience, Meenakshi, I know I will find it. I hear it calling."

"Is it an animal?" I asked.

She shook her head. I couldn't understand what she was talking about, but this was often the case with Sita. I followed as she wound her way through the overgrown trails. We came upon some large birds, they seemed to be water birds, and Sita stopped in front of them. After a few minutes I saw her fold her hands and thank them; then very consciously she went to a nearby stream and started to dig out some roots. "There, I have found it. Now we can return," she said simply, holding a large bunch of roots in her hand.

I followed as she found the way back without any trouble. When we reached the hermitage, she went straight to the hut of the sage, who was explaining something to Janak Baba. "I have brought these for you," she said to the sage, handing him the bunch of roots.

"Thank you, Sita," he said, with a confused look on his face. "I am touched that you thought of me."

"What is this?" asked Janak Baba with a broad smile. "What have you brought Guruji?"

"It is for his stomach," she said. "This will help him."

The confusion on the sage's face turned to shock.

"Stomach?" inquired Janak Baba. Then turning to the sage he asked, "Do you have stomach troubles?"

"Indeed, I do. But how could you know this, Sita? Nobody but my wife is aware of this."

She didn't answer, but instead advised him to boil the roots and drink the liquid, and his stomach troubles would improve.

"Amazing!" exclaimed the sage. "I will certainly do as you advise!"

Janak Baba turned to me, his eye questioning to see whether I could provide any information. "She seemed to know exactly what was needed," I said quietly. "I followed her deep into the forest. And then she stopped to ask where the roots might be."

"Ask? Who did she ask?" he pressed me.

I didn't know how to respond and kept quiet. I turned to Sita, "It was the birds who told you. Is that right, Sita?"

She nodded. "They did direct me to the stream."

Janak Baba and the sage looked at one another. Nobody spoke. "Well, let's see how these roots work," said the sage finally with a small chuckle.

For three days his wife prepared the medicine and then the sage approached Sita and confirmed that he was much, much better. "My stomach is at ease after a long time," he said. "You must show my wife where to find these roots so that I can continue to take this medicine."

When we returned to the palace and Janak Baba relayed this story to Sunaina Ma, she grew concerned. "If word gets out," she said, "people from throughout the kingdom will be coming for healing."

"But isn't that a good thing?" Janak Baba asked. "If she can help people . . . ."

"She is but a small child," protested Sunaina Ma. "Let her have her childhood at least. There will be time later."

"You are right. But we cannot contain her. Whatever she will do, she will do, and there is no way we can stop her."

The following year another incident occurred at a nearby hermitage. I had gone with Janak Baba to care for Sita while he was visiting a sage who had built a hermitage in the middle of the jungle. One evening I looked around to see about putting Sita to bed when I found that she was gone. I searched everywhere but could not find her. Janak Baba was off meditating with the hermitage residents and I hesitated to disturb him. "She will come back soon," I told myself. But she didn't return. Hours later, I saw Janak Baba crossing the courtyard returning to his hut. I had stayed awake, waiting for his return. I rushed out to catch him before he entered his hut.

"What is it, Meenakshi?" he asked when he saw the fearful look on my face.

"Sita has been gone for hours. I don't know where she went, and I can't find her anywhere."

"She will return," he replied assuredly.

"But it is very late and so dark tonight . . ." I began to cry. "I am so sorry I let her out of my sight," I said between sobs.

"Meenakshi, we cannot confine her. I have said that again and again. She will return. Go to sleep."

Janak Baba sat up through the night in meditation. I also sat up through the night, but not in meditation. I was too upset to sleep a wink. When I heard him leave his hut before dawn, I quickly went to follow, my heart pounding.

"I know where she is," he said quietly. "Follow me." He walked some way into the jungle, and there he found her, sleeping beside a family of monkeys, her head resting on the lap of the mother monkey. We approached as quietly as we could, but when the mother monkey heard us she let out a cry and quickly scampered up the nearby tree, the littles ones following her. Sita awoke with a start.

"Pitaji," she exclaimed.

Without saying a word he lifted her into his arms and carried her back to the hermitage. When he put her down in the courtyard, he looked at her with a serious expression. "You should not have gone off without telling Meenakshi. She has been so worried that she didn't sleep all night."

She looked at me with regret in her eyes.

"What happened, Mata, that made you leave in the night?" I asked. "I was so worried when I couldn't find you."

Sita was quiet. Then Janak Baba said, "I know there was a good reason for you to leave, but why didn't you return?"

"That mother monkey was so sad," she said. "One of her newborns had fallen from a tree and died. I felt her sorrow and couldn't help but go to her. When I found her whining I put my head on her lap and that seemed to ease her. Then I must have fallen asleep. I didn't mean to stay out all night."

"I understand," replied Janak Baba. "But let us come to an agreement that you will always let one of us know where you are going so that there will be no cause to worry."

Sita nodded. "I will try, but Pitaji . . . ."

"For a few more years, Sita. I have full faith that you can take of yourself, but there are others who will worry, your mother especially. She would not have been happy had she been here."

For the next few years Sita was careful to let one of us know when she was wandering out. Every night one of the servants would keep watch over Sita. Another one of us would come in the early morning to relieve the one who had been there through the night. Often we would sit outside her door.

There was an incident a few years later that made us realize we could no longer keep such a close watch on her. I came early one morning and found the servant on guard that night fast asleep. Sita's bed was empty. She was nowhere to be found in the palace so I searched the grounds. Something told me to go down to the river, where I found her. She was in the middle of a conversation with the river, and she seemed to be scolding it. I sat quietly nearby. Finally she turned and saw me. Still in her scolding mode, she was not at all apologetic.

"What is it, Mata?" I asked. "What brought you down to the river so early in the morning?"

"Last night the river took the life of an ox. Now what will that farmer do? How will he plow his fields? It was not right."

"How did you know this, Mata?"

"I saw it in a dream," she said. "It was clear as could be. The ox had wandered off and came for a drink but she swept the animal away. Now that farmer must be in a sorry state."

"It rained last night very heavily. Perhaps the ox slipped. Perhaps it wasn't the river's fault at all," I said, not quite knowing why I felt the need to defend the river.

"You may be right, Meenakshi, but still we must help that farmer now."

When we returned to the palace, Sita told Janak Baba what had happened and insisted that they bring a new ox to the farmer. "But how will we find this farmer?" he asked with some amusement at her insistence.

"I will find him," she said. And so Janak Baba asked me to go to Kiran, who was in charge of the animals, and have him bring an ox.

Kiran was an old-time servant like myself. His father, like mine, had served in the household. He was known for his special care of all the animals, and Sita was very fond of him for this reason. She would often sit with him while he cared for one or another of the animals, and she would tell him how to treat an animal if it took sick. I too liked to sit and watch him, when I had the rare opportunity. He spoke to the animals as if they were his children, and I found that endearing. Kiran was a slight man, attractive in a certain way, more due to his manner than facial features. His complexion had a darkish hue, like mine, but I thought this due to the many hours he spent outside in the sun. There was a certain familiarity between us, both having been brought up in the household, although there was also a modesty, and the words between us were few.

Kiran would do anything for Mata, and as soon as I told him about her dream he brought one of our oxen to Janak Baba. He later told me what happened. Janak Baba, Sita, Kiran, and the ox made their way down to the riverside, asking one farmer after another if he had lost an ox in the night. None of them had.

"Sita, perhaps what you saw was only a dream," Janak Baba said after some time. "It seems all the oxen are safe."

"No," she said with determination. "I know it to be true." They trudged further down the river, until at last they came to a farmer who was in a sorry state over the loss of his ox. His was a small plot of land and he had but two oxen to help him plough his fields. The disappearance of one was a great loss indeed.

When he saw the Maharaja bringing him a new ox, he was beside himself with gratitude. But the Maharaja would take no credit. "It was Sita," he said, "who insisted that we come. She saw that your ox had drowned in the river during the night. Take this animal as a gift from her."

Later that day I again found Sita by the riverside, but this time she was remorseful, not scolding. She had come to apologize to the river for her harsh tones. As I sat beside her, I saw a light rise from the river. It hovered over the water for a few minutes and then disappeared back into the depths. Sita seemed relieved by its appearance. Folding her hands, she murmured, "I understand."

"What was that?" I asked in astonishment.

"That was the river goddess. Did you see her beautiful form?"

"No, Mata. I saw only a mist of light."

"She explained to me that death is part of life, and that she took the ox because it was his time to leave his body and take another. She said I should not mourn death because without death there is no birth. I am very sorry for the way I spoke to her."

"Mata, I am sure she understood that your heart was moved by the plight of the farmer."

"Yes, that is why she called me here," she said as she rose to leave. "I will not question her again."

"It is true what she said about death. But this is a hard lesson, Mata."

She turned to look at me. She was thoughtful for a few minutes and then asked, "You were sad for a long time after your father died, weren't you, Meenakshi?" She caught me off guard, and I didn't know how to respond. I nodded. "But that was because you blamed yourself, wasn't it?"

"How do you know that, Mata?" I asked in surprise.

She smiled. "You still feel a little badly, but you shouldn't. You had nothing to do with his death. It was his time to go and nothing could have prevented it."

This conversation was a brief, very natural, matter-of-fact exchange of a few words, and yet it had a profound effect on me. Although I hardly thought of my father's death anymore, it was true that up until that moment I had not fully rid myself of guilt. Sitting in my room that night, I realized that Sita had quietly healed me of these feelings.

A few months later, another incident occurred that reminded us all how keenly Mata felt the suffering endured by the natural world. Janak Baba had been invited to a new hermitage that was being built in the middle of a forest some hours away from Mithila. The hermitage was quite extensive and it was still expanding. Many of the sages from the region were also invited and Janak Baba took Mata along.

One of the servants relayed the story to us when she returned from the journey. After they arrived, Janak Baba was asked to join the gathering of sages to hear how the hermitages were growing in the region. Normally Mata would join him, but this time she held back. She said she preferred to stay in the courtyard. Janak Baba was surprised, as she always loved to join the gatherings, but he didn't press her. For the next few days she kept herself apart, and as the days passed a feeling of sadness came over her, which became apparent to all. Finally Janak Baba asked what the matter was. When she didn't respond, he asked again. Still she didn't respond.

"Sita, I am afraid you are being disrespectful of this hermitage by staying outside when it is known throughout the kingdom how much you enjoy being with the sages." It was rare for Janak Baba to criticize her.

At his words, she looked up at him and apologized. "I am sorry, Pitaji, but it is they who have been disrespectful, and it is hard for me to overlook that."

"How so?" he asked. "How have they been disrespectful? They have made every effort to engage you and have treated you with the greatest honor."

"Come," she said taking his hand. She led him into the forest and showed him all the trees that had been cut down, with only stumps remaining. "They did not even ask permission. They just took what they wanted and thought nothing of how this would affect the other creatures. You have always taught me to be respectful of the forests, not to take more than is absolutely necessary."

Janak Baba was dismayed by what he saw. "You are right, Sita. We must find a solution to this."

"You have taught me, Pitaji, to give back double what one takes from nature and to always take with an attitude of gratitude."

"Yes, this is what I have taught you, and now you must teach these sages. Let us go speak with them." Janak Baba led her into the assembly. The sages were all seated, waiting for their Maharaja to come address them. Instead, he placed Sita in the position of honor and said, "My daughter has been distressed since she arrived here, and I have only now found out the reason why. I will let her explain it to you." With those words he seated himself in the back of the group.

Sita looked around and was silent. Never before had she addressed any group of people, and she had a natural shyness, a modesty and humility that were among her most attractive features. She could speak openly to her father and to those of us in the palace with whom she was familiar, but to address such an honorable group was new for her.

"Come, Sita, explain to them what you have just told me." Still she was silent. Finally she spoke in a voice that was not hers, not her soft childish tone but one that resonated with authority and conviction.

"I was very sad to see the disrespect here." The sage in charge of the hermitage looked greatly surprised and could not help but sputter as he stood with folded hands, "Rajakumari Sita, if any of the hermitage residents have shown you disrespect, please forgive us. It was never intended."

"It is the forest that has been disrespected and all the creatures that depend on the forest for life. You have taken so many trees without thinking of the consequences. This is not what Pitaji has taught me. He has taught me to be respectful of all life, and aren't trees life? Do they not give food and shelter to the forest creatures?"

Everyone in the assembly looked at one another, astonished at her words. "But Sita," protested the head of the hermitage, "we needed space and materials to build our hermitage. Isn't that also important?"

"Have we forgotten that our ancestors were fed and nourished by the forests and are we not taught to give gratitude for this?" Sita's voice became firm and yet the gentleness of her being flowed through her.

"Then what is the solution?" asked another of the sages. "Advise us, Sita. Should we stop building and expanding our hermitages?"

Sita became thoughtful. "No, that is not the solution." After a few minutes, her eyes lit up. "Pitaji has taught me to give back double what we take from nature, and so for every tree cut down, we should plant two. We must be very sure our needs are just, and we must explain our needs and ask permission of the forest before taking anything. If we fail to consider the life in the forest, ours will not be a prosperous future. That is certain."

Murmuring could be heard throughout the assembly and many heads nodded in agreement. "Yes, yes, that is a very good solution," said the hermitage head. "We will implement this at once."

Janak Baba, who had been silent as he observed the dialogue, now stood up and said, "All of the kingdom of Videha will implement this decision so that our young people will learn to preserve the forests and animals and plants that took care of our ancestors." Turning to Sita, he added, "There is a solution to every problem. You must always seek a way to resolve differences and to reconcile opposing needs."

After returning to the palace, Janak Baba described this scene to Sunaina Ma. I was in the room assisting her and overhead their discussion. Sunaina Ma glowed with pride when she heard what Sita had done. "We have no need to worry now about who will rule the kingdom. Sita is more than fit to take your place one day. The people will be overjoyed to see her installed."

Janak Baba shook his head. "As much as I have tried, I cannot see Sita's future. It is as if that vision is blocked to me. But I do know, Sunaina, that she is not destined to rule this kingdom or any other, or to remain in Mithila. You must not have that notion. She has not come to us for that. Yet I do know that she will serve the world. We are here to give her the training she needs for that work."

This episode was the first indication of Sita's transition from childhood. Despite her young years, she was beginning to find her own voice, and she was now to take greater interest not just in visiting the hermitages or wandering into the forests, but also in sitting, listening, and responding to the teaching of the sages.

A year or so later, another story reached the servants, one that we didn't quite understand but that made us all smile. Sita accompanied Janak Baba to visit one of the great sages of the region, who had taught the Maharaja certain sacred mantras. One evening when the sage was explaining the meaning of each sound of a particular mantra, Sita interrupted and asked, "Is it not enough simply to think the words? Why must one recite them out loud?"

"Sounds are vibrations, Sita," he explained. "They affect other vibrations and can bring the desired changes in the external world if the sounds are pronounced correctly. Each sound is attuned to a particular vibration in the universe and a slight mispronunciation can alter the effect tremendously."

Sita was quiet for a few minutes and then asked, "But aren't thoughts also vibrations? Can't thoughts also have an effect?"

"Indeed they do," he explained. "But sound is more powerful than thought. That is why the recitation of a mantra is used to bring about an effect. Just thinking the mantra will not have the same outcome."

Sita thought for a minute and then responded, "But could that be due to the power of one's concentration? If the mind's focus is such, would not a thought have the same effect?"

"Sita is right," sounded a voice from the doorway. "The power of thought cannot be disputed." Everyone turned to see who had interjected themselves into the discussion. A kindly-looking middle-aged women stood in the doorway, dressed in renunciate clothing. Her dark hair, streaked with strands of grey, was swept up atop her head. Her skin was clear with no wrinkles. Her eyes were dark and intense, but also gentle.

The other sages greeted her. "Sage Gargi, welcome. Please come in and join us." Gargi was a great philosopher and expounder of the Vedas, renowned in Janak Baba's kingdom.

Sage Gargi entered the room and took her seat beside Sita. "Sita, we live on the physical plane. In the higher realms, thought alone can manifest what one desires. Here in the material world, a denser vibration is needed. The physical world came into manifestation through the vibration of sound, through the Om vibration. And these wise men are correct: pronunciation is key. It is very difficult to align oneself with the correct vibration; if one's thought is not attuned, the sound will not be perfectly aligned. Thought guides the sound. A pure mind is needed, or at least a very disciplined mind, which is why so few hold the power of mantra. In earlier times, mantra was used to bring benefit to the earth, to bring the rains when they failed to come, for example." She stopped for a moment. "I see, Sita, that you have a question."

Sita didn't respond, but her expression showed she was taking in what she had just heard.

"Come, ask anything," pressed Sage Gargi. "These are important points for you to know. They will be valuable to you later on."

Sita turned to look at the small group that had gathered, a few of whom she knew to be advanced in meditation practices. "There was a long drought in Videha before I was born. Why didn't the mantras bring the rains then?" she asked. They looked at one another without responding. Sita turned to Sage Gargi and asked again, "Why didn't the mantras help when the people and the animals were suffering from lack of water?"

Sage Gargi responded in a low voice, "A very powerful being, Sita, can counter the mantras and make them ineffective. This is rare, but it has happened and did happen then."

"Who would do such a thing?" she asked in amazement. "And who would have such power?"

Again there was silence. No one dared to speak his name. Sita looked from one to another. Finally, Maharaja Janak intervened and said to Sita, "It is getting late. Perhaps it is time for us to retire."

"Pitaji, I must know who is the cause of such suffering, and why?"

"His name is Ravana," replied Sage Gargi quietly. "He was once a highly-respected scholar and a great devotee of *Mahadev* (Lord Shiva), and through long and intense tapasya gained many powers. His mother is a powerful *asura* (of the demon race) but his father is a respected scholar of the Vedas. He could have followed either path, but arrogance and pride overtook him and he sought to conquer the three worlds. He is one of those rare beings who can counter the mantras. He has subdued many parts of the earth and has mastered many forms of subterfuge, but he will not touch Videha now. The sages are safe here."

Sita looked troubled, but she saw her father rise, indicating it was time to end the conversation. She *pranammed* (bowed) to the sages and retired with him.

The next day they left the hermitage. Sita was quiet the whole way back to the palace. Finally her father said, "Sita, do not trouble yourself about what you heard. It is not for you to worry about that now."

"I am not worried, Pitaji. I am just trying to understand why someone with knowledge, a devotee of Mahadev, would do harm."

"He was not ready to handle the power he attained. Power in the wrong hands, Sita, can do great damage." Changing the subject, he said, "I see how much you admire Sage Gargi. Would you like to study with her?"

"Very much," Sita replied with an eager smile.

"Then it shall be arranged."

A few years later I received a great blessing from Sita. Usha and I were sitting in the garden one day watching Mata play with a family of rabbits that often came out of their hideaway to greet her. I was looking at Mata, thinking how beautiful she was now that she was approaching womanhood. She had always been a pretty child, with a clear complexion and eyes that sparkled with life, but her form was changing and she was becoming strikingly beautiful.

As she played with the animals, her long thick hair, dark as a moonless sky, cascaded to her waist and flowed in wavelets over her arms and over the body of a small rabbit she now held close to her chest. Her body was slender and graceful, so light that she barely seemed to touch the earth when she walked. Her large almond-shaped eyes matched the color of her hair and shone with joy. As she had progressed from childhood to womanhood, her eyes had grown deeper, like pools that had no bottom, and they reflected not only the joy that was her being, but also a knowledge, a wisdom, and a deep calm that affected us all. When she looked at you, you knew that she was seeing more than your outer form. She was gazing deep into the inner recesses of your being so that she could alleviate any worry or cause for pain. This was her manner. Her complexion was a few shades lighter than mine and emitted a soft golden hue. Her face, though slender, had a fullness to it and bore no imperfections, no marks. I could not imagine a more beautiful person.

As I was admiring her beauty, Mata suddenly laid the rabbit on the ground and came over to me, seated herself beside me and said in a quiet tone, "Meenakshi, you shouldn't feel that your father did not love you. He loved you a great deal. Love is expressed not only by words, but also by actions."

Caught completely off guard, I was taken aback by her words and didn't know how to respond. "Don't you remember when he would sit by your bed at night and watch until you fell asleep? That was a sign of his love. And when he would bring you along at night to receive Pitaji's blessing before going to bed. That was also a sign of his love." She spoke as if she had been there with me, witnessing these small acts of caring, of which I had taken no note. I couldn't stop the tears from coming to my eyes. As she spoke, images came before me, memories that I had long suppressed. I struggled to keep my composure and my tears in check, feeling as if I were the child and she the adult.

But he never told me that he loved me, I thought.

She replied to my thought. "That doesn't mean he didn't love you." With her endearing smile she added, "Vasundhara Ma does not speak her love for us and yet she loves us, all of us, every creature and plant and even the stones, for they are a part of her, too."

"The earth loves us?" My voice shook as I watched her hands caringly caress the ground beneath us.

She nodded. "Before I was born here, after I had heard Pitaji and Ma calling for me to take birth, Vasundhara Ma appeared before me and said that she would take me to them. She said, 'They will love you just as I do.' That is how I know her love for us, and I will be ever grateful to her for guiding me here." Her expression had softened and displayed great tenderness she spoke these words. Then turning to me, she placed her delicate hand on my arm and said, "And I love you, Meenakshi."

After speaking those precious words, she caught sight of the rabbits again and scampered off. I was deeply touched by her expression of love. Never before had I heard those words "I love you."

Mata stirred something deep within me that day. Usha saw my distracted state and said quietly, "Meenakshi, I will look after Mata. You can go spend some time alone."

I thanked her and retreated to my room, where the tears could flow freely. I allowed myself to be the child again and cry for the father I had lost and perhaps never really appreciated. My tears were also an expression of gratitude for Mata, for the love she had expressed. All the memories of tender moments with my father returned to me, and for the first time I felt his love.

Sometime later that day I made my way to Aditi, who was very ill and in her last days. I told her what had happened. She was in a much weakened state, but she managed to smile and whisper, "Of course your father loved you. You were everything to him, and whatever he did, however stern he seemed, it was his way of protecting you, Meenakshi." She was quiet for a few minutes. "I believe he gave his life so you could advance in this household. Look what blessings have come upon you now. Your father's devotion and loyalty played a large role, Meenakshi. Never doubt that. His sacrifice enabled you to be in the position you now are in. His sacrifice and Janak Baba's love for him."

I looked at her questioningly. She nodded. "So that is why he saved me that day in the river," I murmured. "His love for my father."

"That was his love for you, Meenakshi."

"For me?" I exclaimed in disbelief.

Aditi sighed and gathered her strength. "Have you not noticed his love for all of us, the care he takes for everyone in the household? Despite all his responsibilities, he comes often to check on me, to see whether there is anything I need, to ask what he can do to make me more comfortable, and I am just a servant. It is beyond me to understand such love. And Rajakumari Sita has that same quality."

I nodded, overcome by the emotions that were gushing up. When I could speak again I asked, "But Aditi, how could Mata have known this pain that was long buried in my heart?"

"There are many things about Mata that we will never understand. But one thing is for certain, she has brought joy to this household and to all of Mithila, such as we never had before. She exudes the love that Janak Baba has but does not display so openly. Sometimes I think she is love itself." Aditi's voice had grown very faint, and feeling that I had tired her I started to take my leave, but then I turned and took her hand.

"You have meant a lot to me, Aditi, all these years." She smiled. When she saw the tears gathering, she said, "Do not cry for me, Meenakshi. A new chapter has begun for you, and I must continue with my journey." I knew that this would be our last conversation, so I stayed by her side, but with her eyes she indicated it was time for me to leave. And so internally saying my last goodbye, I let go of her hand and of another part of my past.

From that day I was healed of the pain of feeling myself an unloved child. Some years after this episode, I was to discover that I was not the only servant healed of an inner pain. Many in the household, and I dare say our kingdom, experienced healing of one sort of another from our dear beloved Mata.

SOMA'S ARRIVAL

Some years after Sita's arrival, the Maharani gave birth to a daughter named Urmila. Sita and Urmila had two girl cousins who also lived with them, and so the house became very busy with children. When Sita was around 12, a young servant girl named Soma, only a few years older than Sita, showed up at the palace. The Maharaja took her in without much questioning, and she became Sita's personal attendant. Almost immediately she began calling our Rani "Mata," as did the rest of us.

Soma was an attractive girl, with a round face and broad smile. She was about the same height as Mata, but not nearly as slender. Although she was pretty, her appearance was very modest as she did nothing to enhance herself. She kept her hair tied up at all times, covered by a cloth, as if to keep it out of the way so she could engage in any kind of work. And as I was to discover, no work was too humble for Soma.

There was something very special about Soma, a quality of humility and service, a maturity and wisdom far beyond her years, and a quiet dignity that reminded me much of my father. When I was young I thought my father the ideal servant, who never had a thought of himself, whose every action was for the benefit of the one he served. Soma displayed the same qualities: no task was too menial for her, and she was always the first to perform the tasks that needed to be done. Beyond that, she seemed to know Mata's wishes and thoughts before they were even expressed. If Mata had a desire for a sweet, Soma had already prepared it. If Mata wanted to collect flowers or fruits for a puja, Soma had ready exactly what Mata needed. Mata took this in due course and never seemed surprised by Soma's near perfect attunement with her wishes.

I became very fond of her and found myself seeking her counsel on many matters, although she was young enough to be my child. I began to think of Soma almost as an extension of Mata herself.

It was around the time when Soma came that Mata approached me as we were sitting outside gathering flowers for the evening puja. She suddenly made a motion as if to remove something covering me. "What is it, Mata?" I asked, thinking she was trying to brush some insect away from my shoulders. Suddenly she drew back with a look of surprise on her face.

"I cannot remove it."

"Remove what?" I asked. "Are insects fluttering around me?" I looked at my shoulders and over my back but could see nothing.

She shook her head. "No, Meenakshi. I see a cloud around you, but I can't remove it. I am so sorry."

"A cloud? I don't see any cloud, Mata."

"Never mind," she replied in a soothing voice. "I will speak with Pitaji about it."

In my room that night I pondered over the incident. What had Mata seen that disturbed her? I had come to understand that she had special abilities and could see and know things that none of us could see or know. It was as if she could read our minds and hearts, but she was ever so modest about displaying what she knew. Perhaps she saw the misfortune that had come over my family and that still weighed down my heart, despite the joy of Mata's presence.

Soma had been within hearing distance of our conversation and the next day approached me. "Meenakshi, you must trust Mata. If she saw something amiss, do not worry; she will take care of it."

I nodded. "That is also what I felt," I replied with a faint smile.

"Many of us have received healings from her, and I trust she will . . . take care of it." My voice trailed off. I had grown so close to Soma and at that moment I thought to share with her my family secret—that we had been subjected to great misfortune some generations back—but I could not even find the words to utter. In fact, I did not myself understand it because my father never spoke of the past, so what I could say? I stopped myself as the thought entered my mind that this family matter must stay buried deep in my heart.

Mata's beauty was such now that whenever she went out, people could not help but gaze at her in wonderment. Mata seemed not to notice, but this did not make Janak Baba happy. I overheard him say to Sunaina Ma on several occasions that he wanted the people of Mithila to see her inner beauty, not her outer appearance. The people of Mithila may have treasured her physical perfection, but we in the household saw and loved most the generosity of her heart. If anyone who was suffering crossed her path, or if she heard of a misfortune falling to any family in Mithila, she would be the first to offer aid as if her nearest and dearest had been struck down. Janak Baba saw this and did not discourage it, but what he most appreciated was her mind.

Mata had learned from Sage Gargi the art of spiritual debate, and Janak Baba loved to engage her. Initially he would always win the debate, challenging her with a profound question that she struggled to answer. But this did not last long, and soon she was responding with great insight, or so we, the servants, were told, and Janak Baba would assume a look of satisfaction and appreciation. Then there came the day when she won the debate, posing difficult philosophical questions that he could not answer.

We, in the kitchen, were stunned when we were told that Janak Baba had yielded to his young daughter, saying he had not yet experienced the state of which she spoke.

"You are now my teacher," he said to her.

"Never say that, Pitaji," she replied, placing her fingers over his lips. "I am just your daughter, always your daughter."

He smiled and responded, "Sita, your mind is like a multi-faceted jewel, more insightful than most minds I have encountered. You must always use it to serve the world. There is no other purpose. Never let pride enter. That is the downfall of so many, even of the great teachers."

A beautiful form, a brilliant mind, and a most tender heart, yet Mata seemed oblivious or uncaring of her qualities. Her dress was simple. Her speech was humble. Her love was for the freedom of the forest, to wander at will, to observe the bountiful manifestations of nature and to love and enjoy them all.

A few years after Soma's arrival, Mata began to spend more and more time alone, wandering off into the forest while we were all engaged in other activities. When it would come to our attention that she was nowhere to be found, I would get anxious. Soma always reassured me and would go herself into the forest to find her. On one such occasion, Sunaina Ma had been looking for Sita but she was nowhere to be found. She approached me to inquire about Sita, but I only shook my head. "I have not seen her since last evening," I replied. Looking uneasy, she murmured, "Urmila also has not seen her, and she did not show up for the morning meal. She has been gone a long time."

Then Sunaina Ma inquired of Soma, who responded as I did but then added, "I think I know where to find her."

I glanced at Soma, knowing what she meant. When Sita wanted to walk in the forest to experience its beauty and to be with the animals, she would not go alone. She would always invite her sister, or her cousins, and one of the servants. But when she wanted to commune with the deities in meditation, she would often slip away before any of us noticed. "I believe she left for the forest alone very early this morning," she replied quietly. "I will try to bring her back."

"Please, Soma, go quickly and ask her to return to the palace," requested Sunaina Ma. "A number of sages are coming tonight, including Sage Gargi, and I know Sita will want to serve them their evening meal and sit with them this evening. She must get ready." The sun had passed the midway point in the sky and there were not many hours left of daylight. The sages would soon arrive and Sita always insisted on serving them herself.

Soma left, and I waited anxiously. Not long after this conversation, Sunaina Ma sought me out and asked if Soma and Sita had arrived. I shook my head.

"What could have happened?" she mused. I could see that she was concerned and so hurried to assure her. "I will go and see what has kept them, perhaps an animal in need." Sunaina Ma nodded her head. We all knew of Sita's care for the animals. If there had been an injury or an attack on an animal, Sita would attend to it and not leave until she had done what she could. "Yes, go Meenakshi, and tell them to hurry back."

It had been some years since I had frequented the forest, as it was usually Soma who now accompanied Mata on her walks, so I cautiously entered the thicket of trees and followed the narrow path. I called out to them, at first in a quiet voice and then more forcefully. "Soma. Mata." There was no answer. I continued to call out as I entered more deeply into the groves.

Finally I saw the figure of Soma approaching. She was alone.

"Where is Mata?" I asked in alarm. "Sunaina Ma has sent me to find you both."

The smile that always adorned Soma's face was gone. In its place was an expression of concern. Her face was pale, and her voice vibrated with a slight quiver as she replied, "She is deep in meditation. I think she has entered a very high state and I cannot bring her back. She has not moved since I arrived and sits there still as a rock. Hurry back and ask Janak Baba to come. And bring water and some fruits for when she returns to waking consciousness."

Without a word I turned around and ran as fast as I could over the rock-strewn path, making my way through bramble and heavily-wooded growth. As I neared the edge of the forest, something caught my clothing and, before I could prevent it, I fell to the ground and twisted my ankle. Tears filled my eyes. I could not stop now. I had to get to the Maharaja. "Mata, give me the strength to carry on," I prayed as I forced myself to my feet and with much difficulty made my way into the palace. There I encountered Kiran, leaving the kitchen area.

"What happened, Meenakshi?" he asked in a concerned voice. "Why are you limping? Are you hurt?"

I shook my head. "I must find Janak Baba. Do you know where he is?"

"In the state room, with his guests. They have all arrived. They are ready for the evening meal, but everyone is waiting for Mata." He paused and then glanced down at my leg. "But what is wrong with your foot? You are limping. I can get one of the servants to go to Janak Baba if you need him."

"No, no," I hurried to reply. "I am fine really, but I must go." Taking my leave I did my best to wobble to the state room.

I heard their voices as I approached, but as I reached the doorway, I stopped. Never before had I entered that room without being called there. It would be presumptuous of me to enter, but Janak Baba was needed. What was I to do? I retreated a few steps, undecided, when I heard him call for me to enter.

I tried to steady my steps as I entered the room and pranammed to Janak Baba and the gathered sages.

"What has happened to you, Meenakshi? Why are you limping?" he asked.

"It is nothing," I replied in barely more than a whisper. "Soma has sent me to request your presence. She is with Rajakumari Sita in the forest and says it is urgent that you come."

"Is anything wrong?" he asked in a voice of concern.

"I don't know. She says it is urgent."

Janak Baba closed his eyes and stayed this way for several minutes. Then opening his eyes, he murmured, "It is what I thought. I have long been afraid of the day when she would remember where she came from." As Janak Baba excused himself from the assembled sages, Sage Gargi asked if she could accompany him. He nodded, and calling for Usha, he instructed her to take care of serving the evening meal. Then Janak Baba asked four guards to fire the torches to light the way as darkness had already set in.

As best I could I wobbled off to gather a few fruits in a basket and fill a small jug of water. My ankle was now throbbing. With great pain, I led him to where I had met Soma. She was not there, but when I called out to her she emerged and guided us to where Sita was seated in the immobile position, locked like a lotus flower in an utterly still pond, showing not the slightest flutter of life. I had never seen her like this, and my heart pounded at the thought that she may have left us. A cry escaped from my lips, but Soma put her hand on my arm to still me.

"There is no breath in her," murmured Soma to Janak Baba. "I arrived just after midday but she had been missing since early morning and I suspect has been like this since then." Soma and I retreated a short distance as Janak Baba uttered a mantra and entered meditation. Sage Gargi began to chant Vedic hymns. Several hours passed with him in silent meditation and Sage Gargi chanting. Finally Janak Baba rose and asked me to bring all the sages. "I cannot bring her back, but perhaps collectively we can entreat her to return," he said solemnly.

As Soma saw my condition, she asked me to stay put. She took two of the guards to light the way and returned to the palace. The sages knew nothing of what had transpired and thought it very strange that the Maharaja had disappeared so suddenly with no explanation and had still not returned. It was getting late, and they were eager to retire. They were not pleased with the situation, but when Soma arrived and explained in a sorrowful voice that due to Sita's condition the Maharaja was requesting them to come to the forest and hold their discussions there in her presence, they all nodded, saying they were eager to be of assistance. Soma added, "The Maharaja is hoping that your presence will help bring our beloved Rani back to us."

She led them into the forest where Janak Baba and Sage Gargi were meditating by Sita's side. Some of the servants accompanied them, bringing cushions and torches. The six sages made a semi-circle around Sita and began chanting Vedic invocation. They meditated, then discussed their perceptions, followed by more meditation and more discussion. At one point Janak Baba stopped participating and entered what appeared to be the same state as Sita. He sat there still as rock, without any movement and seemingly without any breath. And so the night passed. Leaning against a tree, I drifted into a semi-sleep state, but as the night wore on the pain in my foot increased until I could no longer find a comfortable position. Soma saw me squirming and realized that I had hurt myself quite badly. Searching for something to wrap around my foot, she finally tore part of her shawl and, despite my protestations, bandaged my leg. This eased the pain enough for me to drift off into a shallow sleep.

At the first rays of dawn, the chanting began again, mingling with the chatter of the assembly of birds. Together they made a most beautiful symphony of sounds. My eyes opened to an almost unearthly scene. The greenery of the forest glittered ever so gently in the early rays of dawn; a soft hue had settled over the forest floor. Many small animals had come close to us in the night to observe this most unusual gathering. It appeared as if we had all awakened to another world, more beautiful than even our earth, if that was possible. I glanced at Sita, hoping that she had returned to the world, but she remained locked in the meditation pose. And Janak Baba was still deep in meditation. The chanting went on for some time and, when it ceased, the sages began discussing the nature of what they had experienced the night before. One of the sages remarked that he had entered a state he had never before experienced. Another concurred.

It was then that I saw Janak Baba slowly open his eyes, a look of extreme joy painted across his face. He listened quietly as the sages continued to comment on the nature of their experiences. Suddenly I saw a movement. Mata had shifted her position ever so slightly. Everyone seemed to catch this subtle movement of her hands, and the sages fell silent with all eyes turned to her. She didn't stir again for some time, but finally her eyes cracked open. The first one she saw was Janak Baba, and she smiled, opening her eyes wider, her face exuding such love. "Pitaji," she whispered. "You are here?"

He also hadn't spoke before this moment. But he nodded and said very slowly, "We are all here, Sita. You could not come to us, and so we came to you to share in your ecstasy." Sita looked around and seemed surprised to see us all gathered, not quite grasping what had happened. And so Janak Baba continued, "You came here early yesterday morning and went into deep meditation. Soma could not bring you back, nor could I. So I brought the sages who had come yesterday to this spot where you are."

For some time everyone sat in silence, as if still enjoying their inner experience, and then Mata noticed the basket of fruits and the pitcher of water before her. Asking the sages to excuse her for not serving them the evening meal last night, she slowly rose and gave each one a piece of fruit and some water. Then Janak Baba asked the guards to guide everyone back to the palace for the morning meal. "I will join you shortly," he said. As I rose to leave, I quietly winced in pain. Mata noticed this and asked me to stay behind with Soma, saying that she would apply some medicine.

When the others had left, he asked very gently, "Where had you gone, my daughter? I could not find you anywhere in the ethers."

She replied simply, "To him."

"To whom?" he asked.

"To the one I will marry. It was he who brought me back. When he uttered the words 'soon we will be re-united,' this body came alive again. Had he not arrived, I would have merged into the great ocean of being."

"I will be ever grateful to him for bringing you back to this world," he replied with deep emotion. "I was afraid you would disappear into the absolute, and my Sita would be with us no more. I am not yet prepared for that."

Sita smiled. "You know I would not leave without first taking your permission. You, who have called me to this world, will be the one to release me." This was the promise Sita made to her father that day in the forest.

Janak Baba smiled. "Let us go have some food with our guests."

"You go ahead, Pitaji. I must first attend to Meenakshi's wounded ankle." As he rose to leave, she added with a knowing smile, "I see you also dove into that blissful sea."

He pranammed and replied very solemnly, "No sage has been able to transmit the experience that I received in your presence last night. If you were not my daughter I would . . . ."

"Pitaji, say no more," she replied, gazing lovingly at him. "What came to you last night was the result of your many years of effort."

Janak Baba seemed reluctant to leave her, but Mata laughed and said, "Don't worry, Pitaji. I have given you my word. I will not disappear from here."

"I will go see to our guests then. But do not stay long. Your mother, I know, is eager to see you."

Once he was gone, Mata directed Soma down a nearby path and described in detail the plant that she would find. Then she reached over to unwrap the bandage that Soma had improvised. I instinctively tried to withdraw my leg, but Mata would not let go of it.

"Please, Mata. It is nothing, really. I just need to rest a bit longer."

"You have been resting all night and look at the swelling. The medicine will help." My ankle was now twice its normal size and the throbbing was relentless. It was difficult to keep the tears from welling up.

"I am your servant, Mata, please," I murmured quietly, trying again to withdraw my leg.

Holding on to my leg, she touched the swollen ankle very gently and said, "And I am the servant of the world, Meenakshi. How can I not take care of your wound when I have the means."

"I am sorry for this mishap, Mata. I don't want to trouble you in any way,"

"Sorry, for what, Meenakshi? It is not your fault that you tripped."

"It is my misfortune, Mata, to have tripped, the misfortune that has followed me from birth."

"Misfortune?" she paused and looked at me thoughtfully and then said, "Ah, yes, the curse. It is true, but you should not succumb to that, Meenakshi."

"Curse, Mata?" I looked at her questioningly, confused by her words.

She didn't respond right away, but then she murmured, "Your father never told you. Perhaps he thought it better." I didn't know what she was referring to and so kept quiet. She looked away as if debating whether to say more. After several minutes, she turned her eyes to me, those eyes that always radiated such kindness and care. "Your father's death was due to the curse cast upon your family generations go. It had nothing to do with you."

I gazed at her, confused by her reference to something I knew nothing about. I was startled by her words but tried not to show the emotions that churned within me.

She continued. "Five generations ago a great sage cursed your ancestor, and that curse was to extend for five generations. You are the last to be affected by this. Your father did everything in his power to try to lift the curse from you, but even Pitaji could not negate what was done. When a great sage utters a curse, it cannot be reversed. The power of the words vibrates in the ethers and brings about the intended effect."

"A curse, Mata?" I muttered in disbelief as if I had not understood her properly.

She nodded.

"For five generations?" I asked. Again she nodded. "But why?" My voice began to tremble. "What could my ancestor have done to bring this upon his descendants?"

She didn't answer right away but finally said, "A misdeed with a young woman whose family was under the protection of the sage. To misbehave in such a way is a very grave infraction." I couldn't believe what I was hearing. "That is when your family lost their standing in society, their land, everything. They were shunned, but the Janak family took in the son of the one who was cursed, your great-grandfather, as a servant. He had a very hard life, and your grandfather as well. The curse weakened with your father, but it left him with a great sadness, and of course the misfortune of losing your brother and mother."

"Brother?" I asked again in disbelief. "I had no notion of a brother. I know none of this!"

"You had an elder brother who drowned in the river, soon after you were born. He was about four when one day your mother took him along when she went to the river to bathe. He fell into the rushing water and was swept away. Overcome with grief, your mother could not forgive herself, and one day the river took her as well."

"I thought my mother died of natural causes soon after I was born." I murmured. "My father never told me about a brother, but that must have been why he never allowed me to go to the river. That is why he never spoke to me about my mother. I never understood him, why he was so austere. I thought it was a lack of love, but it was the sadness of losing his family."

Mata nodded. "Your father tried in every way to have the curse lifted from you. When he lay dying, Pitaji went to see him. As he blessed him, Pitaji said he would fulfil any dying wish. Your father asked that you be cared for, that the Janak family always look after you, and that Pitaji do what he could to ease the curse. Pitaji made him that promise."

"This explains why my father forbade me to marry. He always said it would bring nothing but sorrow to me."

"That was his misunderstanding, Meenakshi. Your children would have been free of the curse. You are the last to feel its effect."

"And that is why Janak Baba came to the river that day," I murmured, as I recalled the image of Janak Baba standing by the river as I struggled in the water, commanding the waves to lift me onto the shore.

Mata nodded. "Pitaji told me that story. He said it was your time to die. The river was about to take you as it had taken your brother and mother, but he could not let that be. He had given his word to your father to protect you, and his word was able to counteract the decreasing power of the curse." Mata fell silent and then began again. "Do you remember when I was much younger we were sitting in the garden and I saw a cloud surrounding you. I tried to lift it but could not."

I nodded, recalling that day when she spoke words that I could not understand.

"When I spoke to Pitaji about this, he explained about the curse that was put upon your family. But he said you were mostly freed of it. The only remainder was a sadness from your father's early death. He had managed to weaken its effect on you."

"But how unjust, Mata, that my father and I should be punished for a misdeed of an ancestor we never knew, however serious that misdeed may be."

"You are right, Meenakshi. This is exactly what I said to Pitaji when he told me this story. I asked him if it would not be better for society to sit in judgement than to have a sage have such power to control a person's fate. He explained that society was not yet ready to assume this responsibility, but that one day it would be so. In earlier times the laws were kept through the words of the sages. But too many now are filled with their own power and are exceeding their boundaries." Mata's eyes assumed a firmness as she gazed off into the distance, as if setting in motion the determination for another way to administer justice. Then, as if speaking to herself, she mused, "I have heard of too many injustices committed by the sages through their curses. Though wise they may be, they also have emotions, preferences, likes and dislikes. Few have risen above that, and only when they are beyond their personal feelings can they truly administer justice. I long to meet such a person. Pitaji is the closest I have found."

I was too shocked to take in fully the meaning of Mata's words. When I turned my head, I saw Soma standing nearby with the basket of medicinal plants and my mind turned to my aching ankle. I again became aware of the pain. Mata saw this and took the plants from Soma. She pounded the plants with a stone, squeezing out every bit of oil, and then she had Soma apply the oil to my aching ankle. "Now you must stay off of your feet. If you apply this ointment every few hours, in a few days you will be much better." Then turning to Soma she asked her to go back to the palace and see if she could find Kiran. "Ask him to come quickly," she said. Then turning to me, she said, "Do not resist, Meenakshi. Kiran can help you back to the palace."

"But, Mata, see I can stand," I tried to raise myself but fell back. My foot was unable to bear any weight.

"Will you disobey me?" She asked in surprise. I shook my head. "Then you must stay off your feet, at least for today." Before long Soma arrived with Kiran. When he saw my state, a look of alarm crossed his face.

"She will be fine, Kiran, do not worry, but you must carry her back to her room. She is not to put any weight on her foot until tomorrow at the earliest, and Soma, you must continue to rub the ointment on her ankle throughout the rest of the day."

I drew back as Kiran tried to lift me. Never had I been touched by a man other than my father, and I resisted. I gazed in shock at Mata, who whispered to me, "It is only Kiran. That is why I called him. He is well known to you, like a brother, do not resist. By tomorrow, you will be much better." As we were leaving, Mata sat down again in the spot where she had meditated through the day and night.

"Mata," Soma protested. "Aren't you coming? You have not eaten since yesterday morning."

Mata smiled. "Do not worry, Soma. I will not disappear again. But I need a few minutes here alone before I return. I won't be long." Her face grew serious. Soma still hesitated to leave her, but Mata nodded, indicating that we should leave. "I will soon follow," she said. We could not but obey, and so reluctantly we returned to the palace without her.

True to her word, Mata appeared shortly in the palace. Something had shifted in her, we could see, but I could not pay much attention as I was so distracted by what she had revealed to me. Soma saw me to my room, where I sat alone reviewing my childhood, the many incidents that now were made clear, remarks by my father that now made sense. It was painful to realize that I was the descendant of a cursed man, a man who had committed a most egregious deed. And I realized how few maharajas would have taken in a cursed family. Had it not been for the generosity of the Janak family, what would have happened to us? A few hours later Soma came to apply the medicine and found me in a sorry state. Tears had overtaken me, and I could not hide my red, swollen eyes and disheveled appearance.

"Meenakshi!" she exclaimed. "Are you still in pain!" I shook my head. I didn't know how much of my conversation with Mata she had overheard and so didn't know how to explain my condition. The more I had reflected on Mata's words, the more the import of her words had hit me. My family had been under a curse. My ancestor had committed a great misdeed for which my grandfather, my father and I had to pay.

"Meenakshi," she asked gently, "is it because of what Mata told you?"

I nodded. "Did you overhear?"

"Yes, I heard some of it. Surely you know that everything Mata does is for a reason. If she has told you this, there is a greater purpose.

Perhaps it is to understand that this curse can be viewed as your greatest blessing. If your ancestor had not been cursed, your family would not have been taken in by the Janak family, and then you would not have come under the protection of Janak Baba. If your father had not lived with this curse, he would not have asked Janak Baba to look after you, and most likely you would not be serving Mata. Is there any greater blessing than to serve her?"

I shook my head and wiped my tears. "You are right, Soma. Since childhood I have been told about some misfortune that visited my family. Now I understand. Mata did right to explain this to me. I don't fault my father for keeping this secret as he was a proud man, and it would have insulted his dignity to reveal this to me. And you are so right. I cannot complain about the turn my life has taken. There is no greater blessing than to serve in this household, and to serve Mata is the greatest gift anybody could want."

We were both quiet. Then I said, "So much has happened today that I don't understand."

"Yes, that is true. Mata has entered a new chapter, and we will be the witness to that. But it is a wonderful development. Do you not see the light that emanates from her now? Her whole being radiates."

I laughed. "Soma, you see what others can't see."

Now it was Soma's turn to laugh. "Meenakshi, do not tell me that you have not noticed the abundance that accompanies Mata. Have you not observed how the flowers multiply along the path that she takes, and how the fruits on the trees increase in her presence? This is part of the mystery of Mata."

I shook my head. "Only you have eyes to see this, but I trust your vision. It is through you that I know something of what Mata is."

"Meenakshi, she is *Prakriti*, nature herself in human body. It is who she is. Where she is, nature flourishes. When her energy is withdrawn, nature diminishes. This will become more apparent now."

I smiled. "Among us all, only you understand her, Soma. I cannot. But I can serve her and love her, and I am content with that." Mata did indeed seem to take on a new air after that night in the forest, one that is hard to describe, as if a new maturity flourished in her.

Some weeks later I was in the room of Sunaina Ma, putting away her personal items when Janak Baba entered. I waited for a sign that I should leave, but none came, and so I carried on with my work. For some time Sunaina Ma had been assisting Janak Baba with his governing responsibilities, and she had been passing on this knowledge to Mata with much success. One never knew when Janak Baba would retreat to the forest for an extended time, and in his absence someone had to carry out the affairs of the kingdom according to his wishes. Sunaina Ma recognized Mata's intuitive wisdom and often sought her advice. Mata took an interest in everything pertaining to the kingdom and participated in much of the decision-making, offering her innovative and creative ideas. On this day, however, Janak Baba sought to prepare Sunaina Ma for Mata's approaching departure.

"We must begin to think of organizing a *swayamvara* (practice in ancient India of choosing a husband from a list of suitors by a girl of marriageable age) as Sita is approaching marriageable age," said Janak Baba slowly, knowing he would meet resistance.

Sunaina Ma gave him a look of disapproval. "Why the hurry?" she asked.

"Her training is now complete. I feel she is ready."

"But I am not," protested Sunaina Ma.

"Will you ever be?"

"You are just setting up the village councils. Let her be part of that and learn. Then we can consider it," she pleaded.

"You have a good point," conceded Janak Baba. "We will move quickly to set up the village councils, but you and I must prepare ourselves, because I feel the time for her departure is approaching."

As Janak Baba was retreating more and more from governing, he had the idea to set up local councils in each village so that the villagers could take care of many local matters by themselves. It was a novel notion, which at first had been met with disapproval from the ministers. But Janak Baba was insistent. I heard him say repeatedly that people must learn to govern themselves.

"But they are not ready," was the frequent response.

"Then we must help them be ready. It is the way of the future. People must learn to administer the affairs of their community."

Even the hermitages were not pleased with the idea. At one gathering of heads of hermitages, the discussion turned to this matter. During a heated moment, Janak Baba turned to Sita and asked her opinion. Soma and I were standing by the doorway waiting to bring in the evening meal.

Sita was quiet and thoughtful. Then she said, "Until now, justice has often been administered through the sages, through their blessings . . . and curses. That cannot continue," she said with a touch of sadness in her voice. "Too many innocents have been affected. Surely we can find another way. These councils can help administer justice."

Sita realized that this would diminish the power of the sages. Their curses kept people in fear of them, and so she added, "Fear is not the way to justice. I think a fairer way is to let the people decide the best means of dealing with a misdeed, and let those who have mis-stepped have a chance to redress their wrongs. That is most important. A curse cannot be undone, but a punishment can be reversed if someone shows true remorse and an earnest desire to correct oneself."

Rarely did any of the sages object to anything Sita said, but on this occasion, they rose in protest, with only a few exceptions. Janak Baba intervened and spoke sternly to them. "I agree fully with Sita, but perhaps society is not yet ready for this. Let us begin by trying to organize these councils, giving each village some limited responsibility for its local affairs. This will be a beginning." He assured the ministers and heads of the hermitages that their authority would not be weakened by this new arrangement. The ministers would have to oversee the new councils, and the hermitages would still set the moral tone for the society. At least for the moment, the power of the curse would remain in place.

SITA'S MARRIAGE

Rajakumari Sita was not destined to rule Videha, although it is what we all hoped and prayed for. She spent many months traveling with Janak Baba throughout the kingdom as he set up local councils, identifying leaders and directing them on how to manage their local affairs. For many of the villagers, Rajakumari Sita's presence was an indication that she was one day to be the Maharaja's successor. Maharaja Janak perceived this expectation and knew that he had to squash it, lest it lead to much disappointment. So the conversation of a swayamvara took place again. And again Sunaina Ma objected, pleading for more time.

"We are doing the kingdom an injustice by allowing the people to believe that one day she will govern here, when we know this to be untrue, Sunaina," Janak Baba told her in a firm voice.

"But then why have you given her this training, this knowledge, if not to govern?"

"She will bring this knowledge wherever she goes. It is for the future, and not just for Mithila."

She sighed. "I cannot image any man worthy of her."

"He has already made himself known to her, and I assure you he is worthy."

"Where is he? Who can this man be?"

Janak Baba shook his head, saying he didn't know, but he recounted what Sita had told him that day in the forest many months earlier.

"We should not stand in the way of their union. Let us organize the swayamvara. I am sure he will appear and Sita will recognize him."

There was nothing more Sunaina Ma could say.

Mata did not object when her father told her it was time to organize the swayamvara. But one evening as they were sitting together, and Soma and I were serving them sweets, I heard Janak Baba mention that ever since he had announced the swayamvara, her mood had changed.

"Will I know him?" Mata asked in an uncertain voice "Will I recognize him?"

"He did appear to you, Sita. You saw his form."

She shook her head. "I heard his voice. I felt his presence, but I did not see a form."

He was quiet for a few minutes and then said, "Sita, everything that has come to you, all the events of your life, seem to have been predetermined, as if you had orchestrated it before being born. I have no doubt that this will be the same."

She smiled. "You have a way of easing my every concern. I will put the matter out of my mind."

The swayamvara was still weeks away. All the rajahs in the Aryan region had been invited. Sita did indeed put the matter out of her mind by spending time in the villages and helping with the seeding of the fields. Janak Baba had taught all the farmers how to use a newly-developed plough that made the readying of their fields for planting so much quicker and easier, despite the heavy labor it entailed. Sita now had the desire to learn the same. One day, just before the swayamvara, she took Soma and me to one of the nearby farms and indicated her desire to help them plough the field. There was great resistance. Allowing the Maharaja to perform this arduous task was one thing, but the Rani? That was quite another! But Mata insisted. Through an unexplained show of strength, she was able to proceed, seemingly without much effort. Several minutes later she dropped the plough and fell on her knees, digging her hands deep into the soil. Soma and I ran to her, thinking she might be in need of help, but she had no such need.

"Look, Soma," she said. "Look at Vasundhara Ma, the gift she has given us. There is vital life in the soil that prevents illness, that keeps our bodies well, life that we cannot see or touch. As long as we keep our soil pure, disease will stay away. This is the gift of Vasundhara Ma." Her face was glowing as she lifted handfuls of dark, rich soil, and rubbed it against her check and then kissed the very dirt that gives us life. "How little do we think of where our food comes from," she murmured. "How little do we appreciate this treasure she has given." Sita released the dirt and stood up. Looking off into the distance, she murmured, "He is here. I feel his presence." She then went back to ploughing.

After she had completed her task, Sita thanked the farmer for allowing her to help and then inquired about the chariot that had stopped while she was in the field.

"It was the two *rajahs* (kings or princes) from Ayodhya," he replied. They had stopped to request water for their horses.

"Ayodhya," Sita murmured to herself. She seemed lost in thought.

"Yes, one of the rajahs noticed you in the field and asked about the woman ploughing the soil. He said that he had never seen a plough like that or imagined a woman could use such an instrument."

"What did you tell him?"

"I told him it was Rajakumari Sita. He seemed very surprised, but he smiled and said he was eager to meet the woman who could accomplish such a feat. Clearly, he doesn't know our Rani," said the farmer affectionately.

A flutter moved through Mata's body when she heard his words. She turned to Soma and I could see the look that passed between them. I wondered if the rajah from Ayodhya was the one for whom she was waiting.

During the evening meal, Sunaina Ma teased Mata about her use of the plough. "How is it possible that our daughter could use such an instrument, when the farmers themselves struggle?"

With a gleam in his eye, Janak Baba turned to Mata and said, "Tell her, dear, how you accomplished such a feat."

"It is a matter of the mind, Ma. I don't have the needed strength in my body, but my mind overcame that weakness. It instructed my body what to do, and my body merely followed. It is the training Pitaji has given me."

Sunaina Ma shook her head. "I am sure the whole kingdom will be speaking of it."

"And the rajahs from Ayodhya," inserted Urmila, who had heard the story of their arrival as it had already circulated through the household.

"They have come?" asked Sunaina Ma in surprise. "Didn't we receive a response from Maharaja Dasaratha that they were away at the hermitage of Rishi Vishwamitra?"

"It seems they have come for another purpose, to view Mahadev's bow. But no doubt they will participate in the swayamvara." He gazed at Sita as he spoke, aware of the quiver that was passing through her. Mata looked away as not to betray her feelings. Suddenly it dawned on Sunaina Ma that the rajahs had seen Sita ploughing in the field. A look of dismay crossed her face.

"They have seen you ploughing, Sita. What will they think?" Mata didn't respond.

"They will think what an amazing daughter we have," Janak Baba was quick to reply. "Whoever wins Sita's hand will have to know who she is and will have to respect her knowledge. As far as I am concerned, that is the only requirement."

"Then why have we set the test to be the lifting of Mahadev's bow?"

"Ma, it is not strength that is needed to lift that bow," said Sita. "I did it as a child. That bow can only be raised by the one Mahadev allows to lift it. It is his will that will prevail. That is the reason for this requirement."

Janak Baba smiled. He had never told this to Sita, but he was pleased that she knew it. It was not strength alone that would determine who her husband would be. It was Mahadev's will and, as he was increasingly coming to understand, Sita's will as well.

It was at the temple that they first met. Mata was performing *aarti* (ritual of light) before the *murti* (statue) of Parvati Ma. He had heard of the temple's beauty and was drawn by the otherworldly singing that drifted over the hills and through the trees of Mithila. It rose to his senses like a celestial song. Mata was dressed in her best finery, as was always the case when she went to the temple. Two servants, Usha and Rohana, carried the fruits and flowers for the puja. Soma was with them.

They did not notice his approach, but they did notice Mata's voice grow softer and softer as she completed the aarti. When she had finished, she turned and saw him standing but a few feet from her. The servants also became aware of the presence of the two rajahs from Ayodhya. Mata froze and, for several minutes, they didn't know whether our Mata was in our world or another. The one who appeared to be the elder of the rajahs also seemed to freeze. Nobody spoke, nobody moved. It was the younger rajah who broke the silence, introducing himself as Lakshman and his brother Ram. Urmila responded by introducing herself and Sita. Still there was silence between the elder prince of Ayodhya and Mata, although they continued to gaze at one another as if in a stupor. No one knew what was taking place between them.

"So you are Rajakumari Sita," Shri Ram finally said. "I saw you the other day in the field. From a distance I could see you lift the soil to your checks so tenderly, with the love of a mother embracing her child."

"Yes, that was me. We teach the people of Videha to love and honor Vasundhara Ma," she replied softly. "She is the source of our strength."

"I would like to learn your ways, so I can bring this knowledge back to Ayodhya and all of the Kosala Kingdom."

"And we are happy to share with you our knowledge," came a booming voice from the back of the temple. "I am happy to receive you, sons of Maharaja Dasaratha." Janak Baba was overjoyed to meet them. After receiving them warmly, he said, "Ram, your fame precedes you. All of Mithila has heard of your deeds. It is a great honor to have you here in our kingdom. And I would be happy to share with you our methods of farming."

That night, as Rohana, Usha, Soma and I were serving the evening meal, Sunaina Ma stopped us and asked with a discrete smile. "I am told you all saw the rajahs from Ayodhya at the temple today. I was not so fortunate to be there. Tell me, how did they look, how did they appear? Sita will tell me nothing. She is silent when I ask about them, as is the Maharaja." All eyes turned to Sita, but she kept eating as if the conversation did not concern her.

Rohana was the first to respond. "Maharani, never have I seen such strength in a man, the older rajah. His arms, his chest, such perfection," she gushed.

"And such beauty," replied Usha. "I did catch a glimpse of his face and saw such perfectly formed features, so well proportioned."

Sunaina Ma pressed her, asking for some description, but she was speechless and could not say more.

"And you, Meenakshi?" Sunaina Ma asked.

"I am sorry to say I was not there."

Turning to Soma she asked eagerly, "How did he appear? What did you see about him?"

Soma didn't answer and so the Maharani prodded her. "Share with us, Soma. It seems they are all referring to the elder rajah, Ram. How did he appear to you?"

"Maharani, please excuse me, but I don't know how to answer your question."

"What do you mean?" she asked. "You were there."

"Maharani, I was blinded by the light coming from his form. The light was so strong, I had to turn my eyes away."

Mata had put aside her food and was listening the whole time to this exchange. Suddenly she interjected with a smile, "Soma sees what I see. But Soma, you must learn to look steadily into the light.

73

If you had, you would have seen his celestial form as I did. Never look away from the light."

"I did turn away but then when I looked at him again, I did see his form, his human form, Mata." Turning to Sunaina Ma, she continued, "I don't really know how to describe him. Rohana is right about his strength. He is not as tall as our Maharaja, but his chest is broader, and every muscle seems defined. And Usha is right about his beauty. The features of his face are quite fine, with a slender, straight nose and full lips. His complexion is like Mata's but slightly more golden. His hair falls to his shoulders and is not quite as dark as Mata's. He keeps it loose so that it frames his face. There is a dignity about him, in the way he carries himself. I was close enough for a moment to catch a glimpse of his eyes, and I have no words to describe them, just as I cannot describe our Mata's eyes."

Sita laughed at her words and then commented, "You describe only his outer form, Soma."

Soma was quiet for a few minutes and then added, "He seemed so . . . so approachable, not at all distant and formal like so many of the rajahs, but very personable, almost modest. So he seemed to me . . . but it is impossible to truly describe . . . ." Her voice trailed off.

Sita turned to her mother and said with a smile, "Everyone will see him differently, Ma. You will have to wait and see how he appears to you."

As they were discussing thus, I recalled an earlier conversation that had taken place before the arrival of the rajahs from Ayodhya when one night over the evening meal, Sunaina Ma had spoken of Shri Ram's achievements, his bravery and courage that enabled him to slay the demoness Taraka. A frown had crossed Sita's face. Seeing her troubled look, Janak Baba had turned to Sita and asked, "Why this dismay, Sita?"

"I wonder if such violence is necessary. And the slaying of a woman, is that not against the laws of nature?"

All eyes had turned to Mata in surprise. In a grave tone Janak Baba responded, "I would never question any deed performed by

Ram. What he did was for the benefit of the whole region."

Mata had not pressed the point, but it was clear that she was not satisfied with his response. Janak Baba had then quickly turned the conversation to Ram's freeing of Lady Ahilya from the curse that had been imposed upon her by her husband, Gautama Maharishi. The story, commonly told, was that the beautiful Ahilya had been tricked and seduced by Indra, the king of the gods. Gautama was angered when he discovered this betrayal and cursed the innocent Ahilya to become like stone. "No sage in all of Videha has had the courage to go near her, yet alone attempt to free her. And who would even have the power to reverse a curse?" he asked, gazing at Sita. "And yet Ram approached her as he would his own mother and freed her from her agony. Is there any compassion greater than that?"

Sita had been visibly moved. "That was a very great deed. She was unjustly cursed through no cause of her own. The story as it is told is not what truly happened, but the important thing is that Ram freed her. How rare for someone to undo a curse! Even our rishis cannot accomplish this. Again we see how these curses of the sages affect the innocents. That someone so pure and wise as Sage Ahilya, who is a rishi in her own right, would be so afflicted, causes me much pain."

"Someday perhaps someone will be able rectify this, Sita. Increasingly we see that the sages are abusing their power, and perhaps it is time for it now to be withdrawn," Janak Baba had then said.

As I recalled this conversation, I wondered if Mata's concern over the killing of Taraka would influence her feelings for the rajah from Ayodhya. But, fortunately, it was not to be so.

The bow of Lord Mahadev had rested in the palace temple for

many, many generations. As the palace was restructured, rebuilt, and expanded over the years, the bow remained where it had been placed so many generations earlier. It was part of the history of our kingdom. Everyone in the kingdom knew that the bow had been given to the ancestor of Janak Baba by Parashurama himself when his work in the world was completed. This was the very bow that Mahadev had given to Parashurama, the sixth *avatar* (incarnation) of Vishnu, to perform his duty of ridding the earth of the violent Kshatriyas, the warriors who had overstepped their bounds and spread conflict everywhere. Parashurama gave the bow to the kingdom of Videha because he said it was the only kingdom where the bow's power would never be abused and never used for warfare, only for worship. He had foreseen then that ours would be a kingdom that lived by the rule of dharma, not by armed force. We would not expand, would not grow powerful, would not conquer our neighbors, and would not invest in armies and weaponry. We would treasure above all else the wisdom of the rishis and be ruled by wise leaders.

Janak Baba had received word during meditation that the lifting and stringing of the bow should be the requirement for Sita's suitors. He knew then that some transition was in store. Whoever lifted that bow would take with him not only the jewel of Mithila, Rajakumari Sita, but also the protection and power of the bow. This would begin the decline of Videha, but he did not mourn. In the movement of time, kingdoms come and kingdoms go. Videha had contributed much and would continue to do so, but it was not in the destiny of his kingdom to lay the foundation for future civilizations. This realization came to him and he accepted it without the slightest concern or care.

The time for the swayamvara was upon us. Rajahs and Maharajas from the entire Arya region came to participate. We were so busy with preparations that there was hardly any time to be with Mata, except to attend briefly to her personal needs. None of us in the household were surprised by the outcome of the swayamvara. From the day when we first heard of Mata's meeting with Shri Ram in the temple, we all suspected that he was destined to be her husband, but still we had to go through the suspense of the competition.

Mata was calm and composed throughout the course of events. I am told that even when other rajahs came close to lifting the bow, she did not display any concern. When Shri Ram lifted and then broke the bow, the family breathed a sigh of relief. But Shri Ram announced that he would come the next day to make sure that Rajakumari Sita accepted the results. She would have a day to reflect and decide her future. Until then, no announcement was made.

The next morning, Shri Ram arrived at the palace with his brother and spent time privately with Mata, Janak Baba, and Sunaina Ma. We never heard what was spoken, only that Mata had accepted Shri Ram as her husband. Word usually traveled very quickly through the palace, and there was hardly anything that we all did not soon come to know. One servant spoke to another, and that one spoke to another, and this is how we heard so many of the stories of our beloved Janak Baba and Mata. But on this occasion, no word leaked out.

Several days later, after one of the evening meals, a servant who had been serving the food called the kitchen staff together and recounted what he had heard during the meal. Janak Baba had remarked how fortunate it was that Shri Ram and Lakshman had arrived in Mithila just in time for the swayamvara. Shri Ram smiled and said it was no accident. When Janak Baba asked him to explain, Ram was quiet for a few minutes but then replied that the battle with Taraka had been very difficult, the more so because she was a woman and it pained him to have to take the life of a woman even though she had killed so many of the hermitage students. That night after the battle when he lay down to rest, overcome with dismay, Ram felt a great presence come over him. It brought a sense of peace and love, healing him of the pain he felt from the battle. It was an overarching presence, and he drifted to sleep in the comfort of its arms, but by morning it was gone and he wondered if he had imagined it. As he approached Mithila, he felt the presence again. When they stopped to get water for their horses and he saw Rajakumari Sita in the field, he knew who it was that had come to comfort him in his distress. Shri Ram then turned to face Mata and told her that when he saw her kissing the soil, he took that as a sign that she had forgiven him for killing the woman demon.

The servant continued his narration. "Mata listened quietly as he spoke. When he had finished she replied, 'I have realized that sometimes a demon takes a woman's form so the warrior will refrain from doing what needs to be done. But you were not deceived. When I first heard the news of her death, I also felt sorry over the deed, but then I realized she was a woman only in outer appearance. The test was to see beyond her outer form to the demonic nature that was inhabiting that body, which is neither male nor female. It was Vasundhara Ma who told me this that day in the field, and that is why I kissed the soil, in gratitude for her helping me to understand this. She had made me aware of a deeper truth.'

Shri Ram seemed touched by her words, but then he added in a serious tone, 'The death of Taraka is not the end. I am afraid many more battles lie ahead, difficult battles.'"

The servant stopped his narrative. "Go on," urged Usha. "What else did he say? What did he mean, and how did Mata respond?"

"I couldn't hear anymore," he replied. "That is all I heard."

"Oh dear," I exclaimed. "I hope for them a peaceful future, full of joy and happiness, not fighting demons."

"None of us should worry," interjected Soma. "Whatever Rajah Ram will do will be for the protection and benefit of us all. I have no doubt that he will succeed in all of his endeavors. After all, he is the one chosen by our Mata."

Now came the wedding preparations, the reception of guests from Ayodhya, and the ceremonies themselves. It was an exhilarating time, but also one of sadness for me as I realized that the time of Mata's departure was approaching. I could not imagine what life would be without her. Janak Baba would retreat more and more into solitude, Sunaina Ma would assume more responsibilities for governing, and we servants would be left without the one who had lit up the palace and brought us such joy. I was just coming to accept this reality when a new widow of hope and possibility opened.

DEPARTURE FROM MITHILA

After the wedding, Janak Baba fulfilled his promise, and he and Mata took Shri Ram to the fields to experience firsthand the beauty of the soil. Janak Baba taught him to use the plough, and Mata taught him about the living qualities of the soil and the bounty of the earth. Janak Baba told Shri Ram about the local councils being set up and he was eager to see them, so they also visited the nearby villages to witness the progress of these councils. Shri Ram took it all in, engaging in long conversations with Janak Baba about the nature of governance. Mata told us that Shri Ram said he learned more about governing from Janak Baba in those few weeks in Mithila than he had in all his years in Ayodhya. He had learned about warfare and the Vedas from Rishis Vasishtha and Vishwamitra, but he had not yet had the opportunity to learn the subtleties of governance and he was glad to learn this first from Janak Baba.

Janak Baba seemed intent on passing on to Shri Ram some of his visions and premonitions for the future. He had seen that the power of Videha would decline and the power of the Kosala kingdom increase. The reach of the Raghu clan had grown immensely under the reign of Maharaja Dasaratha. The capital, Ayodhya, was now an imperial center, extending its influence in all directions. The kingdom of Videha was no match for Kosala except in one regard: it was the seat of knowledge. The coming together of these two kingdoms, the marriage of power and knowledge, would ensure a bright future for the Aryan region. If it could spread its high level of culture and civilization far and wide, the progress of the human species would aid all creation.

Janak Baba knew earth was in a declining cycle and much spiritual knowledge would be lost while material development advanced. It was this to which he wanted to dedicate his last years: helping preserve the knowledge through the dark ages to come. It was almost as if Janak Baba had willed this marriage, knowing the benefit it would bring all humankind. He had trained Sita well, fulfilling the great responsibility that had been entrusted to him. He had exposed her to so many of the rishis and sages in the Aryan region, and she had imbibed their wisdom. He knew that Shri Ram would value this, as well as her care for all creatures large and small, no matter their position in the scheme of things. The last of his great responsibilities was coming to an end, and Janak Baba greeted this time of closure with neither joy nor sadness. His withdrawal had begun.

One evening after returning to the kitchen, Soma shared with us some of Janak Baba's teaching to Ram that she had overheard while serving the evening meal. We all noticed her silence as she entered the kitchen and began her chores. Normally she was quite vocal, requesting this or that servant to do a particular chore, but this evening she seemed not to hear us as she began washing up and organizing the kitchen area. I asked her a question, but instead of responding she stared off into the distance as if she didn't hear me. Finally one of the servants asked what was wrong.

"Wrong? Nothing at all." She fell silent.

"You overheard a conversation while serving the evening meal, didn't you?" Kiran asked quietly. She nodded. He said, "Rohana also overheard something, but she couldn't understand what was being said. It seemed to be a subject of great importance."

"It was not for our ears," Soma replied quietly.

"Perhaps it *is* for our ears and that is why Janak Baba allowed you to overhear it. You know there is a reason behind everything that happens in this household." It was hard for Soma to resist Kiran. Whenever he spoke he made so much sense, and she was so fond of him.

As Soma began to speak, the servants in the kitchen gathered around. "I will repeat to you what I heard. Perhaps you can make sense of it, Kiran. In the middle of the meal, as I was bringing in the last dishes, Janak Baba suddenly stopped eating and began to speak directly to Ram. 'Ram, a king is a servant of his people,' he said. 'When a king grows distant from them, he can no longer serve. All of the families in Videha are known to me. I know their sorrows and seek to alleviate them.' Ram listened intently to Janak Baba, who continued. 'Even in an expanding kingdom, it is possible. An expanded mind can know a population, no matter how large it is. Does not Mahadev take note of each of our thoughts and desires? So it must be for a king in regards to those under his care. That is the responsibility given to us. That is why I regularly visit the villages. Sita often accompanies me as she can read the hearts of the people better than I. She knows the needs of each family. Self-governance, Ram, is what we must aim for. That is the future, for the minds of rulers are increasingly clouded by self-interest, not the interest of their people. I see that this is becoming the reality in many parts of the Aryan region. The only way to counter this is through self-governance.'

"Ram looked surprised and asked, 'Can people govern their villages if they cannot govern their own minds?'

"Janak Baba smiled and replied, 'That is the role of our rishis, to teach people how to govern their minds so that they will then be able to govern their communities. We must plant the seeds, although it will take a long time to bear fruit. There is resistance. The villagers have not been eager for these village councils, as they would prefer to be governed than to govern. They would rather follow than lead, but that will not help in their mental development.

"'My work is coming to an end, and yours is beginning. When Sita departs from here, I will withdraw more and more into the inner realms. You must plant an understanding of dharma in the human mind so that people themselves can resist the darkness that continually seeks to unseat the light. The time is coming when people will not be able to depend on their rulers to guide the way. Each one will need to take responsibility. That is the future, Ram—self-governance. And it must begin with you, for you will set the foundation for the millennia to come. I have tried to plant such seeds among our people, but Mithila is small and Ayodhya will become vast. This is the role for you and Sita together. I understand now that this is why she took birth in Mithila, to bring to Ayodhya the knowledge that we have tried to awaken in the human mind.'"

Soma paused in her narrative for a moment. "I was frozen in my place as I listened to these words of our wise and all-knowing Janak Baba. I saw that Ram and Sita were deep in thought. I then remembered my duties and quickly began clearing the food and withdrew. I don't know whether the conversation continued or if that was the end."

One of the servants looked at Kiran and asked, "What did Janak Baba mean by all of this? What is the need for self-governance when we have such a wise Maharaja?"

"I don't know," replied Kiran thoughtfully. "Not every kingdom is as fortunate as we are to have such a Maharaja. I suppose he was seeing well into the future. Janak Baba's sight is not limited to only our kingdom or our time. His vision is far grander." We all sat in silence for a few minutes, reflecting on these words, and then we gradually went back to our work of getting the kitchen ready for the morning meal. Years later, Soma was to remind me of this conversation.

The dreaded departure of Mata was only days away. Soma saw my despondency and said to me one evening. "Trust Mata, Meenakshi.

She will know what is best and will act accordingly. We must have perfect faith in her."

"I do have faith in her."

She shook her head. "Then why this despair? Would she allow any separation?" I looked at her, confused. What was she thinking? She knew perfectly well that Mata was leaving in a few days and it would be a long time, if ever, before we saw her again.

The next morning, Mata called Soma, Usha, Rohana, and me to accompany her to the forest. I knew it would be our last time alone with her. As we entered the forest, we could not hide our sadness, all of us except Soma, who continued to look as joyous as she always did. Mata, too, was in an exalted mood. As we entered deeper into the forest, Mata stopped at all of her favorite places, touching the trees and wild plants, petting whichever animal approached. She sighed, "I will miss every part of this forest and all of her creatures. But new forests await me and new creatures to meet."

None of us spoke. Mata led us to a place to sit and then said, "I have asked you to join me on this walk because I have a request to make of each one of you." We looked at one another. What could Mata possibly ask of us? Perhaps it was to look after Sunaina Ma? Her sister Urmila was also going to Ayodhya, as she had married Ram's brother Lakshman, so it couldn't be about her. Surely it was about Sunaina Ma, to comfort her after the loss of her two daughters.

"What is it, Mata?" asked Soma.

"I will need to keep a part of Mithila with me when I leave for Ayodhya, to keep the customs and traditions that I have grown up with, and so I have asked Ram if Urmila and I could be accompanied by the four of you, who have cared for us for so long. He has agreed, as have Pitaji and Ma. But I need your permission. Will you accompany me? Ayodhya will be very different from Mithila, very different, I am afraid. You will find yourself in a strange land, away from all you know and love. So think carefully before answering. It is not necessary for you to come. You can stay here and care for the family." Then turning to me, she said, "You have long cared for Ma. If you hesitate to leave her, please tell me." I was tongue-tied and so didn't respond.

It was Soma who replied immediately, in a firm voice. "Mata, where you are, I am. There is no question about staying." Mata smiled.

Usha and Rohana also nodded in agreement. "We are honored that you have chosen us," replied Usha, who was very attached to Urmila. "And we will try to live up to your expectations of representing Mithila."

At those words, I burst into tears. For several minutes, I couldn't speak. Finally I replied, "Mata, I was so afraid you would leave me here. That you would ask me, an old and . . . unfortunate servant . . . ." I almost said "cursed," but stopped, realizing that Usha and Rohana did not know about the curse. Mata placed her hand on mine and replied quietly, "Meenakshi, you are neither old nor unfortunate. You more than anyone represent the spirit of Mithila. You are of this land, of this earth, as I am."

Then she turned to Rohana, who had tears in her eyes. She had a sister and nieces and nephews she would be leaving behind, perhaps never to see again. "Are you sure, Rohana?" Gazing at Mata, she nodded and replied in a steady voice, "Mata, I will come. There is nothing more dear to me than serving you."

"Then it is settled. You must prepare yourselves because we leave in two days." She rose and looked around the forest and said, "This forest has been my world. I have grown up here, learning all I know. It has taught me everything, and I am so very grateful." Placing her hand on her heart, she slowly looked all around and whispered, "I leave with you my love. May you always be protected. I will take the knowledge you have given me to many parts of the world." With those words she turned to leave and we followed back to the palace. As we entered, she turned to me and said, "Make sure you say a proper goodbye to Kiran."

I nodded, but as soon as I got back to my room her words slipped from my mind. There was so much to do to get Mata ready. It was the morning we were leaving when her words returned to me, and so I hurried off to look for him. I found him tending to one of the horses, whose foot had been injured. I stood a short distance away watching him as he tenderly cared for the animal, speaking to the horse all the while. He suddenly became aware of me and turned to face me.

"Meenakshi, is it time? Are you leaving already?" I nodded, shifting from one foot to another. I didn't understand why I suddenly felt so uncomfortable. Perhaps it was because I had never been in the position to say goodbye to a friend knowing that we might not meet again.

He stared at me with sadness in his eyes. "This place won't be the same without Mata," he said.

"I know how you must feel," I hurried to say. "Mata is the life of the palace. But Janak Baba and Sunaina Ma will still be here. And as Mata said, she will never leave Mithila. It will always be in her heart."

"I probably will not see you again," he said quietly.

"I don't know, Kiran, what the future holds, but do take good care of all the animals. I know you will. That will make Mata happy." With a slight wave of my hand I hurried away, not sure why this brief exchange gave me such an uneasy feeling.

I didn't have time to give this conversation much thought as my mind was ruminating over all that I was leaving behind. I returned to my small room for one last goodbye. Memories of my father flooded my mind, my childhood with him, his severity with me, my lack of understanding. I was sad to leave behind the places I had known with him. And the other servants, with whom I had grown up, had become my family. I loved Mithila, everything about it. Then I thought that Mata must be experiencing the same. She would be leaving Sunaina Ma and Janak Baba. As I was reflecting thus, I heard a voice. It was Soma standing at the door.

"You can never leave Mithila, Meenakshi. Mithila is in you, as it is in me, Mata, and all of us. Mithila will always be with us, wherever we are. Be assured of that."

"Is it time?" I asked. She nodded. Everyone had gathered in the courtyard by the departure gate. Gathering my few belongings, I looked around the room and said goodbye for the last time.

Many of the goodbyes had already been said. Soma and I joined Rohana and Usha with the others who would be part of the retinue leaving for Ayodhya. Shri Ram was by his chariot with his brother. We waited now for only Sita and Urmila to emerge with Janak Baba and Sunaina Ma. Some time passed, and we waited. Finally they emerged. It was a tearful parting. Sunaina Ma had the hardest time. She took off a bracelet from her wrist and put it around Urmila's wrist and said, "This bracelet will always protect you." Then she took off an amulet that she wore around her neck and placed it around Sita's neck, saying, "My mother gave this to me when I left home for married life. It was her most precious possession. Wherever you go, keep this with you," she said between tears.

Janak Baba drew his daughters into his arms and silently embraced them, then gave them each a parting blessing. To Sita he said, "Remember always who you are and why you have come. You have gained what you need from Mithila, now you must share it with the world."

She nodded. "Pitaji," she uttered, but he placed his fingers on her lips.

"No words. I know what is in your heart."

Then he came to Shri Ram and stood silently before him.

"I have grown to love Mithila," said Shri Ram with great affection and also a touch of sadness. "I have learned much from you and would have been glad to spend all my days here."

Janak Baba smiled and replied. "I have given you my knowledge, Ram. Use it for the benefit of the world." Then spontaneously he took the hands of Sita and Ram in his own and said, "you are now one. The love you will manifest will be the foundation for the future and will sustain this world for millennia to come. I have no doubt about that."

Unexpectedly, he next came to us, the four servants who were accompanying Sita and Urmila. "Do you think I would let you leave without a blessing?" he asked as he drew us to him. "You also are my daughters. Take good care of Sita and Urmila as you always have, and take good care of yourselves." As he released us, he turned to me and said quietly, in such a loving way, "You have given your father every reason to be pleased. You have exceeded his expectations, and I have no doubt that he is aware of this. Through your devotion, you have brought him great honor."

Those words meant more to me than anything he could have said to me. At that moment I realized what it would mean to leave Janak Baba. He had been our protector, our sustainer, the one we turned to in every matter. He was my link to my father and my past. I was now leaving behind that link and heading into the unknown, with only my love and faith in Mata to guide me. What lay ahead, I didn't know. But as I turned to look at Mata and felt the joy flowing from her, I knew this was not a choice I was making. Like her, I was destined to leave behind my beloved Mithila and begin a new life in Ayodhya.

ADJUSTING TO AYODHYA

Mata had cautioned us that life in Ayodhya would be very different from Mithila, and that it would take time to adjust. "Everything is more formal there," she had said. "We have to follow their customs and regulations. We will not be able to wander as freely as we have in Mithila. At first we will be foreigners, but that will change over time. You will have each other, so you will be able to keep the feeling of Mithila alive in your hearts. You must never forget the freedom we have had here, and someday perhaps we can bring some of that freedom to the people of Ayodhya. That is my hope."

Despite these words of caution, we were unprepared for what greeted us in Ayodhya. The city was much larger and grander than Mithila. Its wealth was on display everywhere. It was the capital of an expanding and prosperous kingdom. Guards and soldiers lined our route, evidence of the military might of the kingdom. It was more than a little intimidating. Elaborate ceremonies greeted us along the road to the palace, and when we arrived, we were astounded at its size. I had thought the palace in Mithila was grand, but it was nothing like that of Ayodhya. I wondered how we would ever find our way about, but we were not to have the freedom to roam the palace. We were assigned to rooms in the back of the palace, and our movements were limited to Sita's quarters. That was fine with us, as our only care was in serving her. We knew it would not be possible to integrate with the other servants.

As we were putting away Mata's belongings, Soma turned to us and said, "We must not call Mata by that name when we are in the company of others. They will find that disrespectful."

"What do we call our Mata then, if not Mata?" asked Usha.

"We don't call her anything. I have noticed that the servants here do not address the family directly, but if we must address her, we simply call her Rani."

"And when we are alone with her?" I asked.

"When we are alone with her, we will be as we were in Mithila." She paused. "And I have noticed that the other servants here cast their eyes down when in the company of the family and do not speak until they are spoken to." Soma then added with a pained look on her face, "They are also not addressed by their name, but simply as servant."

We looked at one another. "I don't think we will be in their company much, so I am sure this will not be a problem," I hurried to say. "I want to make sure that nothing we do or say in any way reflects poorly on Mithila. We must remember we are representing our Janak Baba and Sunaina Ma."

Mata's days were busy with many functions, and it was only early in the morning, during rest time after the noon meal, and then again late at night that we had any access to her. The meals were elaborate affairs, as the household consisted of many more people. We were not needed in the kitchen or to serve the meals. In Mithila we each had served many different functions in the household, but here in Ayodhya our duties were restricted to caring for Mata and Urmila's personal needs.

I missed the intimacy of Mithila. I missed seeing Janak Baba and Sunaina Ma and the other servants with whom I had grown up. I missed seeing Mata throughout the day in one manner or another, hearing her laughter, which had filled the palace, and sharing stories of her various doings. The palace of the Raghu clan was a much more somber place. I wondered how Mata was faring in the new environment, but we had little occasion to ask. When we saw her she seemed radiant, and on the few occasions that we saw her with Shri Ram, we could see the blossoming of their love. They both seemed engrossed in each other's presence. But Soma saw something else. One day I asked her whether she had any notion of how Mata was adjusting to Ayodhya.

Soma said, "There is great joy for her here, but also unease. I can tell by her few remarks that she senses the disunity in the palace. And this causes her pain."

"Disunity? What do you mean?" Maharaja Dasaratha and Mata had formed an instant bond and his affection for her was known to all. Likewise, his three queens all doted on her. What disunity could she be referring to?

"Do you not feel, Meenakshi, something lacking here? A certain harmony that existed in Mithila, which I think was due to Janak Baba's nature. Here, the Maharaja seems torn between his wives, and although they put on the appearance of closeness, I sense something else. And if I sense it, no doubt Mata does as well. I hope she is able to heal whatever problems exist here."

I grew thoughtful. I had heard certain backbiting among the servants, but Mata had warned us not to get involved in the household politics so I had closed my ears to such talk. "We must remain above politics and gossip," she said. "After all, we are foreigners here. In Mithila, we don't have such divisions."

"There is something else," continued Soma. "I feel that she is longing to touch the earth, to be with the animals and plant life. She hasn't left the palace since we arrived. I am sure she will soon call us with some plan."

Soma was right. A few days later, as we were helping Mata take off and put away her ornaments, she turned to us and in a low voice asked us to meet her in her dressing room just before dawn. "I have not yet met the river. We will slip out of the palace and go to meet her, quietly, before anyone stops us. Bring all we need for the puja."

Rohana, Soma, and I arrived just before dawn and found Mata

dressed like us, with her head cover hiding her hair and part of her face. No one would suspect who she was. We each had a tray of flowers and lights for the river goddess. Usha stayed behind to care for Urmila.

"Let us go by the back gate. There are fewer guards there," Sita said.

So we crept down the hallway and stairs to the back gate, where we were stopped by two guards.

Soma spoke. "Rajakumari Sita has asked us to offer a puja to the river. We won't be gone long."

"They are the servants from Mithila," said the other guard. "You can let them go."

Once out of the palace, a sigh of relief came over all of us. We walked along the river until we found a secluded spot, and there we offered the river goddess flowers and candle lights while Mata chanted mantras and invocations. The first rays of dawn were approaching when Mata entered the water and quietly spoke to the river goddess. Before we knew it, Mata was submerged in the water. Coming up for air, she called to us, laughing and splashing. "Come. The river Devi wants to play with us. She is the younger sister of Ganga Ma and is very playful." Rohana and Soma slowly entered. Since the time of my near drowning, I had kept my distance from the river, not wanting to test my fate. Soma bobbed up and down; giggling, she told Mata how wonderful it was to be out in the open.

"Sarayu Devi knew I needed this time to be free of all formalities; that is why she called me here," Mata said.

"She called you, Mata?" Soma asked.

"Yes, for many nights I have heard her calling me. Just think, I have been here so many months and have not yet come to meet her properly. But I couldn't see how to slip away until the idea came to me last night."

We did not stay too long by the river, just long enough for the sense of freedom and joy we had known in Mithila to return to us. As we re-entered the palace, we found Shri Ram waiting by Mata's dressing room, a gentle smile on his face.

"Had I known you were longing for the river, I would have brought you there myself," he said to her. "I know you are not accustomed to being so restricted. We will go to the forest soon."

Mata indicated that she would not need us to help her dress, and so we three slipped away so they could be alone. In a few days' time, Soma accompanied Mata and Shri Ram to the forest. When they returned, she told us how Mata insisted on getting down from the chariot, taking off her shoes and walking into the forest. "It is not the same to go by chariot," she said. "One must feel the earth." Soma waited by the chariot for them.

"They were gone hours," she said. "I am sure Mata was familiarizing herself with all the animal and plant life. But when they emerged from the forest, Mata was quiet," said Soma. "Later she told me of signs of human encroachment. 'A balance must be found,' she said, 'between the growing needs of human beings and the other species. Without such a balance, the harmony that exists naturally will be destroyed.' She is right," Soma mused. "Mata ensured such a balance in Mithila, but here in Ayodhya, she does not have the same right to speak out."

We looked at one another, understanding perfectly well what Soma was referring to. In Mithila, Mata's voice was second only to that of Janak Baba. Everyone respected her wisdom, but things were very different in Ayodhya, and life was far more complex. Here, many different opinions were expressed, and there were competing power centers. The spread of Aryan culture was prioritized at the expense of other species. But there were things that we did not know then. It was only on the night of her departure that Mata shared with us the underlying causes that led to the event, which though dreaded by us, was welcomed by the rishis and sages who were at the forefront of spreading Aryan culture.

"How happy Mata is. I have never seen her more joyful," I expressed to Soma a few weeks after the visit to the forest. We had just returned one morning from helping Mata dress. There was not the hint of a smile on Soma's face. Rarely had I seen her so serious. "Don't you agree?" I asked. Her face softened and she nodded. I found her quietude disconcerting and so pressed her.

Looking down, she replied, "You see Mata's external expressions, Meenakshi, the face she shows to the world. I see what is taking place underneath the surface."

"What do you mean?" I asked in alarm.

"Her joy is indeed bubbling over because that is the imprint she wants to leave when she departs from here. She wants to leave some of her joy in this house that will be overcome with sorrow."

"Depart? Sorrow? What on earth are you referring to Soma?"

"Have you not noticed the bitterness that has taken over Maharani Kaikeyi? Have you not seen her dark looks?"

I stared at Soma in confusion, dumbstruck by the implication of her words. "Never mind," said Soma. "Let us enjoy what time we have."

"What do you know, Soma, and who has told you?" My voice was incredulous, but also harsh. Mata had warned us not to get involved with the gossip of the household servants, and Soma of all people was very attentive to these instructions. She hardly mingled. It could not be that she was susceptible to malicious talk. She looked away. For the first time ever, I saw tears gather in her eyes. Nothing could calm my thoughts that day. It was not until the evening when Soma and I went to put away Mata's ornaments and clothing, my mind was calmed by the joy that flowed from Mata. Even Soma seemed back to her normal self.

That night in my small room, I reasoned that although Soma had special insight into Mata, had an inner connection to her that none of us could match or even understand, this time she was wrong. She was imagining something that didn't exist. I put it out of my mind. It was only a few days later that we learned the kingdom of Ayodhya was about to be turned upside down, not from an external foe, but an internal one.

Those few days were tumultuous. The Maharaja had taken ill. It was his heart, they said. As much as Mata tried to help him with medicinal plants, his strength did not return. Then there was talk of his decision to coronate Ram right away. The auspicious day and hour were approaching when suddenly everything turned. Maharani Kaikeyi's mind had been twisted by her servant, a bitter and manipulative woman, and a long dormant jealousy and anger emerged in the queen. Years earlier Kaikeyi had saved the Maharaja's life in battle and he had promised to fulfil two wishes whenever she requested. Now she asked him to honor that commitment made long ago. When he asked what the two wishes were, thinking them to be desires he could easily fulfil, she requested that he coronate her son, Bharat, instead of Ram, although Ram was the eldest, and Ram was to be exiled for fourteen years.

We servants heard rumblings of this turn of events, but it was not until Mata called us to her that we understood what was in store. She was departing with him. She stood before us and said, "Ram has agreed to go into exile, and since there is no possibility of a separation, I will go as well." Then she added in a most gentle voice, "Where Ram is, there is Sita, and where Sita is, there is Ram." She waited for this news to sink in. We were speechless. I am not sure if we displayed any emotion, as we could not quite fathom the meaning of what she was saying. She looked at us intently and continued. "I am afraid great sorrow will come upon this kingdom, and it will be vulnerable to outside threats. There will be those who will seek to take advantage of Ram's absence. I have no doubt that from wherever we are, he will protect the kingdom, but I must also do my part. I will depend greatly on the four of you to help me fulfill my responsibilities here." She fell quiet.

"Then we are to stay here, Mata, without you?" I asked questioningly. I had assumed that we would return to Mithila.

She nodded. "Urmila will be here. You must help care for her. And you must maintain my presence here the best you can."

"How long will you be away, Mata?" Usha ventured to ask in a shaky voice. Mata didn't answer right away, but then replied in a quiet voice, looking away from us, "Fourteen years."

"Fourteen years, Mata!" I exclaimed in dismay. "How will we possibly survive that long without you?"

"You won't be without me, Meenakshi. You will have to learn to see beyond my physical presence. It is easy to serve me when I am here with you, but now you must learn to serve when my physical presence is no longer here."

"I don't understand," I said in trembling voice.

A faint smile crossed her lips as she replied, "You will, one day."

"When do you leave, Mata?" Soma asked in a steady tone.

"Tomorrow morning."

"Then I must go get ready." She made a motion to leave, but Mata put her hand on her arm and shook her head. "Soma, this time you cannot accompany me. I need you here more than I will need you in the forest. You must help maintain my presence in this household. I need all of you here. You can serve much better by maintaining my presence and trying to uplift the spirit among all the people here who will soon be thrown into a state of disarray."

"Must it be so soon, Mata?" I asked in consternation. "There is no time for us to prepare."

"There is nothing to prepare, Meenakshi. Now, I will share with you what must be done. Come with me." She led us to an open hallway outside of her room where she had constructed a small shrine. A large bowl was placed beside the shrine. Closing her eyes and uttering some words, Mata placed her hand over the bowl. It seemed that flames shot out of her open palm and into the bowl. She spoke in a very serious and steady voice, "I have put my energy into this flame. Watch over it. Don't let it diminish while I am gone. Your prayers and care for it will ensure that it does not go out. This flame will form a protective shield for the palace. But you must care for it and guard it as you would care for me. No ghee is needed, only mantras, day and night." She recited the mantas she wanted us to chant. "I will be in this fire, and when the time is right, I will draw it back into my being, and it will self-extinguish. Then you will know the work that Ram and I are setting out to accomplish is complete, and our return will be imminent. Through this flame I will be able to spread my love through this kingdom, and you will be able to send your love and prayers to me, for it is this love that will protect us all."

None of us spoke. By now it had sunk in that Mata was leaving us. I don't think any of us, except perhaps Soma, understood what she was saying, but we did understand that she was giving us certain instructions that we must follow.

"Usha," she continued. "Care well for Sister Urmila. She will go into deep meditation to help Lakshman with the tasks he will have. Stay by her side at all times. Soma, you must be a vehicle for my love to sustain Kausalya Ma, Ram's mother, who will undergo great suffering in his absence. Serve her as you would serve me." Soma nodded. "Rohana, bring my love and peace of mind to Sumitra Ma, Lakshman's mother. She is spiritually advanced and will rely much on Mahadev. Assist her with her pujas." Then Mata turned to me. As she looked at me thoughtfully, I asked. "Mata, how can I serve you while you are gone." My voice was cracking.

She replied slowly. "Meenakshi, I will need you to look after Kaikeyi Ma." A look of horror crossed my face, but I didn't utter a word. "She will need the most care, for she will be disdained and abandoned by all. When she returns to her senses, she will be unforgiving of herself. Ram loves her a great deal and will want to help restore her sense of dignity and self-worth."

"Mata, after what she had done? She is the cause of all this sorrow!"

Mata shook her head. "It only appears that way. She is but a vehicle for our departure, and yes, her mental weakness allowed her to be used in this way, which is why we must not abandon her." She looked from one of us to another. "There is a greater plan that we are fulfilling. Behind every misfortune is a hidden blessing. This journey through the jungles is necessary. Hermitages are being attacked and destroyed. Without these centers of learning, the sacred Vedas will not be preserved for the coming ages. A new civilization is yearning to be born. We must all do our part in helping with that birth."

She told us we must all get rest as the day of departure was but a few hours away. I could not sleep at all that night. I lay in bed hearing again and again the words Mata had spoken to me: "Behind every misfortune is a hidden blessing." She had told me this earlier in Mithila, adding that one only needs to search for it. "It is the attitude, Meenakshi, with which one encounters life, that determines whether one can turn a misfortune into a blessing." But I could not find any hidden blessing in what was about to befall us.

Later I heard that the Maharaja had been up all night pleading with Shri Ram not to leave. When Shri Ram explained again and again that he had no choice but to fulfil his dharma, the Maharaja then pleaded with Sita not to leave with him. Maharani Kausalya asked what they would say to Janak Baba when he learned that his daughter had gone into exile. Sita responded calmly that she had already asked for and received his blessing.

"He has come?" asked Maharani Kausalya in disbelief.

Sita had shaken her head and replied, "His physical presence is not required for me to communicate with him. I would never take such a step without his blessing." There was nothing we servants from Mithila could say if Janak Baba had given his blessing. We had to assume it was for the greater good.

Dawn came too quickly. Everyone gathered in the courtyard to see them off. Shri Ram, his brother Lakshman, and Mata Sita were all dressed in ascetic clothing. Instead of rain, sorrow drenched the ground and the earth seemed to cry out. We were all heavy with pain, but Mata looked calm and radiant, as did Shri Ram. The four of us servants stood off to the side as the three ascetics said their goodbyes to the family. I didn't think we would have a chance to speak with Mata, but she stepped aside and came to us, taking our hands one by one. "You have all served me well," she said quietly, "and I know you will continue to do so. My love will always be with you."

The thought came into my mind that I would not see her again, as I was aging and not in the best of health. Fourteen years seemed an eternity to me. Mata looked at me and I heard her voice inside say, "I will see you again, Meenakshi. I promise you that." Then with a parting glance, she turned and walked away. Many of the people began to follow them. Usha and I started to go as well, but Soma placed her hand on our shoulders and held us back, shaking her head. "Mata would not want this," she said. "We must get back to our duties and continue as before."

"Without Mata," I said mournfully.

"No, with Mata," she replied firmly. "Let us not forget her words to us. We must maintain her presence, which means we must care for her room, her clothing, her jewels, everything. Especially the fire. Let us go now to recite the mantra she taught us. We must believe she is still here."

DEATH IN AYODHYA

It took some time to settle into the new reality. Soma was the only one who had the presence of mind to instruct us on our activity. She divided the time that each of us was to spend caring for the sacred fire. She decided who would prepare Mata's clothing and ornaments for the day, who was to clean her room, who was to place the flowers and which flowers to use, who was to help with the pujas that Mata performed each day. In this way, we managed to keep Mata's presence with us, but we were also mindful to carry out the new duties that she had assigned us.

Soma brought great comfort to Kausalya Ma, and I sought to do the same to Kaikeyi Ma. That was perhaps the most difficult endeavor of my life, because I could not deny that I harbored great resentment toward her, and it took many weeks before the waters of compassion began to flow in me. Her longtime loyal servant had been exiled for having twisted the Maharani's mind, and none of the other servants of the household would go near her.

The Maharaja did not recover from his illness and the other two Maharanis were too absorbed with his health to take any notice of Maharani Kaikeyi, and so it was left to me to take care of her meals. I would not have offered to serve in this capacity had not Mata requested this of me. Each morning I knocked on her locked door, called out and left the food. I would return hours later to find it untouched. I would do the same each evening. This went on for days until one morning when I went to her room to collect the morning meal, I found the tray was gone. It was the same for the next few days. Then one day when I knocked and put down the tray, I noticed that the door was unlocked and slightly ajar. I pushed it open and cautiously entered the darkened room. I looked around. The room was in complete disarray, as was the Maharani.

At that moment I forgot all of her dark acts, and for the first time felt compassion for her, although I kept my distance, as I feared to come too close. I kept my eyes lowered as Soma had instructed me to do. The Maharani motioned me to approach. Crinkling her eyes as if she didn't recognize me, she asked, "Is it you who has been bringing me the food each day?" I nodded. "Who are you? Are you a new servant?" I didn't know how to answer. I was still new to Ayodhya but I could not consider myself a new servant. Suddenly she realized who I was. "You are one of the servants who came with Sita from Mithila, aren't you?" I nodded. "Then why have you taken care for my meals? Don't you know what I have done? Don't you know I am the reason that you are bereft of your Rani?" Her voice was rasping, harsh, and growing louder. I drew back as fear overtook me.

"Maharani, it is Rajakumari Sita's instructions that I am following," I replied in a hoarse whisper.

She looked shocked. Then breaking into tears she shouted, "Leave me!"

I don't know how I gained the courage to ask if I could be of service, but the words just came out of my mouth. "Maharani, please let me clean your room and help you with a bath and to dress." She was completely unkept and the room had a terrible odor as a result of being closed up. But when she shouted "Leave me" again, I quickly retreated.

My nerves had been undone by what I had just experienced. Shaken, I hastened to Mata's sacred flame. "I am trying, Mata," I whispered to her. "I am doing my best, but she is unreachable." Tears had formed in my eyes, and I wiped them.

Just then I heard Soma's quiet voice. "You are fulfilling Mata's wishes."

"She is vile, filled with venom," I said to Soma, wiping my tears. "I don't understand why Mata wanted me to serve her."

"Just for that reason. Yes, there is venom in her, no doubt, but Mata wanted us to free her of that venom, and only love can do that." She added, "Her servant has been banished and nobody else in the palace will go near her. She will starve if someone doesn't care for her. I am happy to do it, Meenakshi. I can take this burden from you."

I shook my head. "Never have I failed to take up a task Mata has given to me. If I fail now, how will I face her, Soma? But if you could have seen her. She looks like a madwoman, with her hair unkept, unwashed, and her clothing half undone, and the room has such a stench. She won't let me clean it. I don't know what to do." As I described the scene, a look of compassion came over Soma's face.

"Poor woman," she murmured. "She had truly lost her mind. I don't blame her. I am sure her guilt is overwhelming. But you must have patience and persistence, Meenakshi. Isn't that what Mata would say?" I nodded. Soma placed her hand on my arm, "Meenakshi, you are trembling. Fear has overtaken you."

"Never before have I felt such fear, Soma, not even when I was drowning in the river. I was ready to let go of my life then. But this feeling is something I have not known before. There is a darkness in that room, a darkness that frightens me."

"There is a darkness that runs through this palace now, a darkness because of what was done. But we all must resist that." She paused and then continued. "That last night after you and the others had left Mata, I stayed with her a little longer so she could give me instructions. Before I left I asked her if she had fear of what lay ahead. Do you know what she told me?" I shook my head. "These are her words. I will never forget them. 'Soma, this human body will know fear and deprivation. But it will also know strength and conviction and courage, and it will overcome all the obstacles it faces. It is time for me to put to use all the knowledge I have gained from

Pitaji and the sages who have blessed me.'" These words quieted my trembling. Then Soma added, "We also have been blessed by Janak Baba. Don't you remember that last blessing he gave us? That alone is enough to keep us safe. There is nothing for us to fear here."

And so I kept bringing the food. If the door was locked, I would leave the food outside the door, and if it was slightly ajar, I would enter and leave it by her table. The days passed. One day I entered and she spoke to me, "You may clean the room now."

I looked up at her and saw that her senses seemed to have returned. I could not deny that I felt great timidity in her presence. "May I help you with a bath, Maharani?" I asked. She nodded, and so my service to her began, although few words were ever spoken between us. Some months later a new servant arrived at the palace who was assigned to care for Maharani Kaikeyi and I was relieved of this burden. Soma came to tell me the news.

"I am no longer needed there?" I asked, with some hesitation in my voice.

Soma nodded. "I thought you would be glad, but you seem sorry. Have you become fond of her?"

I shook my head. "But then I have failed Mata. It was she who gave me this assignment," I sighed.

"Mata never asks us to do more than we can manage. I suspect it was Mata herself who arranged for that new servant so you would be relieved of this responsibility."

"How could she have? She is far from here."

"Meenakshi, she is never far. I have told you that so many times. She is aware, so aware of everything that takes place. I have seen that over and over."

Maharaja Dasaratha died. Bharat, the brother of Shri Ram and son of Maharani Kaikeyi, distraught over events, left for the jungle to inform Shri Ram, Lakshman, and Sita. He went to plead with them to return. Everyone thought he would be successful.

"Perhaps they will return now," I said to Soma. "Maharani Kaikeyi seems to regret her actions and will welcome them."

Soma shook her head. "They cannot return. Their work is only just beginning." I held on to hope, but when Bharat returned alone from the forest, sadness settled over the palace again. The only smiling face was that of Soma.

"How can you smile, Soma, when he did not succeed in bringing them back?" I asked her.

"But he did," she exclaimed. "Do you not remember Mata's saying that Ram would find a way to instill his presence in the kingdom to protect against the forces that would seek to weaken Ayodhya? That is what he has done. He has sent his sandals to sit on the throne. His presence is here, just as is Mata's. Do you not feel it, Meenakshi? It is a great blessing for Ayodhya."

I looked at her glumly. I tried to feel Mata's presence as I mumbled the mantra she had taught us before the sacred fire, but I could not say that I felt anything. I felt only absence—the absence of her laughter, her care, her love. It was difficult for Usha and Rohana as well. The meaning seemed to have been sucked from our lives, although we went through the routine of taking out Mata's clothing and ornaments each morning, arranging new flowers for the puja, putting away her clothing and ornaments at night, speaking to her all the while. We would tell her things that happened in the palace that day, report news of the Maharanis, the brothers, and Urmila. If there was no news to report, we would share our thoughts and dream up stories.

Soma seemed the only one to receive messages from Mata, and every now and then she would report the events that were taking place in the forest so far away. "How do you know this?" I once asked her.

"Don't you remember that Mata said Agni Dev (the fire deity) would carry her messages to us? He is doing just that. The flame is a sacred gift from Mata. Distance is of no concern. She is sending messages to all of us, but you haven't learned to quiet your mind and listen, Meenakshi." She was right. I received no messages. We didn't know whether Soma was making up the stories or whether by some miraculous event she was receiving news directly from Mata. It didn't matter. Rohana, Usha, and I eagerly took in these stories of Mata's travels. We wanted to believe them.

One day, about three years after Mata's departure, I found Rohana seated by the sacred fire in tears. She had received news from Mithila that her sister was very ill and suddenly she missed home terribly. I tried to console her, but to no avail. What could we do? We were not in charge of our own fate. She could not decide on her own to return to Mithila. Soma arrived just as I was explaining this to her. When she took stock of the situation, she offered to speak with Maharani Kausalya, and so it was arranged that Rohana would return to Mithila. We had become like a family, sisters in a foreign land, and her departure left another hole in our small circle. I dared not admit that I also longed to return. So many times at night I envisioned being back at the palace, but I realized that with Mata's absence and Janak Baba in retreat, it would not be the same. We could not recreate the past. It was gone, yet I longed for those days.

Two years later Usha was the next to leave. She left us not for the calm and joy of Mithila, but for the peace of the celestial realms. She took sick and died very suddenly, and then it was just Soma and I who were left to keep alive the sacred fire and Mata's presence. It was not long after that my health began to go. My eyesight was failing, but I dared not tell anyone, not even Soma. I didn't want to burden her with additional care, and I was still able to manage.

One morning when I awoke before dawn to recite the mantra by the sacred fire, I tripped as I was leaving my room and had a bad fall. It was a struggle to get to the fire, but I managed. I found Soma there. She had arrived before me. I looked at her in surprise. The mornings were my time, her watch was sunset and during the night.

"You are here?" I asked.

"I sensed that you were not well, and so I came," she replied. We both stood there reciting the mantra, and then I turned to go back to my room.

"Let me help you," she said. Grateful for the assistance, I put my hand on her arm. She led me back to the room and told me to stay there the whole day and rest. She would take over my duties. Despite my protestations, she insisted on bringing my meals and checking on me throughout the day. That evening she came to sit with me. "You are losing your eyesight, aren't you, Meenakshi?" I nodded. "And you didn't tell me. How long has it been?"

"Many months," I replied in a cracking voice. "But it seems to be getting worse now. I didn't want to burden you, Soma, but now I am frightened. What will become of me? What use will this household have for an aged, blind, and cursed servant from Mithila. Surely I will be turned away."

"Do not speak of the curse," she replied sharply. "Didn't Mata once tell you that you are neither aged nor cursed?" Then in a gentler voice, she added, "Do you not yet realize that the curse has been your greatest blessing."

I looked at her. Those were almost the same words Mata once spoke to me. "You sound like Mata," I said.

"I will find a solution," she replied. "Mata always told us there is a solution to every problem, and so there must be a solution to this." Several days later, Soma came with a medicinal liquid and dropped it into my eyes. "Every few hours we must apply this," she instructed.

"Who gave you this treatment," I asked suspiciously.

"Mata," she replied.

"Mata?"

She nodded. "She came to me in a dream and told me where to find this plant. I had to look far and wide for it. She instructed me what to do and said in a few weeks your eyes will grow stronger.

I have told the other servants that you are ill and need a week to recover. We will see how you are then."

"But the fire, Soma, who will assist you?"

"I don't need any assistance, and the truth is that the fire doesn't really need our mantras. Mata did that for us so we could feel our connection to her. Just as the flame manifested through Mata's will, so it will sustain itself through her will until she returns. But we must continue with the mantra because those were her instructions and the minute we part from her words, I fear some ill will befall this kingdom."

In a week's time, my eyesight was noticeably improved, enough for me to return to most of my normal duties. Several weeks later, my eyesight, if not fully recovered, was good enough for me to perform all my functions. It was around that time that Soma approached me and told me that she wanted to take me someplace just before dawn. She would not tell me where.

"Why this big secret?"

"A surprise. Something that will bring joy to your heart."

I awoke earlier than usual, recited the mantra before the sacred fire and was ready when she came to my room. The two of us quietly left the palace. I followed as she led me to the Sarayu River, where we walked along its banks. I could hear the quiet sound of women's voices chanting.

"What is that?" I whispered.

She smiled. "This is what I wanted to show you. Do you remember that spot?" She pointed in the direction where the sound was coming from, and through the early rays of dawn I recognized that we were in the vicinity where Mata had taken us to meet the river goddess when we first arrived in Ayodhya.

I nodded. "That is where Mata played with the river devi."

"Now, look and listen," she said. "In that same spot, the women of Ayodhya are praying for Mata. I have seen them come here for years, just before dawn. At first it was one woman. She came alone, and would chant and sing to the river devi, beseeching her protection for the Rani from Mithila who had gone with their Rajah Ram into exile. Then over time a few more came, and now there are a dozen there, all praying for the protection of our Mata. It moves me so to see their care for her, a foreign Rani they hardly know."

"Soma, you are right. My heart is bursting at this display of love for her. No greater gift could they give us."

"One day, when she returns, she will thank those women."

"But Soma, isn't it odd that they are praying at the very place where Mata entered the waters."

Soma smiled. "Not at all. Mata was not just playing that day. She was sanctifying the place so that this could occur. I believe she had foresight and wanted to create a place where their prayers could reach her, and where she could reach them and bless the women of Ayodhya."

"Should we go to them?"

She shook her head. "We are from the palace. Let their prayers be undisturbed. We do not know if the palace would approve of women being out so early on their own. We are only let through the gates because we are the servants from Mithila."

It gladdened my heart to think of those women singing by the river, and often at night when I felt tired, lonely, or sad, the memory of their song lightened my spirit.

Seven years had passed since Mata's departure and my body was becoming more and more frail. Privately I did not think I could survive another seven years until Mata's return, but when my mind thought this, I would recall her last words when she said that she would see me again. Perhaps I had imagined it. I had not heard her speak those words out loud; I had merely heard them in my mind. One day I shared this concern with Soma.

"You did not image that, Meenakshi, because I heard those words as well. I heard her say that she would see you again, and so it must be. There is nothing that can change that."

"You heard her speak to me in my mind?" I asked astonished. Soma looked away, and I didn't know whether she was saying that to comfort me or whether she really heard the words.

"Go to the river, Meenakshi. Go to that spot where Mata took us. You will find your answer there."

It was several days before I could get away, but finally I managed to go alone one morning and stand at the very spot where we servants had accompanied Mata, where the women of Ayodhya now came in the early morning to sing and pray for Mata. The spot that was now sanctified. I slipped off my sandals and for the first time entered the river. If only I could bring back those days in Mithila, I thought to myself, those days when we were so carefree. Suddenly the burden of all the years of absence came over me and I could not restrain the tears. Sinking down onto my knees I let the water swirl around me. It was past dawn and the women were now gone. I was alone in the water and could wash my face with my tears.

I quietly cried, "Mata, I am trying to wait for you, but my body will not. I will not last until your return. I am so sorry, Mata, that I will not be here to welcome you."

As I spoke these words, I heard a voice quiet as a gentle breeze brushing over me, almost inaudible. "Did I not promise that you will see me again?" I could not tell if the voice was coming from inside me or from the external world, but something made me turn around, and there I saw her standing at the edge of the river. I was speechless. My tears ceased and a quiet joy entered my heart. "Then welcome me home now, Meenakshi," she said in a gentle voice.

"Mata, you've come back?"

With a faint smile she said, "You will catch a chill, Meenakshi, if you stay in the water like that." Just then I noticed my body was trembling from the cold. She walked a few steps into the river and helped me rise. Then she took off her shawl and wrapped it around me.

I wanted to express my love for her, to tell her that I would serve her throughout eternity, but the words would not come. No sound emerged.

She nodded as if receiving my love and added, "You do not

need to see this body to know I am with you, not just for this life, Meenakshi, but for all time." Then with a broader smile, she turned and walked into a small gathering of trees. I tried to follow but stumbled and couldn't get to her. A few minutes later I made my way over to the trees, but she was nowhere in sight. I stood for a few minutes in awe, perplexed by what had just happened. Then slowly I returned to the palace in a daze. When Soma saw me, she exclaimed, "Meenakshi, how did you get Mata's shawl?"

"Mata wrapped it around me when she saw how wet I was from the river," I replied in a stunned voice. "The water was washing over me. She said I would catch a chill. She took it off from her shoulders and wrapped it around me herself."

"Come with me." Soma took me by the hand and led me to Mata's room. "This is the very shawl I laid out for her today. It is missing. All the other clothing is here. Are you sure you did not come to the room and borrow it?"

"Soma, would I ever do that?" I exclaimed, horrified that she would suggest such a thing. "But those are the very clothes I saw her in. Look, Soma, the hem of her clothing is wet. She was standing by the edge of the water. How did it get wet if her clothing was here in the room? And if you laid out this shawl, how did Mata have it? I don't understand."

Soma nodded, a smile creeping across her face. She replied quietly. "Now I understand. Mata wanted you to know that your experience was real. You really saw her. She came to bless you. This is her sign to you."

The experience brought such peace and comfort to my heart. The weeks passed. One day I was too weak and tired to rise from my bed. Soma came to see me. She seemed to know what was in store. "I hope all your desires have been put to rest."

I nodded, and whispered faintly, "My only hope is that in the future I can continue to serve her." I drifted off to sleep. When I awoke I found Soma still sitting by my side. "I had the most beautiful dream, Soma. We were back in Mithila, you and I, with Mata in the forest. Do you remember the forest?" I asked in a faint voice. She nodded. "How I wish we could be back in Mithila with her."

"Do not think of Mithila, Meenakshi. You are in Ayodhya now, and here is where we have to serve Mata, here in Ayodhya."

"But I never felt at home in Ayodhya."

"You will, Meenakshi, you will."

"And will you be here . . . .?" My voice trailed off. I no longer had the energy to speak.

Soma was quiet for a few minutes and then replied, "I will be. I will be here." I gazed at Soma, too weak to speak. She had been such a dear friend, more than a friend really. In her presence I felt close to Mata, as if she was reaching me through Soma. "Why did she come?" I gathered the strength to ask. "That morning by the river?"

Soma shook her head slightly as she looked out into the distance. "It was out of love. That is who she is. Love itself, and that love extends to all, to every creature. She makes no distinction because we are all her children." Then turning to me she said softly, "The purpose of Mata's birth is to awaken that love, the love that permeates the celestial worlds, to awaken that love on earth. And this is what she is doing every moment of her life."

I didn't understand. I knew nothing of the celestial worlds. But then I remembered Mata's words to me as she was departing Ayodhya. "You will see me again," she had said. And so now I realized Mata had come because she had given her word. A great sigh passed through my lips as if all my burdens of this life were being lifted.

I didn't have to wait for Mata anymore. Soma would be here to receive her. I had seen over the last few years how Soma had gained a respected place in the household. All the servants now came to her for advice and guidance. Even the Maharanis depended on her. She would not be alone. Unlike me, who had never integrated into the household, she was a part of Ayodhya now. I alone had maintained my Videhi identity. But still, the thought of leaving her was difficult.

A deep bond of affection had grown between us.

"Soma, you will wait . . . for Mata . . . ." My faint voice trailed off.

"Meenakshi," she said gently, gazing into my eyes. "I have never been waiting, because Mata has never left me."

I smiled. Soma was unlike the rest of us. She was a mystery, one I could never fathom. But her words gave me comfort, and they were the last words I heard before my eyes closed to the world.

One life falls away and leaves its imprint in the sand, giving rise to another life, taking along the memories, the memories, which do not die, which are not washed away. They simply sink to the bottom of the mind's sea and rest there, folded in the many layers of mental sediment until called forth to help the soul on its journey toward full awakening.

Part Two

AYODHYA

REBIRTH IN ANCIENT AYODHYA

I was born into a *kshatriya* (warrior caste) family in the last declining *treta yuga*, the second of the four great ages of humankind. My father worked in the administration of the kingdom of Ayodhya. He was a most loyal servant to the Maharaja, Shri Ram, and worked untiringly to achieve the tasks set for him. My mother was a modest woman and took a back seat in our family, bowing to the desires and demands of my father. Of all their children, I was the youngest and only girl. Much of my growing up years were spent alone, as my brothers were much older and were married while I was still young, so I naturally drifted toward my mother and helped her with various chores. From an early age I found great satisfaction in serving my parents. In fact, I had come to think that was how I would spend my life.

Every now and then my father would remark to my mother, "Anasuya will make a very devoted wife. Her nature is to serve." I was pleased to hear the second part of this remark, but not the first, as from an early age I was intent on not marrying. The very thought gave me great anxiety.

It was a time of growth and expansion, prosperity and innovation in the kingdom, and my father traveled a great deal, often to the far reaches of the kingdom. By the time I reached the age of seven or eight, our beloved Maharaja Ram had died, leaving his two sons to rule in his stead. I had the opportunity at that time to be educated at a new *gurukula* established for young girls. Gurukulas typically were schools where male students lived near or with the guru.

The education of girls had been a passion of Maharani Sita, although she didn't live to see its implementation. After her death, Shri Ram made it a priority to establish a place where girls could go for learning. There had been much resistance, but he persisted, and in the end won the consent of the sages and rishis to start a small non-residential school for girls. Learning had begun to flourish under Shri Ram's rule. Before that it was reserved for brahmins, princes, and others of high standing. But with the marriage of Mithila and Ayodhya, a new interest in knowledge had emerged. It was said that Maharani Sita had come to balance Ayodhya's growing might. Power without wisdom could indeed lead to unwanted results.

It was not just learning we were to acquire. We all lived in the shadow of what had happened to Lanka, when their ruler, Ravana, one of the most knowledgeable and scholarly figures of the time, grew arrogant beyond control as a result of his power. It was more than scholarly learning that was needed now. We would learn humility, devotion, and service, and these were the prime qualities of our Maharaja, Shri Ram. He was an example for us all, as my father never ceased to remind the family.

Our Maharaja had encouraged the education of girls, and although my father was reluctant to send me to the gurukula, as I would be the first girl in my family to attend, my father felt it was his duty to do so. The experience turned out to be a mixed one for me. After several years in the gurukula, our teacher one day recited the narrative of Shri Ram and Rajakumari Sita. At the point in the story when Sita is captured by Ravana, I cried out, "No, it is not true," and ran from the group. Nothing could convince me that this part of the story was true. My father was called and I was taken home, quite shaken. After that I refused to attend the gurukula.

My father tried to reason with me. "What do you think led to the great war," he asked one day, "if it was not the kidnapping of Maharani Sita?"

"I don't know," I cried. "But I am sure she was not kidnapped. I am sure of it." It then became a rule in my family never to discuss this part of the story. As far as I was concerned, the Maharaja and Maharani had gone into exile, completed their time in the forest, and then returned after fourteen years. Yes, there was a war and Ravana was defeated, but it had nothing to do with our Maharani. Somehow I felt that the part about the abduction of Sita was a betrayal of her, a diminishment of her abilities. Surely she could have protected herself, I thought. One with the courage to enter the jungle and live there for fourteen years was not without the means of self-defense. Besides, Maharaja Ram would never have allowed this to happen. So my thinking went, but I could never quite express the emotions roused by this part of the story.

After my withdrawal from the gurukula I began to spend more time helping my mother in the kitchen. I remember one occasion where my mother and I had prepared a wonderful meal. As one of the servants was carrying the tray of food to the room where we normally took our meals, she tripped and everything spilled to the floor. Immediately I ran to clean it up. My father entered the room as I was on my hand and knees wiping up the mess. He addressed me sternly, asking me to get up from the floor and let the servant take care of the cleaning. I was dismayed as he had never spoken to me in that tone before. My mother, seeing my hurt expression, took me aside and explained that my father believed everyone had a proper place in the household and we must respect that. I should not be performing the tasks assigned to the servants. I did not understand this and the incident stayed with me for long after.

My favorite place in Ayodhya was the sacred River Sarayu. She was a beautiful river, clear as a crystal and swift as a bird, with her wavelets whispering a captivating song as she hurried by. It gave me deep inner comfort to sit by her side and listen to her music. I could stay there for hours if permitted, but rarely did I have the occasion to do so. With so many foreigners now entering our city for trade and exchange, it was no longer considered safe for young girls to be outside alone. Whenever I had the opportunity to visit my friend, the river Sarayu, I had to be accompanied by a member of our household, which took away some of the pleasure for me. Deep inside, I felt the river had a message for me, a very personal message that could only be conveyed if I were unattended. I waited for the opportunity for this private audience, but it did not happen, and so the message was never transmitted to me. As I grew older, I laughed at my childish idea that the river would speak to me, and eventually this concept faded from my mind.

I had hidden within me a stubborn streak. Although I was compliant in most matters, when something struck me deeply, like the story of Maharani Sita's capture, I was uncompromising. A similar response emerged when the time came for the discussion of my marriage. There was an acquaintance of my father's who also worked in the administration of the kingdom and who had a son not much older than me. My father thought this a good match and had from time to time mentioned it to me. I didn't take it seriously and so never responded, but one day he brought up the subject in a more determined manner. I was now of marriageable age. When I heard the serious tone in his voice, I burst into tears and declared that I would never marry. It took him some time to calm me down.

"Why such an outburst?" he asked in astonishment. "All girls dream of marrying a good man."

With a heaving chest I pleaded, "Please don't force me, Pitaji."

Seeing the fear in my eyes, he sought to comfort me. "I would never force you to do anything, child. But I want to understand your feelings. Why this reaction?"

"Because . . . because I know I will die if I marry, or my children will die." Tears were pouring down my contorted face.

"Die! What nonsense. Who has told you this?"

"Something terrible will happen to me. I just know it." I was trembling like the earth when things go awry.

Seeing my condition, he took me in his arms and said, "I would never let anything happen to you."

This scene was repeated several times before I saw my parents become truly alarmed. I myself did not understand my emotions. I only knew that deep inside me I felt something terrible would happen if I married. And the very thought sent waves of fear through my being.

Finally, one night I heard my father ask my mother to find someone who could heal me of this fear. My mother took me from one healer to another, tried all sorts of medicinal plants, and even called Brahmin priests to perform special pujas, but nothing could erase the fear that stalked me. Then one evening I overheard a conversation between my parents. My mother was explaining to my father that she had heard that one Mithila attendant of the Maharani still lived and was said to have healing powers.

"But she is far away," my mother explained. "She still lives near the hermitage where the Maharani spent her last days. I don't know if she would see us, or whether she can help, but perhaps it is worth a try."

"We have no other option," replied my father. "There is a deep-seated fear, perhaps from a past life, and we must find a way to resolve it if she is to find happiness in this life. Perhaps the blessings of our Maharani will flow through this woman."

"She would be quite old now. She may not even be alive any more. The woman who told me of her said it has been a few years since she has received any word of her. I don't know much about her, except that it is said the Maharani had conveyed to her much knowledge of the plant medicines. And people from here used to travel all the way there for healings. I am told her name is Soma."

I was listening quietly outside the room, not wanting to make my presence known. But when I heard my mother say the name Soma, a slight expression of surprise involuntarily escaped my lips. My parents fell silent when they heard my murmur. Realizing that I had unwillingly revealed my presence, I entered the room. My parents looked at one another, unsure of what to say to me.

"Pitaji," I pleaded, looking at my father. "I want to overcome this fear as much as you want me to. Please, let me go meet this woman. I feel that she will be able to help me."

"Yes, of course. Your mother will take you. It is a long journey but you will be sent with supplies and guards so that you can safely make the trip."

My heart began to flutter at his words. Did I really have my father's blessing to go meet the woman who had cared for our Maharani for most of her life? Feelings that I had had for the Maharani since childhood, but which had been put aside during my growing-up years, now re-emerged in full force. She would be able to tell me what had really happened to the Maharani in the jungles of the south. I alone, it seemed, among all the people of Ayodhya had refused to believe the story of the kidnapping. She would confirm my intuitions, of that I had no doubt, and then I could refute this story to all. Perhaps she also could help me understand why I had such a fear of marriage.

When my mother saw the glow of hope on my face, she cautioned me. "Don't get your hopes up, Anasuya. We don't know if she will meet us or even if she is still alive."

It was too late. My hopes had been raised and I lived the next few days in anticipation of meeting Soma. We set off some days later for the journey, which took place without incident. As we traveled through forests and villages, I wondered why the Maharani had chosen to live in such an isolated place rather than in the comfort of Ayodhya. I had never traveled outside of the city before and every detail struck me. I wondered at the village life, the animals, the thick forests. The journey gave me a taste of the extent of our kingdom. Previously my universe had been contained within the walls of Ayodhya, but now I was discovering the world beyond. It made me wonder what it must have been like for the Maharani and Shri Ram to have traveled all the way to the ends of the land, to such distant places I could not imagine. In my wildest dreams,

I could not have envisioned the world that lay beyond our narrow streets and peopled markets.

My father was a respected administrator in the government, and we knew we would be well received at the hermitage near the place where Soma was known to dwell. My father had already sent word of the reason for our journey and our intention to meet Mata's attendant, Soma. The day's light was quickly fading, and we had to race against time to reach there before being fully enveloped in darkness. When we arrived at the hermitage I was surprised by its modest appearance. My mother had warned me that we would have to accept whatever accommodations were offered, as ascetics live a simple life. The *guru* (spiritual teacher) of the hermitage came to greet us and received us warmly. After having us shown to our modest but clean room, he invited us to join him for the evening meal. It was then that my mother inquired about Soma.

"Is she still alive?" my mother asked.

He nodded with a smile. "Very much alive, but aged."

"Does she receive visitors? We have come all this way to see her." Then my mother added, "I am told she has healing powers."

He laughed. Without confirming or denying, he replied, "It has been many years since Devi Sita left her physical form. At first many people used to come see Soma. Now hardly any visit. Whether the people of Ayodhya came for healing or not, whether they received what they came for or not, I cannot say. I know for sure that Soma would deny any healing power. She would say that whatever is given comes from her Mata. That is what she called Devi Sita. Now only the wandering ascetics come by. I hear that she continues to feed them all, despite her age. No doubt, she will insist on feeding you as well," he chuckled. "But you may take your meals here, and you are welcome to stay as long as need be.

"Whether your daughter receives healing or not, I am sure the visit with Soma will be well worth your long journey. Well worth it. But I must warn you, she spends most of her time in silence these days and doesn't speak much. It seems as if she has already entered the other world. Every now and then I am able to visit her, but we just sit in silence. Sometimes she does not even open her eyes, and I am not sure she is aware that I am there. Yet her body persists. Once she told me that she will only leave when her Mata comes to get her. She is waiting for that moment."

I couldn't sleep that night, although it wasn't due to any lack in the accommodations. Everything was suitable. It was a nervousness, an anticipation that I couldn't explain. I sat outside the small guest hut my mother and I shared, gazing into the starlit sky, when suddenly I was overcome with emotion and inexplicitly my chest began to heave. I let the tears flow, from no apparent cause. On the journey, I had already decided that after this visit, I would acquiesce and agree to the marriage my father wanted, even though I, my husband, or my children might die as a result. Whatever would come, I would accept it. I could not go on with this tension with my parents, causing them such worry and concern. I would hide my pain deep in my mind so they would no longer know of it. But I knew that this issue was not the cause of my tears. They were not tears of sadness or fear. They seemed to be tears of relief, relief from what I didn't know. All I knew was that I felt deeply comforted in knowing that I was to meet this attendant Soma. I waited through the night for my mother to awaken, and when she did just after dawn, I was already dressed and ready to go.

"Let us take our meal first," she replied, trying to slow me down. I nodded, but my mother could sense my eagerness and so did not take much time in preparing herself. After our meal, one of the residents of the hermitage offered to lead us to the hut where Soma lived. It was not a long walk, but we had to enter the forest to arrive there. Soon a clearing was in view and we could see a small abode built near a series of rock outcroppings. My nervousness increased as we approached the hut. Our guide left us once it was in sight, and as we approached the door, I stopped. My mother also paused.

"Would you mind, Ma, if I went in by myself?"

She smiled and nodded. "Of course not. I will wait outside." I pressed open the door. The early morning sunlight had just begun to stream into the room, chasing away the remains of darkness, and I could perceive in the corner a woman seated on the floor. A beam of light fell on her form and before me I saw a beautiful young woman with dark hair streaming down the sides of her round face, her head covered simply by an orange cloth. That vision lasted only for the briefest second. As I stepped closer, the beautiful woman transformed into a very aged figure seated in meditation, her eyes closed, her deeply-lined face still as the silent sky.

My breath seemed to stop the moment I saw her. Emotions roiled my insides like a rumbling sea. I didn't know whether to laugh or cry, to stay or leave, to remain in the spot where I stood until invited in or to approach closer. The minutes passed and still I didn't move. Perhaps it was the brilliance of the morning rays that brought her back to this world. It was only when I heard her feeble voice say, "Come, child, you may enter," that I took another step forward in the small room where she was seated.

FINDING SOMA

Itook a few steps toward the elderly woman seated in the corner and then sat down and pranammed to her. No words emerged from my throat. I thought to introduce myself, but I didn't know what to say.

"Come closer, child, so that I can see you," she encouraged me with the hint of a smile. Her eyes were merely half open and I could tell that she was only gradually returning to the world. I inched closer to her, thinking perhaps her eyesight was not very good, until I was right in front of her. When she saw me, her face crinkled and a look of confusion shot across her eyes, which were now fully open. For a few minutes there was silence, and then she finally whispered, "It is you." A full smile broke across her face like sunlight piercing a clouded sky. The confusion was gone. I saw her taking in every detail of my face as she gently ran her fingers over my checks until she came to a very small birth mark on my lower right check. She rested her fingers there and nodded. Then she ran her hand over my thick dark hair that was gathered in a full braid resting over my shoulder and chest. "How thick and beautiful your hair is," she remarked with a smile. "How lovely you are, child." I had never thought about my appearance and didn't know whether I was attractive or not; I knew that in my father's eyes I was beautiful, because since childhood he had called me his "little beauty," even when I grew to quite a tall stature.

Just then my mother entered and properly introduced us. As Soma and my mother exchanged a few words, I began to feel more comfortable and took in the sight of her.

Soma was indeed aged. Her long strands of grey hair, thinned by time, were wound together in a narrow braid that seemed to fall well below her waist. She was dressed in a simple orange cloth like the residents of the hermitage; the cloth half covered her head. Her face was thin and deeply lined, yet, as she returned to the outer world, I could see a youthful sparkle in her eyes. With a faint smile, Soma kept shifting her glance from my mother to me, as my mother explained about our family and our situation. As she listened, Soma emitted a gentle and loving energy. I was transfixed by the feeling of care that poured from her eyes and smile and the nod of her head. She hung on every word my mother spoke, taking it all in, as if she were receiving word from a long lost family member. Never had I seen anything like this before.

"So you are named after the great sage Anasuya. Mata loved her very much and would be very pleased with that," she said softly, turning to me.

"Yes, after Anasuya, the devoted wife of Rishi Atri," replied my mother, as if to correct her.

Soma smiled. "Is that how she is now known in Ayodhya, as a devoted wife?" She shook her head. "Sage Anasuya is as great as any sage who ever walked this earth. She undertook such tapasya as few of the male sages could do, and this earned her the adoration of the three great devis. Through her tapasya she helped to create many things on this earth that would shape it for generations to come. She had the heart of a mother and the wisdom of a *jnani* (one who seeks liberation through knowledge). Her wisdom and love were perfectly balanced, which is why she was able to help Mata prepare for what was to happen in Lanka."

At the mention of Lanka, waves of pain rose up in my chest, and I struggled to hold back my emotions.

"You have touched upon a very sensitive subject for my daughter. She refuses to accept the captivity of our Maharani."

Soma had been conversing with my mother, but now she turned to look directly at me as if studying me. She didn't speak for a few minutes Then she said, "I understand. It is perfectly natural for her to feel that way. Perhaps though it is because she hasn't heard the true story." Turning to me, she said, "Tell me why you feel the captivity didn't happen."

I struggled for words, but couldn't reply. She encouraged me. "What is it you feel?"

"I don't know myself what these feelings are . . . ." I stuttered, "but I feel . . . I know deep inside . . . I just know it is impossible that anything could have happened without her will, her consent. She was not helpless and had all the resources to defend herself. That is what I feel and have always felt since childhood," I muttered.

"And you are absolutely right, my dear," she replied with a smile. "It was Mata's will that enabled Ravana to capture her. She knew that one of them had to enter the heart of the asura kingdom, and it had to be her. She accepted this responsibility. But there is so much more to the story. So much I have to tell, but few are interested these days. People would rather hear of the growth and wealth of the kingdom than of Mata's sacrifice, which brought such benefit to them, to all of us."

"Please do tell us," I asked in a pleading voice. "I must know the truth."

Soma smiled. "Have patience, child. First I must feed you. Mata will not be pleased if I do not feed you first."

"Please don't trouble yourself," insisted my mother. "We have already taken our meal at the hermitage."

"I know what they provide at the hermitage," she replied with a smile. "I will fix some food and a very refreshing drink, something to cool you during this warm time of year. Soon the heat of the sun will be upon us. It is no trouble at all. It is Mata who will be serving you through me. Surely you will not refuse her." My mother hurried to assure her that we would not. She helped Soma to her feet and held her arm as Soma led us to the kitchen area outside behind the hut.

Soma's words had already given me considerable ease of mind. Although I was eager to hear her story, I didn't mind waiting. We were in no rush. We watched as she fixed a light delicious meal of vegetables and wild grains, accompanied by a refreshing drink made from crushed berries. The meal far surpassed what we had had at the hermitage. As we were eating, Soma caught sight of a lone ascetic passing through the forest trail. She motioned to him to join us for the morning meal.

"Soma never fails to feed us," he said, gladly taking a seat and accepting the food Soma offered.

"What would Mata say if I did not? I have to answer to her, you know."

He smiled. "We ascetics reap the benefit of that. Often we receive alms at the hermitages, but nobody feeds us like Soma."

"That is Mata's command. She often said to feed all who come, not with the leftovers, but with the best there is."

"Is that how it was in Mithila?" I suddenly asked.

She nodded. "It was Janak Baba and Sunaina Ma who started this practice. Their household and their kitchen were always open to the sages, the ascetics, any wanderer. It was a custom Mata brought to Ayodhya." She smiled as if reminiscing. "Sometimes in Mithila, so many would come that there would be nothing left. Those of us who worked in the kitchen didn't know what we would do, but just at that moment a farmer would arrive with supplies for us. More would always come just in time. Janak Baba used to say that this was the way for all to benefit from the gift of giving. Mata practiced this until the last day of her life on earth, and I will continue it until she comes for me."

"I hope that won't be anytime soon," replied the ascetic as he finished his meal and cleaned his hands and face with the water Soma had brought him.

"I am ready any time and have been. I often wonder why she leaves me here."

"Perhaps it is to keep feeding us and to pass on your stories," he replied gratefully as he took his leave.

Soma grew quiet. It seemed her mind was still on the past. A few minutes later she picked up the thread of her story. "During the long drought, many people in the kingdom suffered, and it caused Janak Baba great pain. That was when he opened his kitchen to anyone who came asking for food. One day a couple was turned away by a new servant because she saw that there was barely enough for the household. Janak Baba called her to him. When she explained to him her reason for turning them away, he wasn't angry, but he told her that in the future he and Sunaina Ma would go without food if there was any shortage. No one was ever to be turned away. He insisted on finding that couple himself and bringing them food. This incident took place before I came to the palace, before Mata was even born, but another servant told me this story, and it has stayed with me until now.

"Mata once explained that it is against the laws of nature to hoard food. Nature is designed in such a way that there is enough for everyone if no one takes more than their share. It is greed that causes shortages, and the drought was caused by greed, no doubt, greed coming from the south, from Lanka." Soma's face tightened as she spoke these last words. "What happens in one part of the world affects all others. This is a little known truth. Ravana was sucking the resources from everyone." She fell silent.

"It must have been difficult to leave Mithila," I commented quietly. Soma turned to me and asked in surprise.

"How could we leave Mithila? It was so deeply embedded in all of us. Mata used to say we never left Mithila. Mithila came with us wherever we went. But I will admit it was difficult to be physically parted from Janak Baba, who was a father to everyone. I dare say he was connected to every person in the whole kingdom." She smiled. "I remember that last moment when we really had to say goodbye. He took all four of us servants who were accompanying Sita into his arms and said, 'You, too, are my daughters.' But when he said his last goodbye to Mata, something transpired between them that even to this day I do not understand. I think they were affirming that their contact would now take place on the inner planes because Mata often received messages from him. The night before her departure from Ayodhya he came and blessed her, and the same was true before . . . before the captivity.

"When we left Mithila, it was Sunaina Ma who was the most distressed, as she was losing both her daughters. She gave each of them a piece of jewelry that she had received from her mother on her wedding day when she came to live in Mithila. This touched Mata deeply. The only piece of jewelry besides her hair comb that Mata took with her during the exile was the pendant she received from her mother. That pendant was very precious to her, and later she gave it . . . Oh, but that is a story for another day." Soma looked up at the sky. The sun was nearly in its midday position.

"Surya Dev (the sun deity), you are surely spreading your heat. Come, it is getting too warm. Let us go inside. Then we won't be distracted by the many animal visitors that come here. They come in memory of Mata and receive the offerings of food I leave them. She belongs to them as well."

As we followed Soma back inside, she continued to speak. "Before we arrived in Ayodhya, Maharani Kausalya surprised us all by bringing artisans from Mithila to decorate Mata's rooms so they would be like the ones at home, and she sent her cooks to Mithila to learn how to prepare our food specialties. She wanted Mata to be as much at home as possible, and that moved Mata a great deal. Even before she set eyes on her, the Maharani said she had come to love Mata." She paused and then added, "Mata was very beautiful, but she never paid much mind to that. She often said that everything in this material world will one day fade and dissipate, so we should not give it too much consideration." Soma laughed. "She was right. Just look at this old body I have to carry around."

Once we were inside, she returned to her seat in the corner. For the first time I looked around the small room that composed her hut. I had not noticed anything when I first arrived, so taken was I with the sight of Soma. In a corner of the room was a bed of straw and grass, with a cloth thrown over it for a cover. In the corner where Soma sat was a small area for puja, with a statue of a woman that looked like Maharani Sita, decked in flowers. Many flowers and items from the forest—leaves, stones, and such—beautified the puja area.

My mother was glancing around the room to see where we should sit, but Soma had already taken two cushions and placed them close to her. A cover of woven cloth was placed over most of the dirt floor, and a number of woven cushions were piled up by the puja area, clearly awaiting her guests.

"Perhaps you are tired," my mother said. Much time had been taken up with the preparation and eating of the food, and my mother was concerned that we had tired her. "We can return in a few hours after you rest."

"Rest? I have no need for rest," she replied shaking her head. "I will answer the questions that have drawn you here. Come, sit beside me." She closed her eyes and was quiet for a while. Then, with eyes still closed, she began to speak. Her voice had changed, and it was as if another was speaking through her.

"When Mata and Shri Ram left for the forest, I knew there was a far deeper reason for their departure. It was not for the purpose of keeping Maharaja Dasaratha's promise to Maharani Kaikeyi, or due to her jealousy, or even the wickedness of the Maharani's servant; those were external causes, the outer conditions that enabled their departure. If it had not been that, another set up circumstances would have appeared. The design for these events took form long ago in another realm, but we will come to that later. Those conditions formed the perfect scenario for them to leave the confinement of Ayodhya so they could fulfill the deeper purpose of their birth." Soma opened her eyes and looked at us, perhaps to see if we understood what she was saying. My mother nodded. I waited to hear more.

"I knew this to be true because Mata left me hints, hidden seeds that I had to uncover for myself. Before she left, she lit a sacred fire and asked all four of us servants from Mithila to keep it alive until her return. She said it would spread a protective cover over the kingdom, allowing a part of her presence to remain. She had put a part of herself into that fire." Soma turned to look at me when she spoke these words. "Over time I discovered there was more to the fire. Often when I would sit before the flames and close my eyes, I would see images of Mata and Shri Ram from their journey and I would hear conversations. I could follow them to some degree and know their whereabouts. Mata had left me a doorway through which I could reach her, and throughout her journey, this doorway never closed, until . . . until Lanka." Soma paused. "I never spoke to anyone about this, nor shared any of the things I saw or heard, except when there was a special message for someone. Sometimes I would say that I saw it in a dream. I realized that Mata wanted to send messages back to Ayodhya and to receive word that all was well. Just as her link with Janak Baba had never been broken, she knew I could not survive without my link to her.

"That is how I came to know of the great tapasya of Sage Anasuya," she said. "When I sat before the flame one night, I could hear parts of their conversation when Shri Ram and Mata visited the hermitage of the sages Atri and Anasuya. I heard Sage Atri say that he hoped his wife would be a model for women so they would pursue deep spiritual practices and do their part in helping to shape the earth and its future. I heard these things. It was she who brought to earth the great Mandakini River so that the inhabitants could have a constant supply of water and the blessings of the river devi. She has many other such accomplishments that are not commonly known; she was very modest about her spiritual achievements.

"When Shri Ram and Mata were in Chitrakut visiting Sages Atri and Anasuya, they were shown a large, magnificent cave by one of the hermits in the area. 'You can take rest here, Ram, and you can have privacy in this cave,' he said. The cave satisfied all of their needs, except there was no water source. One day when Mata was thirsty, Shri Ram was about to go fetch water for her when they heard the gushing of water.

"Ram said, 'Sita, see how nature fulfills your every wish. Look at the spring that has come to satisfy your thirst.' The spring grew into a clear pool of water and out of the water rose a devi.

"'I am the River Godavari,' the goddess said. 'I have come to seek your blessing, Lord, and yours, Mata.' And so they gave their blessing.

"'May you always be full and plentiful,'" replied Ram.

"'And may you nourish all the life around you,' added Mata.

"Godavari pranammed. 'So it will be. Now I will head south, where I will meet you later. I will leave this pool to satisfy your thirst and where you can bathe in private.' With those words she disappeared into the water again.

"While sitting by the flame Mata left, overhearing these conversations, I realized that Mata wanted me to understand the deeper purpose of their exile. She had told me before she left that the sages were helping to preserve the teachings given by the devas and devis during an earlier age, and that their work would help set the foundation for religious learning to guide society through the succeeding ages. Shri Ram knew from his time at the hermitage of his guru, Rishi Vishwamitra, that he would be called upon to help secure this foundation; when he first set eyes on Mata, he recognized that she was the one to help him accomplish this mission. He knew that she alone would be able to withstand the difficulties and trials that lay ahead of them. Their success was of paramount importance, but as they traveled through the jungle visiting the hermitages, they learned that the *rakshasas* (unruly flesh-eating creatures) were creating great obstacles. They had untamed instincts, and their appetite was fed by human meat. They would often attack at night, devastating the hermitages. Shri Ram knew they would have to travel deeper into the jungle to realize their objective, and it was Mata's knowledge of forest foods and medicines that enabled the three exiles to survive their ordeal."

Soma's eyes had closed during her talk, but now she opened her eyes and looked at us to see whether we understood what she was saying. My mother nodded, but I could not. I hardly could take in what she was saying, it was so counter to all that I had heard since childhood. I had learned a far simpler story of jealously and the protection of honor by keeping one's word. Any deeper complexities I could not fathom, but this did not stop Soma from continuing her narrative.

"The spread of Aryan civilization was already determined, but who could clear the path? It was not only ridding the jungles of the rakshasas, those fierce eaters of humans; the forest communities also needed to learn to cultivate the earth. With the coming decline of forest foods, cultivation was going to be essential for survival. Mata taught them knowledge of seeds and diverse foods, so they could live on plant foods and not human flesh. She taught them to read the signs of nature, the direction of the winds, the timing of the flight of birds, and so many other things.

"While Shri Ram was trying to bring some elementary governance to their communities, she was teaching them how to express gratitude toward Vasundhara Ma, the Earth. She gave them the knowledge she had gained in Mithila. After every battle, for every community that lost their leaders, their fathers and husbands, Mata would bring them food and prepare a feast, and she would help them heal. In this way many communities were transformed all along their route. Again and again I saw this take place. But as they moved further south, the difficulties grew, the battles became more intense, and I began to feel anxiety." Soma had been looking off into the distance as she spoke, but now she closed her eyes again and fell silent. After a few minutes she resumed her narrative.

"After their marriage, the love between Shri Ram and Mata was like a newborn bud, just opening. There was a special beauty to this time, and everyone who was in their presence felt the intense attraction between them. It was all-encompassing, and each and every one of us in the household and in the city was part of this circle of love. It was so personal, as if each one of us had found our very special love mate. It was such a joyous time. That is why the Maharanis finally had to accept that Sita could not be parted from Shri Ram and allowed her to accompany him during the exile. They didn't know Mata's true purpose and the extent of her capabilities, but they saw how perfectly Mata and Shri Ram completed one another. As they journeyed through the jungles, I could see their love deepening, reaching new levels of unity.

"The principle of sharing that Mata had imbibed in Mithila was very much part of her nature. She could not do otherwise, so she continued to feed whoever was in need, even when they had little. Sometimes if there was not enough, she would do without. One day Shri Ram noticed this and asked why she had taken no food. She didn't answer. He insisted that she take his food, but she refused. 'When you eat, I am filled,' she remarked. 'And the same with me. I nourish myself through your mouth, Sita,' he replied. It went back and forth like this. She told him he needed his strength in case a battle should arise. He told her he had no strength if she did not eat. His strength came from her, he said. She looked at him and didn't know how to respond.

"Lakshman was observing all of this. He intervened and told Mata that Shri Ram would not eat unless she did, so he pleaded with her to take his own food, saying he was not hungry. She refused for the same reason. Should there be a battle, brother Lakshman would need his strength. Finally, Shri Ram asked if she would accept half of his food. After quietly considering the situation, she agreed. Then Lakshman insisted she take part of his food as well, and in the end she was laughing, saying she could not possibly eat all they had given her. Such was the love between the three of them. Scenarios like this played out in many ways, at many times.

"At the slightest wound to Shri Ram's body, she would cringe in pain, and the same for him. There were times during the journey when Mata became very ill. The first time, she tried to hide it, but it was impossible to keep anything from Shri Ram. He insisted she cease all work and lie down. Mata instructed him which plant medicines to gather and how to prepare them. Day and night he sat by her side, feeding her the medicine and wiping down her heated body. He felt the illness as if it had ravaged him as well, but he would not admit this in her presence, lest she become concerned.

"On one occasion there was a need for him in one of the villages, but she was ill and he would not leave her. She tried to insist that he go, but he refused. She battled with the illness all through the night so that she would be well enough the next morning for him to leave. Indeed, Mata's will was indominable, and she recovered in a few hours' time. Their journey through the jungle provided them time to deepen their unity, which would be critical for what lay ahead. They learned to read one another's thoughts and emotions. Mata once told me she saw threads of light connecting them, and their thoughts could pass from one to another through these filaments. They were like different rays of one jewel, and the concept of separation did not exist until . . . until the captivity. But that was also a necessary part of the unfolding."

Soma stopped here and went into silence. Her eyes slowly shut and after some time we realized she was in meditation. We waited an hour but then realized she would not soon return. My mother indicated it was time for us to leave, and we quietly withdrew.

My mother didn't speak on the walk back to our guest hut at the hermitage. I was grateful for that because I was too deep in thought myself to want to talk. In just one day it seemed my whole world had been turned upside down. I didn't understand much of what Soma had said, but I did grasp that the story that we, that all of Ayodhya knew, was only a half-truth. There was so much more that we didn't know, and Soma had only just begun to share her knowledge. Back at the hermitage, I looked over at my mother as she lay on her bed. Her eyes were shut. I asked, "What are you thinking, Ma?"

She opened her eyes. "I am thinking what a blessing it is that we have been able to meet Soma. She has caused me to question so many things, but I would not even know how to describe what we have heard. What will I tell your father? We came to find out why you have such a fear of marriage, and now I wonder if that was the real reason for our journey here. And you, my dear, what did you feel?"

"I feel such love for her, I cannot explain it. And when she spoke of Maharaja Janak, I . . . something deep in me stirred." I became teary as I spoke. My mother didn't answer. She closed her eyes and said "Let us rest before we are called for the evening meal."

The evening meal at the hermitage was very simple fare. The guru joined us and asked how our time with Soma was. "Did she speak with you or was she in meditation?"

"She spoke a great deal," my mother replied.

"And did she tell you stories of Mithila?" he inquired with a broad smile. When my mother nodded, he turned to me and asked if I would share one with the hermitage residents. "They don't often have the opportunity to meet Soma, as I keep them very busy here," he said. I repeated what we had heard about how the Maharaja had shared the food of his household during the drought and what he said about greed causing shortages.

"And he is very right," confirmed the sage. "Excessive wealth causes poverty. It blocks the flow of nature's resources. When too much accumulates in one place, shortages arise elsewhere. When a river flows unimpeded, everything is distributed as need be. But if there is some blockage, and too much silt accumulates in one part, the flow is disturbed and disease can result. This is a truth about nature that has not yet been learned by most of us. The animals seem to know this well because they do not take more than is needed. They do not know greed. Only we humans display this dangerous quality. Maharaja Janak was very wise. He understood well the laws of nature and built his kingdom upon those very laws. He valued knowledge above power. As the years advance, we will see the position of his kingdom weaken, because knowledge will not be the prime value of the future. It will be power. One of Devi Sita's main lessons for us is to know and live according to the laws of nature. That is why she retreated here to raise her sons, so they could gain this knowledge. She chose not to remain in the palace with all the comforts there; she knew to follow the example set by her father, who after her departure retreated to the hermitage in pursuit of knowledge."

All of the hermitage residents were listening attentively. "So it was her choice then?" asked one of the residents.

The guru laughed. "Of course. Everything that happened in Devi Sita's life was by her choice."

I wondered about the meaning of his words. Ayodhya was a center of power for the whole region, a growing power. Were we not knowledgeable? Did we not honor knowledge? And what was this knowledge he was referring to? I was too timid to ask the guru but inwardly resolved that I would ask Soma these questions before leaving.

SOMA'S TALE

I entered a deep sleep that night and didn't awaken until the morning sun poured in through the small window in our hut. My mother was already dressed and ready to go.

"You have slept so long, Anasuya," she said. "You needed the rest from our long journey, so I didn't wake you, but I am afraid we missed the morning meal at the hermitage." The heritage only served two meals a day, one in the early morning and the second in the early evening. That meant we would have to wait quite a long time before eating.

"I can do without, Ma. Let us go quickly to Soma."

Within a short time we were on our way. The heat of the day was already upon us and the forest cover gave us only modest relief. When we arrived and pushed open the door, we were surprised to find Soma's room empty. My mother and I looked at one another, wondering where she could have gone.

Within a few minutes we heard her cheerful voice from outside. "I have been waiting for you. Come around the back. I have fixed a meal for you. I would not want you to go the whole day without eating. Mata would not approve of that."

"Soma, we did not want you to fuss over us," my mother protested. "And in this heat . . ."

"You do not know the pleasure I receive in serving you and your daughter," she quickly replied.

This time she had fixed a grand feast. Several ascetics were just finishing up and saying their goodbyes to her. "You have come just in time," she said to us. "I have fed everyone I need to this morning, and only you remain. So you can have a leisurely meal, although Surya Dev will soon chase us inside."

I was hungry indeed since we hadn't had a proper meal since the morning meal the day before. The evening meal at the hermitage had hardly filled me, and I eagerly consumed the food Soma set before me. When we finished, we went inside and took the same places we had assumed the day before. Before she began, I touched Soma's folded feet and said, "Mataji . . . ." The word came out of my mouth as I sought to express my gratitude.

"*Nay, nay*," she said gently, taking my hands into hers and looking into my eyes lovingly. "To you, I am Soma, and will always be. To you as well," she said to my mother. "Everyone calls me Soma, for there is only one Mata."

"Soma, I am so happy to have met you. Meeting you has satisfied a deep longing I have felt since childhood." Soma smiled and nodded.

"This visit means a lot to both of us," my mother hurried to say. "But we do not want to tire you; please let us know if you do not feel like sharing your stories today."

"What else am I here for but to narrate these stories? When I am no longer here, who will know them? Few will then know who our Mata truly is . . . ." Her voice trailed off and she went into silence again. We waited patiently. After some time she began to speak, her eyes gently closing . . . . Here is the story she told us:

The sages Atri and Anasuya requested Shri Ram and Mata to head south into the Dandaka forest to rid the area of the violent creatures so that the forest communities could live in peace. Before seeing them off on their journey, Sage Anasuya took Mata aside and said, "I have nothing to offer for your journey but the fruits of my meditation. These I give to you for your strength and protection." Mata was very moved by this gift and told her she would never forget her time there. She told me later that she often felt Sage Anasuya's presence during difficult times as they traveled south.

They spent years battling the rakshasas and helping communities develop farming skills. Finally, heading further south, Mata, Shri Ram, and Lakshman came to the Panchavati forest. How Mata loved this region by the Godavari River! She told me that the river became like her daughter. Whenever she sat by her side, Godavari Devi would send her gifts— beautiful flowers floating by, or medicinal plants suddenly peering out along the banks. Godavari fed them the whole time they were there. Mata told me that in all of their journey, she had never seen such an array of colorful flowers, made more striking by the special light in this area. The land was rich in fruits and abundant foods, and water was everywhere— rivers, streams, lakes. Yet, despite the outward beauty, something was amiss. Both Mata and Shri Ram felt it as soon as they arrived.

Not long after they built their hut and settled in, the sages in the region spoke to them about the disturbances that were growing out of control. One day several sages came together to welcome them, and spoke about their grief. Shri Ram listened carefully as they told him that this area was of special significance to Ravana, the king of Lanka. His commanders had made the area their base and were taking many of the local resources for themselves. If anyone complained, all the villages around would suffer. Ravana's men would drain whole rivers to punish a village for resisting their rule, leaving the entire area without water. They made Panchavati the center from which they sought to infiltrate the north and thereby expand their territory.

"So we have moved into their base, have we?" smiled Shri Ram. "We will be wary."

"Has he grown so powerful now that you sages all fear him?" Mata asked in surprise. She remembered Ravana from her childhood in Mithila, when he had once come to her father demanding the bow of Lord Mahadev, but he was not so powerful then and had gone away humiliated. "Can mantras not be used to ward him off?" Mata asked.

One of the sages replied, "He is the only one we have ever known who has the power to counter mantras, to render them ineffective. Through his commanders he has taken down whole forests, destroyed rivers, tortured animals, kidnapped our women, and I am very sorry to say that our mantras are of no avail, nor are any of our weapons. We have heard that he has even gained power over the devas, and has threatened to burn out the sun and to blow up the moon with his weapons. He has threatened all kinds of destruction; we all live in fear of what he could do to this earth, nay, to the whole solar system and beyond. We believe he could destroy it all. We have seen evidence of this power, and we dare not test him."

Sita glanced at Shri Ram in alarm, but his demeanor was as calm as ever. "We are here now," Shri Ram said gently. "Please do not worry. Perhaps he is the reason we have come to this place."

Mata fed the sages and they took their leave. After they were gone, she voiced her concerns to Shri Ram and Lakshman. "If left unchallenged, he will destroy what has taken millennia to create, these forests and rivers, for which so many beings have sacrificed. We cannot allow that. What has given him such power and what is behind his lust for control?"

"Sita, everything will reveal itself in time . . ." Shri Ram began to reply, but Lakshman interrupted him.

"We should not wait any longer. We should attack him."

"What will be the cause of our attack?" asked Shri Ram, looking calmly at Lakshman. "Do not forget, Lakshman, that he is also a great scholar and devotee of Mahadev. To attack a devotee of Mahadev, we must have a clear cause that no one can question."

"The destruction we have just heard about . . . is that not cause enough?"

Shri Ram shook his head. "No, Lakshman, Ravana has covered his tracks well. His ways of retribution and destruction are such that he cannot be named as the cause, although the sages know well his role, we can prove nothing. We have no obvious cause for such a confrontation, which will be very violent and cause many deaths, with much destruction to the harmony and balance of the earth. We do not even know the effects of his weapons . . . or ours for that matter, if we release them."

Sita began to tremble. "Ram is right, Lakshman. I dread the destruction that such a war will cause. We must find another way to restrain him, unless we have clear evidence that he is behind these attacks."

"Then I will provoke him!" cried Lakshman. "I will make him come out of the shadows so that all will know who is behind this effort to control the earth."

"Calm down, Lakshman. Our path will reveal itself in time," Shri Ram replied with his characteristically even demeanor and soothing voice. "Ravana may have gained control over the celestial beings, but no one, not even he, can stop the law of cause and effect. The damage he has done will return to him. He will bring about his own destruction. He is now seeding the means for his own demise."

The next day Shri Ram, Mata, and Lakshman went to see Sage Agastya and his wife Sage Lopamudra, who had a hermitage not far away by the side of the Godavari River. Sage Lopamudra was known as a great philosopher and writer of hymns, as well as having extraordinary spiritual powers in the invisible realms; she excelled at battling the asuras, who often operated in the dark unseen worlds. Her mudras were as powerful as any weapon and could disintegrate the form of any asura, but she used her powers wisely and sparingly, once having stated that even the asuras have a right to life as long as they didn't disrupt the natural order.

The two sages verified what the others had told them. "Ravana has mastered the illusionary arts, and many of the most powerful mantras cannot counter his ill effects. But we have been able to call forth little known mantras that may be effective," revealed Sage Agastya. He and Sage Lopamudra shared these mantras with Shri Ram and Mata. "Use them sparingly," Sage Lopamudra cautioned, "and only when all else fails. As with all mantras, pronunciation is key. When misspoken, they can produce disastrous effects. Ravana has gained his power partly by manipulating the mantras. But he does not know the ones we have shared with you because they have only recently been revealed. I cannot stress enough the need for caution. Ravana has spies everywhere and is known to enter people's minds and steal their thoughts. If he would take these mantras . . . ."

Shri Ram and Mata looked at one another. Shri Ram turned his eyes to Sage Lopamudra and replied, "These mantras will be well hidden in the deep recesses of our mind and will only be recalled in times of utmost need."

By now there was only a little more than a year left of their exile. When Mata arrived in Panchavati, she was so taken by its natural beauty that at first she thought it would be a restful year before they began the journey home, even though an ascetic had warned them that the last year would be the most difficult and dangerous.

Cognizant of the warnings, Shri Ram cautioned both Mata and Lakshman to be on guard. "We mustn't take the warning of the sages lightly," he said. "And we must recognize the danger Ravana and his generals pose to us and the whole area." Turning to Mata he added, "Often you travel deep into the forest looking for special foods and medicines. I know how you love your freedom to explore the forest, but for the immediate future, do not wander far without me or Lakshman." His tone was serious. Mata normally would resist such restrictions, but this time she acquiesced. And she kept to it for the most part, wandering only down to the Godavari River.

It didn't take long before Shri Ram had his first encounter and killed one of Ravana's generals. Then another came, and he was killed as well. One after another fell before the arrows of Shri Ram and Lakshman, but the battles were brutal and Shri Ram saw that they were using weapons he had not encountered before. As his concern increased, so did Sita's.

Soma paused and opened her eyes. "I could feel it here in Ayodhya. I could hardly sleep. And I was not alone. For many years during the exile, a small group of women from the town would go down to the Sarayu River just before dawn, to a very special place where Mata had once bathed, and there they would sing to the river and request her protection of Mata. When I first learned of this, a few years after Mata had left, I was very moved that these women from Ayodhya, who hardly knew the rani from Mithila, were praying for her. As the years progressed, more and more women from the town joined together at the river for morning prayers. I took much comfort in them and would go quietly to listen. I never made myself known. I sat just close enough to hear their voices. They used to sing the most beautiful songs to Rajakumari Sita that would bring tears to my eyes. This greatly helped me to get through those last years." Soma closed her eyes again and picked up her narrative.

With the killing of Ravana's generals, the atmosphere in Panchavati grew tense. Mata noticed many disruptions in nature among the forest creature, the plants, and the rains. Things were off-season. Because of these disruptions, she had a hard time accessing the natural world. The birds that usually flocked around her now stayed hidden. Previously when she bathed in the river, fish would come into her hands, but they were mostly absent now. She asked Godavari Devi what the cause was, and the river responded that Ravana's men were again threatening to drain the rivers, and the river creatures had become as fearful as had the forest creatures. An atmosphere of fear embraced the whole region. Mata did not know what she could do to help the situation.

And then came Surpanakha, the sister of Ravana. Mata never knew whether Surpanakha had been sent by Ravana to stir up trouble or whether she had come of her own accord. Whatever the reason, her arrival in Panchavati created discord in many of the hermitages, as she would take a beautiful form and ensnare the young men through her charms and deceptions. When Mata and Shri Ram visited some hermitages, they heard stories of the most promising students being lured away by a beautiful woman, who would then abandon them and leave them in despair.

Due to these disturbances, Lakshman developed a sense of unease and was unable to sleep. Throughout their journey they had developed a system where Lakshman would stay up through the night and keep guard. Shri Ram and Mata would awake at dawn, and at that time he would go into the hut to rest while they bathed and meditated, and then Mata would prepare the morning meal. He didn't need much sleep, only a few hours, but since arriving in Panchavati he hardly slept at all, which was beginning to affect his discernment. This weighed heavily on Mata. She tried all sorts of remedies to no avail. One morning she awoke with a strong sense that she would find the right plant on the other side of the river, which was just a short walk from their hut. After the morning meal, as Lakshman was trying to rest and Shri Ram had gone to take care of a nearby village, she decided to venture out alone. She reasoned it was not too far and she wouldn't be gone long.

Mata arrived at the river and wondered how to cross. Just then her daughter Godavari indicated a place where it was shallow enough for her to walk across. She crossed and began searching for the plant. Again Godavari intervened and directed her to one of her tributaries where the plant she was seeking grew in abundance. Mata walked deeper into the forest looking for that stream. Her search was rewarded when she found what she was looking for by a shallow stream. After gathering a basketful of plants, Mata started for home. Suddenly, amid the chatter of the birds, monkeys, and other forest sounds, the steady rhythm of a woman's voice wafted through the thick moist air and reached her ears. The chanting sounds revealed a longing, an almost aching cry that called out to Mata. She could not resist following the voice.

She reached a small broken-down hut, badly in need of repair. A young woman sat outside before a murti of Parvati Ma, encased in an abundance of flowers. The woman was singing to Parvati Ma in a moving, mournful tone, the sacred sounds woven with a sadness so tangible that it brought tears to Sita's eyes. Mata approached quietly so as not to disturb her and sat a few feet behind the woman. As she listened to the chanting, she entered a state of meditation. Suddenly the chanting stopped. The sound of a small pitiful cry brought Mata her out of her meditation. The woman had risen and was staring at her in fear. She began to back away.

Mata responded immediately. "You have no reason to fear me," she said, rising from her seat. "I was gathering plants nearby and heard your beautiful chanting. I could not help but come to see who was calling out to Parvati Ma with such longing." Mata now had an opportunity to view the woman, who had a disheveled appearance, with her abundant hair unkempt and flowing freely around her face. She was thin, almost gaunt. One could see the remnants of beauty in her young face, the bloom of youth prematurely faded. Her eyes were hollow, sunken from tears and the absence of sleep. Mata's heart went out to her. Who was this young woman and what had led her to such despair?

Mata's words did not ease the woman's fear and she continued to back away. "Who are you?" she asked in a trembling voice.

"I am Sita. I am staying not far from here with my husband Ram and brother-in-law Lakshman."

"That cannot be," the woman cried in a fearful voice. "Please do not test me. Tell me who you truly are and what you want from me." A sigh rose in her chest and she began to weep.

Never had anyone doubted Mata's identity before. She was perplexed but replied. "It is true. I am Sita. I am living with my husband and brother-in-law in a small hut not far from here at the edge of the forest. But my dear child, what has caused this great fear in you?" Seeing that words alone would not erase her doubts, with her calm and loving eyes Mata silently entered her heart and gently lifted the fear from the woman's mind. Smiling, Mata held out her hand to her. "Look into my eyes and you will know that I am truly the one I say I am."

The woman wiped her tears and with some hesitation looked into Mata's eyes, those loving eyes that healed all who gazed into their depths. "Yes, I do believe you now," she slowly reached out to accept Mata's hand. "That other woman, her eyes were not clear and tender, like yours. There is no deception in your eyes."

Suddenly she realized that she was truly standing before Sita and had doubted her identity; she was overcome with remorse. Sinking to the ground, she touched Sita's feet and exclaimed, "Mata, please forgive me for doubting who you were. I never could have imagined that I would have the honor of meeting you. I do not deserve this honor, and . . . and I have nothing to offer you."

Mata was so moved by the woman's appearance and words that she could not speak for several minutes. What had happened to this woman to bring her to such a state? Gently lifting her, she said, "Your trust is the only thing I seek. I feel your pain in my heart, but I do not know the cause. Perhaps if you share with me your story, we can together remove the root of your suffering."

"I am afraid, Mata, that is not possible." She looked off into the distance. Seating herself again before the murti and staring at

Parvati Ma, she fell silent. Mata sat beside her and waited for the woman to begin. Finally she spoke in a halting voice: "My name is Chandrika. I was married to a promising young sage. Our guru so believed in my husband's abilities that he began to send his students to him. After some time we established a small hermitage not far from our guru, and as word spread, more students began to come. I saw the way they admired my husband, and I took great pride in him. Perhaps that was my weakness . . ." she murmured. Her voice grew firm, almost bitter. "Then one day she appeared. She said her name was Maya, daughter of a great sage. She came with an offering of food, which of course we could not refuse. She was beautiful and very clever, that soon became apparent. A most entrancing fragrance followed her wherever she went, captivating the students, who jumped to fulfill her every desire.

"After a few days of seeing this, I became alarmed. Beneath her beauty I could discern a smirk as she gained this strange power over everyone in the hermitage. I tried to warn my husband, but he chastised me, saying she was a celestial being who had chosen our hermitage because of his level of spiritual attainment. I began to feel something I had never felt before from my husband, almost disdain for me, as if I had become a hindrance. This wounded me greatly, and so I stopped protesting. As she showered attention on my husband, I could see his pride mounting, but I thought that because of his years of meditation he would not succumb to her wiles. I tried to believe him, that she was a celestial being. I don't know how long she was there. It seemed like years, but I think it was only weeks, perhaps not even. I awoke one morning to find her gone, my husband with her.

"I was distraught. With her departure the spell was broken, and the students began to speak ill of my husband. They all left, every one of them. They went to the hermitage of our guru, but I could not return. I could not face him. I blamed myself for what had befallen my husband. Perhaps had I been a better wife, had served him better . . . I don't know. Without the students I could not sustain the hermitage. I had no place to go.

"One day I wandered into the forest thinking that I could find my husband and bring him back to his senses. But then I began to hear a voice inside my head urging me to end my life, to give my life to the river. Finally, unable to withstand that taunting voice, I went to the river's edge and was about to throw myself into the rushing water, when I heard another voice pulling me back to life. I knew it to be Parvati Ma. It was she who saved me and guided me here so that I could devote my life to spiritual pursuits in this hut. She saved my life, for whatever it is now worth."

Tears again filled Chandrika's eyes, and the waters rose in Mata's eyes as well. She felt Chandrika's pain, the agony of a deserted wife, the abandonment, the humiliation. Internally Mata gave thanks to Parvati Ma for saving this woman's life.

Chandrika continued, "Since that time, I have learned that my husband was not the first. This woman, whoever she is, this demoness goes from hermitage to hermitage presenting herself as the daughter of a great sage, finding the best of the students and luring them away. Many women have ended their lives in the river as I sought to do. Why Parvati Ma saved me, I do not understand." She then fell silent.

Mata was bereft of words as she allowed Chandrika's suffering to pass through her. Finally she asked, "And so you live here alone?" Chandrika nodded. "But it is not safe," protested Mata. "Brutal rakshasas still terrorize the forests. Are you not fearful of them?"

Chandrika shook her head. "What more can they do to me? I have lost everything that I have held dear."

"What has happened to your husband?"

"I don't know. I don't know if he is dead or alive." Her voice was expressionless.

"I will try to find him . . . ."

Chandrika shook her head before Mata could finish. "Forgive me,

Mata. I will try to follow whatever guidance you give me, but I beg you, do not ask me to return to him; for the sake of my honor I can never return to him, and that causes me pain because I love him still, despite his arrogance and disdain for me." Mata understood, but her mind was still on the thought of reconciling the couple.

"What would you do, Mata?" Chandrika asked in a beseeching voice, lifting her eyes to Sita. "You, who are the guide for us all, admired and respected for your unconditional love but also for your dignity as a woman. What would you do if you found yourself in my situation?"

Mata was taken aback by the question and did not respond right away. She could not imagine such an occurrence. It was inconceivable that her beloved husband Ram would succumb to such seductions, he who was beyond reproach, the living example of dharma. But she felt the pain in Chandrika's heart and experienced not only the betrayal and loss, but also the affront to her dignity, disrespected by her husband, abandoned by the students and by their guru. That a woman who once must have commanded the respect of the whole hermitage should be reduced to such a state saddened Sita.

"I cannot imagine any condition that would lessen my love for my husband, but I also would not tolerate any condition that would cause me to lose my dignity. From a very young age, I learned from my father, Maharaja Janak, that a woman must uphold her dignity, her self-respect, at all costs. Indeed this is true for all human beings. No matter what happens to us, we must retain our self-respect. Whether you return to the hermitage or not, whether you reconcile with your husband or not, that is less important than regaining your self-confidence and belief in yourself."

Mata placed her hand on the woman's hand and said, "You are a brave and noble woman and have my admiration. You have done no wrong. Do not deprecate yourself, for in doing so you do a disservice to all women. We all must strive to be an example for others. It is not I who am the model. I simply seek to do my part. Each one of us must stand as an example. To be in control of ourselves and to retain our dignity, that is all that is asked of us. We cannot control the behavior of others, and we are not responsible for it, but we are responsible for our own behavior and attitudes. Do not do yourself a disservice by thinking your life is of no value. The disrespect your husband showed you reflects on him, not you, and sadly he will have to suffer the consequences. Perhaps he already has."

"Then you do not object to my remaining as a forest hermit?" she asked timidly. "I was afraid you would try to convince me to return to my husband."

Mata shook her head. "If you had left your husband of your own volition, it would have been different. But circumstances have brought you here and you are in the best of hands with Parvati Ma as your guide. But come, let me prepare for you a soothing drink to lift your spirits. I found these plants in the forest. They have a very calming effect." Mata went over to the fire pit and brought the dying embers back to life. Chandrika filled a pot with water. As Mata began to heat the herbs, she found some food items and began to prepare a simple meal for Chandrika. They sat together for some time, until Mata could see the effects of the brew.

By the end of the meal, Chandrika was smiling. There was so much Mata wanted to do for her, but she restrained herself. "I will leave the rest of these plants with you, Chandrika. Heat them and drink the brew morning and night. You will feel better and your meditation will improve. I will come visit you again, but before leaving I will share some meditation practices that I have learned along our journey. They may be helpful." And so Mata shared with Chandrika what she had learned from Sage Anasuya about focusing on the breath to calm the mind.

"Mata, how can I ever thank you? You have given me new life. Parvati Ma saved my life but you have given me a reason to live, to preserve my dignity so that I can provide hope to other women who find themselves in my situation."

Mata smiled. "You have also taught me something, Chandrika.

I would have encouraged you to return to the hermitage, but you have shown me that a woman must have the strength and courage to carve her own path in life and choose her own future. You have chosen to be a hermit, and I will pray that you receive the knowledge and wisdom to guide your path."

Mata took her leave and began to head home when she realized she had given away all the plants she had collected for Lakshman. They were the reason she had gone to the forest in the first place, and she couldn't return without them. Retracing her steps, she again sought out the spot where she had first gathered the plants. It was getting late. After filling her basket once more with the plants, she quickly followed the path out of the forest, crossed the river, and reached their small abode just before dark. She was sure Lakshman and Ram would be concerned about her as she had been gone nearly the whole day. When she reached the hut, she found Lakshman alone, nervously pacing back and forth.

"There you are!" he called in a concerned voice when he saw her rushing down the path to their hut. Then seeing that she was alone, he asked where Ram was.

"Isn't he here?"

"I assumed he was with you. After you left I tried in vain to get some rest. When I couldn't sleep I came out to find that neither of you were here. You both have been gone a long time. I was very worried."

"We were not together. I went to find medicinal plants for you," replied Sita absentmindedly. Her mind was still preoccupied with Chandrika. "I have found the plants that will help you sleep." Withdrawing to the kitchen area, she stirred the fire and began to heat up water so that she could prepare the brew for Lakshman.

Not long after, Shri Ram arrived, but he was in a quiet, almost withdrawn state. Throughout the evening meal, both Shri Ram and Mata were silent, responding with one-word replies to Lakshman's inquiries. Finally, Lakshman could not stand it any longer. "Why are neither of you speaking tonight? Whatever happened to the two of you today, I wish you would kindly share it with me."

Shri Ram was the first to reply. "I am sorry, Lakshman. Yes, something did happen today that disturbed me. On my way home from the village this morning, I came across the body of a young man floating face down in the river. He was dressed like an ascetic. I pulled him from the river so he could have a proper cremation and went to find someone who might have known him. I came upon two of his students, who told me some details of his story. At first they refused to help, claiming he was unfit for a proper cremation, but at my urging they reconsidered and we were able to perform a cremation for the poor fellow."

"What had he done that his students would refuse him a cremation?" asked Lakshman in dismay.

Suddenly Mata murmured, "It was him, her husband." Both Shri Ram and Lakshman turned to face her. Mata had been silent throughout the meal but now she spoke up. "He was a young teacher held in great esteem, but he fell for the seductions of a beautiful and powerful asura and abandoned his wife, leaving her distraught and humiliated. He ran off, leaving everything behind, but then this demoness deserted him. Now his poor young wife has nowhere to turn."

"How do you know his story?" asked Shri Ram, astonished.

"Because I was with his wife today." Mata then relayed the events of that day and what she had experienced. "Chandrika will be distraught when she learns of her husband's end. I must go to her tomorrow and inform her."

Shri Ram was thoughtful. "I will accompany you. I fear this woman who has been creating disturbances in the hermitages is no ordinary woman. She clearly has great powers of deception. We must find out what her motive is."

"I will be on the lookout for her, brother," said Lakshman.

But Mata did not get to return to Chandrika. Early the next morning, a villager came to inform Shri Ram and Lakshman that there had been a massacre at a neighboring settlement the night before. None of the villagers had survived. He said the people in his village were preparing to leave the forest in search of safer ground, closer to one of the hermitages. As Shri Ram and Lakshman prepared to go in search of the forces that had committed such a heinous deed, they asked Mata to stay in the hut.

Mata was restless. She knew not to return to Chandrika—it was a long walk deep into the forest—but she had to see whether Chandrika had learned of her husband's death. Having no other way to communicate with her, Mata went into meditation. Chanting one of the sacred mantras she had learned from Sage Lopamudra, she felt herself leave her body. She then found herself by the side of the woman hermit she had visited the day before. Chandrika could not see her, as Mata's body was one of light too subtle to be perceived by the human eye. A young man, no doubt a former student of her husband, was reciting to her the events that had led to her husband's death. Tears filled her eyes and her chest heaved in pain as she heard the sad news. After the young man departed, Chandrika looked distraught and Mata longed to reach out to her. She spoke, but Chandrika did not hear. Instead she fell at the feet of the murti of Parvati Ma and let her tears flow. Mata then saw Parvati Ma emerge from the murti and take a visible form.

"Child," she said tapping Chandrika on the forehead. "Look and see, Devi Sita has come to console you. Take her guidance and you will be well." She then disappeared back into the murti.

Looking around, Chandrika was now able to see Mata, who said with compassion, "Ram himself performed the cremation. Your husband's actions led to this outcome. You must free yourself from any attachment to him. Let go of your past, Chandrika. You are beginning a new life and if you persist you will achieve success."

"I have no strength left, Mata, no will to live," she replied tearfully.

"Then I will give you some of mine."

"Mata?"

The bright light that encompassed Mata's spiritual body expanded until it encompassed Chandrika as well. "You will be protected, and you will be able to continue with your *sadhana*, your spiritual practice, and achieve many spiritual rewards."

"I love him still, despite everything."

"You will meet again under better circumstances, but for now you must let go of your attachment if you are to progress. The clinging to him will hold you back, and him as well. Ram has released him from his suffering. Do not hold him back."

"Will she go unpunished then, this evil woman?" Her tears had by now stopped.

Mata didn't reply right away. Finally she said, somewhat mournfully, "Nobody escapes their deeds, Chandrika. She will not go unpunished. Hers will be a living death. She will prefer death than to live as she will have to live."

Mata felt herself being pulled back into her body; giving Chandrika a last loving glance, she again found herself seated in meditation inside her small hut. When Mata realized what she had said to Chandrika, she was taken aback. She didn't know why those words had come out of her mouth. How could she know what the fate of this woman would be when she didn't even know who the woman was? But Mata didn't dwell on this. A calm returned to her as she realized that Chandrika would recover and progress.

The day passed and Shri Ram and Lakshman did not return. They were low on water and she would have to go to the river to fetch more for the evening meal. Cautiously, looking to all sides, Mata went down to her daughter Godavari to get some water. After filling her pots, through the sound of the swiftly flowing water, she heard her daughter's voice say, "Beware, Mata. Danger is near." She turned and started to head back to the hut when she smelled the most beautiful fragrance. Never before had she smelled such a captivating scent. "These must be new flowers my daughter is sending me," she thought, when suddenly the words of Chandrika came back to her about the fragrance that accompanied the demoness who seduced her husband.

She is near, thought Sita, returning to the path and quickening her steps. What harm could she be dreaming up now? Suddenly the thought of Lakshman came to her. He was tired, his body worn from lack of sleep. He could be vulnerable. She would have to make him a strong brew of the healing herb and let him sleep the night. Ram and she would stay up for the watch that evening.

When Shri Ram and Lakshman returned it was well past dark. Shri Ram and Lakshman had found the small band of rakshasas who were terrorizing the forest settlements and a battle had taken place. Shri Ram had escaped with only a few minor bruises, but Lakshman had a wound in his shoulder. Mata quickly tended to it and then brought them the evening meal. In her concern for them she failed to mention that she felt the demoness near.

There was tension in the air over the next few days. Mata could not get the memory of the scent out of her mind. At first it had been most appealing, but now it repulsed her. She tried all sorts of ways to erase the odor, bringing her favorite flowers to her kitchen, using fragrant herbs in her cooking, but nothing would erase it.

Suddenly Soma paused in her narrative. I had been listening with closed eyes, trying to visualize the events that she was describing, but when she paused I opened my eyes and could see the pain etched across Soma's face. Tears were drizzling down her cheeks.

"You must forgive me," she said in a shaky voice. "It is very hard for me to narrate the events that come next. They are the most painful for me as I could not do anything to help. I could not serve my Mata when she needed me the most." Soma placed her face in her hands and shook her head. "That is the greatest agony for me, that I could not be there to endure what she had to endure."

I looked around. We were no longer alone. Several ascetics had come into the hut while we were listening to Soma. One called out, "Do not exert yourself, Soma." Then turning to us, he explained, "She always suffers when she comes to this part of her narrative. It is best to let her rest and gather her strength."

"Perhaps we should leave you, to let you rest," my mother interjected. Soma shook her head. "Just give me a few minutes and I will continue." The heat of the sun was beating down and nobody seemed to want to leave the hut, which had a surprisingly cool breeze passing through it. Soma closed her eyes again and sank back into meditation. We all waited. It took some time for her to emerge and continue her narrative.

SOMA RELATES SITA'S
JOURNEY INTO LANKA

One evening, a few days later, as Sita was preparing the night meal, she overheard Lakshman ask Shri Ram if he noticed the wonderful fragrance in the air that evening. Shri Ram shook his head. He had not noticed anything unusual. Lakshman continued to muse with a smile, "I wonder which unknown flower is emitting that beautiful smell?" Mata nearly dropped the pot she was holding when she realized that the fragrance had now entered the area around their hut. She had no time to think of a response because just then she heard a female voice.

Mata listened as the woman who had entered their garden introduced herself. "I am Maya, daughter of a great sage who is not known in these parts. My father and I are visiting one of the hermitages, and hearing that two hermits are living here alone, I have brought you food that I have cooked with my own hands."

Lakshman welcomed her. He told her that dinner was being prepared and she was most welcome to join them. Mata peered out from the kitchen area and caught sight of the young, beautiful woman who had entered, the fragrance that she had come to abhor trailing along, overpowering all the other scents. Even at this distance, she could feel the magnetism that emanated from the woman and immediately knew her to be the demoness of whom Chandrika had spoken. When she saw Lakshman accept the pot of food from her,

Mata rushed out and immediately took the pot from him.

Maya looked at her wryly and said in a sarcastic tone, "I didn't know you had a servant with you. I had heard two hermit warriors were living in these woods. Nobody mentioned a servant."

Shri Ram stiffened and replied in a cool tone, "Let me introduce you to my wife, Sita. You may join us if Sita has no objection." Mata nodded her assent and then returned to the kitchen. Her heart was pounding, and she was unsure of what to do. What trouble was this woman stirring? What if it were Lakshman she was after? Or her husband? That could not be, she reasoned.

She remembered her response to Chandrika when asked what she would do if the demoness twisted her husband's mind. Mata shook this thought away. "It could never be," she silently affirmed to herself. She had no reason to believe that this woman was going to trouble them. But what to do with the food she had brought? Already the meal for the evening was prepared. Instinctively she threw out the food behind a nearby tree and, after washing the pot, filled it with food she had prepared. It was already dark and the faded light from the fire was not bright enough for the woman to see that she had replaced her gift of food.

Mata returned to where the others sat and dished out the food. Lakshman and Shri Ram hungrily ate it all, thanking the woman profusely for the delicious meal. Taking second and third helpings, they easily finished all the food in the pot. Neither Mata nor Maya touched the food. They simply watched as the men ate. Maya watched them intently, chatting all the while. At first, she inched closer to Shri Ram, but when Shri Ram rose and seated himself on the other side of Mata, she began to approach Lakshman. Not suspecting any dangerous event, he readily responded to her conversation and flirtations. But eventually he grew tired of the conversation and suggested it was time for all of them to retire. Maya looked at Lakshman and then Shri Ram. They had eaten all of her food, and there was no effect.

Suddenly she looked at Mata, who was smiling knowingly at her. "You replaced the food I brought, didn't you?" she asked accusingly, her voice rising. "Is this how you treat a guest who has brought you food?"

Mata asked in a stern voice, "Who are you really, and what have you come for?" When Mata spoke these words, Shri Ram realized that this woman was the one causing disturbances at the hermitages. She was the one responsible for that young ascetic's death, for Chandrika's sorrow. "What do you want here in this forest?" asked Mata. "We will not be fooled or beguiled by you."

The woman's face turned red with anger. At that moment, Mata saw her true form and she cried out, "Surpanakha!" She had never seen Ravana's sister, but somehow she knew the woman to be her.

"I will teach you to disrespect me, you farmer girl." Surpanakha lunged at Mata, her hands circling Mata's neck as Mata gasped for air. Shri Ram tried to reach Mata, but before he could free her, Lakshman grabbed his knife and threw it at the woman, badly disfiguring her face. She let out a bloodcurdling scream. With blood pouring down her sliced nose, she cursed them and ran off before they fully realized what had happened: her parting words as she pointed her bloodied finger at Lakshman— "And you, you will suffer a most painful death!"—reverberated through the air.

They were all agitated by what had taken place. "Who is that woman?" Lakshman asked when he regained his bearing.

"The sister of Ravana," whispered Mata as Shri Ram sat her down and began massaging her neck. Surpanakha's fingers had left deep marks, and she felt sore and depleted. "This will not be the last of her, I fear. She was the one who lured away Chandrika's husband, the man you found dead in the river. And how many more she has killed that way we can only guess."

"I know," he replied. "Her arrival is a warning. We will soon face Ravana. It is inevitable now. He will not accept the wounding of his sister without a response."

"I am sorry about her disfigurement," Mata said. "It was something that I foresaw." Mata then told Shri Ram and Lakshman about her experience a few days earlier when during meditation she found herself seated beside Chandrika, comforting her after she learned of her husband's untimely death. "I told her that the law of cause and effect will bring to the woman who deceived her husband the fruits of her actions." She added, looking at Lakshman, "But if that is true, then what we have just done will also bring the fruits." Tears came into Mata's eyes and in her mind she resolved that she would never let anything happen to Lakshman. After all, what he had done was for the purpose of defending her.

"It is I who am responsible," replied Lakshman. "I threw the knife that wounded her, and I will gladly take responsibility for protecting you, no matter what price I have to pay."

Shri Ram tried to calm them both. "Whatever comes from this series of events will be borne by all of us. There was no choice but to protect you, Sita. Lakshman did what he needed to do, and what you saw that day with Chandrika was merely the outcome of Surpanakha's deeds, just as that poor man's death was the outcome of his deeds. It is true that it is a great offense to harm an unarmed woman," said Shri Ram soberly, "even a demoness, even one who has committed such atrocities. But we have had to kill and maim women demons before, and we have had to pay the price. So we will this time as well."

"She was not unarmed, Ram," replied Mata. "Her delusionary powers were her weapons. This was a just battle."

Shri Ram nodded. "Now we must brace ourselves for what lies ahead."

Lakshman continued to look troubled, and Shri Ram sought to allay his concerns. "You did what you needed to do, Lakshman. Had you not intervened, Sita could have been seriously hurt, or worse. It all happened so quickly. Lakshman, you and I were not alert. Only Sita saw the danger that this woman posed, and exchanged the food she had brought us for her own cooking. As soon as I tasted the food, I recognized that it was Sita's. We must be even more attentive now, because the negative forces have come right into our midst. They are among us."

The next morning when Mata went to the kitchen to prepare the morning meal, she found three dead birds on the ground in the spot where she had poured out Surpanakha's food. Lifting the birds, she spoke to them in a sorrowful tone, "I am so sorry. I should never have poured that poisonous food where you could reach it." Shri Ram found her there, mourning over the dead birds.

"This is what would have become of us had we eaten her food. I never should have poured the food here, where the birds could eat it." He placed his arm around her. "This is no time to mourn, Sita. Before this is over, many will die."

A few days later they were seated around the fire, eating the evening meal, discussing the inevitability of soon encountering Ravana. "We should not wait. We can't just sit here. Now is the time to attack, before he attacks us," said Lakshman impatiently.

"Lakshman, what I said before still holds true. We cannot attack him without just cause."

"He sent his sister here to poison us. Is that not just cause?"

"How do we know he was behind her actions? Do we have evidence of that? And we defended ourselves against her, wounding her badly. It is not in our hands; it is not our place to attack him," replied Shri Ram.

"Then what do we do, just sit here and wait?" There was anger in Lakshman's voice. He was always the one to rush into action. Shri Ram was the one to see the larger picture and to know the right moment.

Like an echo in the wind, Sita's voice entered the conversation. "It won't be long now." She had been sitting quietly listening to their discussion, when suddenly the words came out of her mouth. Shri Ram and Lakshman turned to look at her.

"How do you know that?" Lakshman asked.

Sita rose from her seat and turned away so they wouldn't see the concern on her face. "I feel it. I feel his presence approaching." She looked up at the sky. "The winds have changed course. The flocks of birds are in confusion as to which way to fly. The small forest creatures are not visiting our garden. They are in hiding. The rivers are rushing with unnatural speed. Fear has enveloped the whole region. Don't you see the signs, Lakshman, the signs of his approach?"

"Isn't that reason enough for us to attack?"

"No, Lakshman," replied Sita, her face still turned away. "We must wait. The cause will come for which an attack is justified. It is not just Ravana that we will face, but all of the negative forces that he is gathering round to disrupt the progress of Earth and her creatures. These all must be countered, and it will exact a great toll. No, Lakshman, we must wait for a just cause. Ram is right, so right."

As Mata finished speaking, an image passed briefly through her mind—the image of a celestial being who greatly loved Narayan, the supreme deity who had incarnated on earth as her beloved Ram, and Narayani, Sita herself, his female counterpart and equal. She saw this devotee of great repute fall away from them, fall into a great abyss. She reached out her arms but couldn't stop him. He kept falling. A quiet gasp escaped her lips as this image crossed her mind. Lakshman did not notice, but nothing escaped Shri Ram. The same image had come into his mind, but it also had quickly vanished. They glanced at each other in astonishment but said nothing. In order to dismiss the thought, she began clearing the remains of the meal. Shri Ram followed her into the kitchen area. Neither of them spoke for quite some time as Sri Ram helped Mata wash and put away the cooking utensils.

Mata was the first to break the silence. "I have met Ravana." She spoke calmly as she looked into Shri Ram's eyes. "He had come to claim Mahadev's bow from my father, and I saw the way my father dealt with him. Clever as Ravana is, my father outwitted him at every turn, and he did not get what he sought. This angered him greatly. Before he left Mithila, he told my father he would pay a heavy price for refusing him what was his due. My father looked at him calmly and replied, 'Ravana, you will get your just due, in time, in time.' I had not thought about this incident in a long while, but now his words have come back to me."

"That was many years ago," replied Shri Ram gently. "He has grown very powerful since then and, from what we have heard and seen, he has mastered the deceptive arts. He can enter people's minds and twist their thinking, making them do horrendous acts. There is perhaps no one more dangerous. I myself am unsure as to how we can deal with him, but deal with him we must or he will set the world on fire to achieve his ends. I am afraid the time is approaching."

"My father was insistent that I be with him during all his conversations with Ravana, even though I was merely a child. I have wondered about that. My father never did anything without a reason."

A tender expression crept over his face. "Sita, you were your father's support, his source of strength. You gave him the power to be who he is, just as you do for me."

Mata had grown serious at the memory of her father's exchange with Ravana, but at these words of Shri Ram a loving smile crossed her face. The remembrance of her father always brought her joy, as did the expression of Shri Ram's love. How fortunate she was to have these two men in her life!

After Shri Ram went to sleep, she crept out of the hut and sat under the night sky, recalling again how her father had kept her by his side during his encounter with Ravana, which had begun in a friendly tone but had turned threatening after Janak refused him the bow. Rather than being frightened, she had felt indignant at the way he had treated her father. She had never heard anyone speak so disrespectfully to him. Later her father told her that in the end Ravana would have to pay a price for his arrogance. He explained that he didn't care how Ravana spoke to him, but it was the arrogance he showed toward the forces of nature, to the gods, who Ravana claimed would one day bow down to him. Mahadev had granted him many boons for his long years of austerities, but there is always a danger in the receiving of boons. If they are misused, one's downfall is inevitable. Surely, Ravana must have been a great one in the past, her father had said, but greatness can lead to pride, which has grave repercussions.

Why had her father kept her by his side to witness this, she wondered. Everything her father did had some deeper purpose, a hidden meaning. She had seen Ravana walk away defeated by her father, angry and flustered, but as Shri Ram had said, that was long ago and he had far more power now. If she were to face him, would she be able to prevail against him as her father once had? After some time Mata went back inside the hut and fell asleep. Just before dawn she had a dream of Janak Baba standing by her. He said, "You have the inner strength and the knowledge to do what must be done. You will succeed." She awoke pondering these words.

As the first rays of dawn peered through the window, she felt her daughter Godavari calling to her. Not wanting to disturb Shri Ram, she made her way to the riverbank. The Devi emerged from the river and seated herself beside Mata. "You know, Mata, that you must face him, and you must face him alone. You are the only one who can awaken in him the love that is buried deep inside him, covered by hurt and pain and by his deceits. But this cannot happen without your consent."

"My consent is there. I give it," she whispered. The consent to meet him, yes she would do that. To reason with him, use her mental acuity and her spiritual skills, the sacred mantras she had learned. She would do all of that.

"No, Mata. It is not that which is required."

"Then what?"

"You must enter the heart of the asura kingdom. It will test all of your skills and your will. Only there can you relieve Vasundara Ma, Mother Earth, of the pain she is suffering. Only in this way can you free us from his demonic rule." The devi, overcome with sorrow, slipped back into the rushing waves, her heart breaking for Mata, who was soon to be tested in such a difficult manner.

Scenes of a terrifying battle came to Mata's mind, and she realized what lay ahead for Shri Ram. Her chest pounded and tears cascaded over her cheeks. Then she heard the calm voice of Shri Ram calling her name as he approached. Quickly drying her tears, she tried to assume a more composed countenance. "Sita, you should not have come here alone, not now, at this time when danger is near." He took her hand and asked, "What is it that has made you so upset?" Still she didn't respond.

Finally she replied in a hoarse voice, "If we should be separated, I don't want you to fear . . . to fear what might happen to me."

The look on his face grew grave. "I know that you are capable of taking care of yourself, Sita. I know that you have access to all the spiritual resources you might need, in any situation. But I . . . ."

She placed her fingers over his mouth. Gazing deep into his eyes, she said, "We cannot be separated, for we are now one. Isn't that so?"

He feigned a smile. He took her hand and held it tightly as they both turned their eyes to their daughter Godavari. She was calm now. Her waves had ceased. She was happy to see their unity. Before they got up to return to their hut, Shri Ram took some water in his hand and said to Mata, "We should not allow fear to enter us. With your daughter Godavari as my witness, I affirm that you are the star that guides my life. No matter what happens, I will always find my way back to you. There is no force in the universe that can keep me away or that can overpower you, Sita, for it is your love that sustains not only me but all of the universes." With those words he closed his eyes, whispered a mantra, and then sprinkled the water into the greater body of the Godavari River.

Mata did the same, saying, "And you are the calm that stills my tears, that heals the pain I feel for the world. In your eyes I find again my true self."

Godavari Devi received the water they had sprinkled over her and with the words "So it is," she disappeared into the depth of the gently flowing waters.

Mata had given her consent, and so events began to unfold. The next morning, dark threatening clouds cast their shadows over the land. The birds were all in flight. It was not the season for rain.

"Another storm is brewing," said Mata, looking up at the sky. "But it is not the season. This is the third storm we've had in ten days' time. Nature has been thrown in confusion." She could not shake off her concern. Shri Ram did his best to cheer Mata. He himself was not in the best of spirits as he could feel the negative forces surrounding them, but he did what he could to amuse her. At one point he looked up and saw a golden deer peering at them from a distance.

"Look there, Sita," he said. "A golden deer, like we used to see in Mithila. We have not seen one like that since we left Mithila so many years ago."

"Where is it?" asked Mata, looking in all directions.

"Straight ahead. Can you not see it peering through the leafy branches?"

Mata shook her head. "Are you sure it is real?"

"Look, there it goes."

"I don't see it, Ram."

"I will catch it for you. It will bring you much joy to have that deer as a pet." As he grabbed his bow and started after the deer, a wave of fear came over Sita. She tried to call out to him, but no sound emerged. She tried to run after him, but her feet would not move.

Lakshman came out of the hut. Seeing the distressed look on her face, he asked what was wrong. Her voice returned and her feet were now able to move, but Shri Ram was nowhere in sight. She told Lakshman where Shri Ram had gone.

"Don't worry. He will return soon," he comforted her.

When he didn't return she grew nervous, and then she and Lakshman heard his voice cry out to them as if he were in pain. Both Mata and Lakshman were greatly unsettled, but Mata thought it might be a demon imitating his voice. Lakshman didn't know whether to stay or go check on Shri Ram. Finally Mata said he should go. Reluctantly he left her, pleading with her not to leave the hut. She thought that she should accompany him and not stay alone, but her feet would not budge and her voice fell mute.

She retreated into the hut. From the open doorway she saw *him* approaching. It was Ravana, disguised as an ascetic begging for food. Mata had never refused food to anyone, and it was not within the realm of possibility for her to refuse him now. This was the being who had once gravely insulted her father. She would have to confront him alone, as her daughter Godavari had foreseen. At that moment Mata realized that this confrontation would be far more than a conversation. She would have to enter the very entrails of his demon kingdom and his demon mind if she had any hope for a positive result.

As she slowly stepped forth from the hut with a bowl of fruits in hand, she knew she was stepping into the darkness that he inhabited. She thought she was ready, but when he grabbed her by the wrist, she cried out in agony. She cried out Ram's name, but at Ravana's touch the link was broken and she could no longer reach her beloved Ram. She was now in Ravana's field, far from Ram's reach. This was something that she could not have known beforehand. She did not realize that the golden threads that wove them together, and which allowed instant communication between them, would be broken. Mata was now beyond the reach of her beloved husband or brother-in-law, far from the assistance of any creature.

Soma ended her narrative as the tears poured down her face. She opened her eyes and wiped them, apologizing. "I can never tell this part of the story without weeping," she explained. "The pain that Mata went through still pierces me so many years later."

Both my mother and I were also teary-eyed. As we all sought to gain control of our emotions, my mother began to express her gratitude for sharing this story. "I am sure you need some rest, Soma. I know that I do. I must have time to absorb what you have told us."

Soma nodded. "Will you stay for the evening meal? I can fix it for you now."

"We must get back to the hermitage. They will be expecting us. But we will come again tomorrow if you will receive us."

"I am happy to have you as my guests. Tomorrow I will share with you what took place in Lanka during the captivity. I will tell you about Mata's great sacrifice."

My mother and I took our evening meal by ourselves that night as the head of the ashram had left for a meditation retreat. I was glad for the time to be alone and quiet. My mother also didn't feel like speaking much. We ate our sparse meal and went to bed.

I had slept very soundly the night before, but this night I couldn't sleep. As Soma had narrated her tale, the scenes had drifted across my mind, making me feel as if I had been there myself. Devi Sita, Shri Ram, and Lakshman had come alive for me, and now I felt as if I knew them personally, as if whatever they had gone through I had also experienced. The terror of being grabbed by Ravana had entered me and shaken me to the core; I could not free myself from the feeling. I waited impatiently for the dawn to come, tossing and turning, at times pretending to sleep. At the first rays, I was up and ready to go. My mother saw my state and realized I hadn't slept and so agreed to go to Soma without taking the morning meal.

"Prepare yourself, Anasuya. I am sure what Soma will narrate today will disturb us greatly. None of us have heard what took place in Lanka, only that our Maharani was tortured and that Shri Ram and his army rescued her. That is all we know. I am sure there is much more to tell and Soma will relay it."

I quietly replied, "I don't think my fear of marriage was the real reason that we came here, because . . . because, I have wanted to tell you that I will agree to whatever marriage you and Pitaji decide for me. There is something else that drew us here, Ma, and I don't know what it is."

My mother took my hands in hers and smiled, "Perhaps it was to help you re-establish your connection with Maharani Sita. You loved her from the moment you were born, but you never knew her. Now through Soma, you are coming to know her again."

SITA'S SACRIFICE

"**H**ah!" exclaimed Soma as we sat before her in the early morning. Her voice, which previously had been so soft and gentle, now boomed through the air, and it startled us. I nearly jumped from my seat. "He thought he had tricked Mata, but the trick was on him!"

The sorrowful tone of Soma's voice of the day before had turned to one of defiance. "He didn't know that her entry into Lanka was essential for his defeat. It was he, not she, who had fallen for the trap! She didn't know what lay before her, but she knew that she had come to earth for this, to rid earth of the growing negative forces that would derail all of earth's life from its destined course. Her entry into Lanka was Mata's great sacrifice, undertaken for the sake of us all."

"So then it was by her design," murmured my mother in disbelief. "There has been talk of this, but no one in Ayodhya has paid much heed to those rumors."

Soma rose slightly from her seat on the floor and turned her eyes to my mother, speaking slowly in a determined voice, with a steely look replacing her soft and gentle demeanor. "What I am about to tell you is not known to the people of Ayodhya, for they are not ready to hear of the trials of their Maharani, but only of the bravery and victory of their Maharaja. I don't blame them for this. The tide is turning and the feats of women will not be spoken of in the future. Women are receding into the shadows now. I have seen this and so has Mata."

Her face softened, and she continued.

After Mata returned to Ayodhya, she never spoke of her time in Lanka, I suspect not even to Shri Ram. The only one she spoke to about her trials was Hanuman. Born into the Vanara race (a branch of the early human family), Hanuman's monkey-like form was taken by Mahadev in order to help Ram and Sita complete their mission. There was a deep bond between Mata and Hanuman, a very precious bond indeed. Hanuman was like Mata's child, a devoted and loving child. He would travel to the ends of the universe for her if need be. It was he who told me these stories after Mata had left her body. Mata rarely spoke about her own achievements and told him it was not necessary to make public what she had to endure; she said that those who needed to know, would know. I am passing on this narrative to you and your daughter to share as you see fit, and to the others gathered here, who have heard these stories before."

I looked around and saw that a group of ascetics had come into the small hut. I had been so engrossed in Soma that I had not heard them enter. They sat quietly with closed eyes and folded hands.

After speaking these words, Soma slowly sank back onto the floor, and with closed eyes began rocking gently back and forth. She picked up her story where she had left off the previous day.

After Mata had been dragged onto Ravana's *vimana* (aircraft), she was able to shake herself free of his grasp. The fact that he had laid a hand on her created a response that I never saw in Mata—anger! That was not a natural state for her, but anger arose and she lashed out at him. "How dare you lay a hand on me! I will go into your demon nest, but I will go willingly, not as your captive. Never, Ravana, will I be your captive!"

He drew back at the fire coming out of her. Mata told Hanuman that she didn't know what came over her, but this fire had arisen and her whole body was burning with great heat. She could not calm herself down until she remembered the words she had spoken to Shri Ram the day before: "You are the calm that stills my tears, that heals the pain I feel for the world." At the thought of Shri Ram coming back to the hut and not finding her, she collapsed in anguish. She told Hanuman that she had to fight to prevent herself from losing consciousness. She knew that she had to remain alert.

Then she saw their dear friend Jatayu, a vulture, flying after them. He had heard her cry out Ram's name and saw her being dragged onto the vimana. He bravely tried to battle Ravana, who slashed his wing and left him mortally wounded. Jatayu fell to the ground. Mata cried out in pain as if her own arm had been severed. Then Vayu, the deva of the wind, swept over her and she heard his words: "My dear, this is your first loss, but it will not be the last. Many sacrifices will be required to accomplish the task you have set for yourself." This brought back her resolve.

It did not take long before they arrived at Lanka. Ravana wanted her to be seen as a captive and tried to chain her wrists, but she fought him off. She said that had she not agreed to go along, no chains in the world could contain her. When they landed, she stepped down from the vimana, amazed at the crowd that had come to greet them—soldiers, members of the household, and Surpanakha, with a huge grin on her wounded face. As Mata entered the courtyard, Surpanakha spat on her and said this was her revenge.

As if walking in a daze, Mata passed through a large entranceway, the courtyard, and out into an enclosed garden. She had regained her composure and was thinking of finding a place of refuge. On the far side of the garden she spotted a large Ashoka tree that seemed to call her. She seated herself beneath the tree and pressed her back against the bark as if to secure herself in the life of the tree. A group of fierce-looking female guards surrounded her.

One of the guards brought her a basket of fruit and cup of water, and of all the guards, her eyes were the only ones that wore anything close to a kindly expression. "You must be thirsty, Rajakumari Sita, drink and have some fruit."

Sita took a deep drink of water and went into meditation. Her mind began to feel foggy, and she struggled to keep herself alert. She needed to re-ignite her connection to Shri Ram, so he would know what had happened to her and where she was. Repeating his name over and over again, she tried but could not feel his presence or response. Whenever she had called out to him in the past, immediately there had been his reassuring presence, the calm to still her emotions. She struggled to retain her composure, to keep herself from thinking the worst—that something might have happened to him when she heard him call out her name. Perhaps he had died and that was why she could no longer feel his presence. But no, she reasoned, even death could not separate them.

Hours passed and Mata struggled to feel Ram's presence. Night set in and still she didn't move. The kindly woman guard again brought her food and drink, but Mata refused. She realized that the water she had drunk upon her arrival had been tainted and had clouded her mind. She would have to refrain from taking anything to drink or eat. That much she knew. During the night her desperation grew, and she called out to Parvati Ma. With Shri Ram now beyond her reach, the only one who could guide her was Parvati Ma. From the depths of her being, Mata called to her.

Soma opened her eyes and spoke directly to the ascetics who were seated behind us. "Mata had come to Lanka to enter Ravana's mind and to clear him of his anger, lust, and thirst for power. But she didn't realize the extent of his mental abilities: how he could create illusions that appeared all too real. She had to face these illusions now as he attempted to capture her mind and weaken her resistance. He relished the challenge because he knew she was a woman of great abilities and to conquer her would add to his achievements, but he didn't realize the extent of her capability. The battle of the minds began."

Deeper and deeper Mata sank into the dark until she was engulfed by swirling black space. Gradually shapes took form, and she saw before her a desolate landscape, completely barren with no signs of life—trees burnt to ashes, dried-up rivers, volcanic lava bleeding from blackened mountains with its red glow providing the only light. The sun, moon, and stars had disappeared behind a thick veil that was suffocating any life. Wandering through the landscape, which went on and on, she could find no way out.

Finally she asked in anguish, "What place is this that reeks of death?" She could barely see a few feet ahead of her when suddenly she stumbled upon a pile of corpses, half decomposed, faces and limbs partially eaten. Gasping, she drew back. She heard them call out to her, and drew closer. "What has happened to you?" she cried. "Who has done this?"

The corpses rose and began to speak all at once. Mata watched as the corpses turned into women who had been abused and disfigured. The realization came to her that these were the women who had been tormented by Ravana—some he had killed, others died by their own hand after he abused them. "Help us, Mata," they called out. Her horror turned to compassion and she touched them one by one, pressing her hands across their half-decayed faces.

"Let me take this suffering from you, daughter," she whispered as she went from one to another. Standing among the abused women, her voice rang out, "Ravana, see what you have done. One who abuses a woman will reap the result, I guarantee this."

The figure of Ravana appeared and began to laugh, a deep loud laugh that pierced Sita's ears. "You have found my trophies, Sita.

They were created for my pleasure." Sita let go of the woman she was holding and saw them all turn to dust. Ravana too disappeared amid a cloud of laughter.

Was it an illusion, or was it real? She couldn't tell. She fell back onto the ground, weak and disoriented. Then with great difficulty she lifted herself and began to walk. There must be a way out of this desolate place, she thought. Suddenly a beautiful forest appeared. Her heart leapt up; she was free! As she entered the forest, she saw her beloved Ram resting by a sparkling lake. A cry of joy escaped her lips and she began to run to him. Then she saw a beautiful unknown young woman lying beside him, and he was playfully stroking her hair. He was telling the woman that Sita was dead and she would now be the Maharani of Ayodhya. Mata's cry of joy turned to a cry of pain.

That scene disappeared, and before her she saw the palace in Ayodhya. Ram was seated on the throne with the beautiful woman beside him. People were coming and touching their feet. "No, No…!" Mata cried. "I am not dead, Ram! I am alive. I am alive." But he didn't hear. Falling to her knees, her chest heaved in pain, tears rushed forth, and before her eyes she saw the form of Ram turn into Ravana. Again his tortuous laughter rent the air.

Mata put her hands over her ears and turned her eyes away, but wherever she turned, there was Ravana's form. Each form had beside him a beautiful woman. Suddenly he grabbed the women and began to abuse them. They tried to escape but he held them down, ripped their clothes, violated them, and left them wallowing in pain. One by one he pursued and abused them. Sharp pains racked her body as if she were in the bodies of these woman, as if this were being done to her. Her heart was shattering and she felt death was certainly near.

That scene disappeared and again she found herself alone in darkness. "This is an illusion," she told herself. "It is not real. He has trapped me in an illusionary world. I must not succumb to these false images." She ran to all sides of the dark space, seeking to escape, but she was enclosed by walls of glass. Wherever she looked, Ravana's face glared out at her, mocking, taunting. "What power is this?" she murmured. She turned in every direction but could not find a way out. Exhausted, she fell to the ground.

Mata called out to Mother Earth, but this was not earth. She grabbed a handful of what appeared to be earth in her hands and saw there was no life in it. It was a dead world, a world of illusion. Then she saw Ram again sitting on the throne with two young children in his arms. She recognized them to be her children, and she cried out to him. She ran in his direction, but could not advance any closer. No matter how hard she ran, he remained at a distance. At the sight of the children, she longed to embrace them, to look into Ram's eyes and say these are our children. She called and called, but he seemed not to hear.

In total horror, she watched as he took out a sword and began chopping the children to pieces. She turned her face away and said, "This is not real. It is an illusion." Once again her beloved husband's form turned into Ravana, and his laughter consumed the air. She found herself in a sea of dismembered and disemboweled corpses of children. Their mothers stood on the shore, crying out to her to help. Mata looked around at the savagery and, with tears pouring from her eyes, called out, "What evil is this? What mind has created this horror?"

The answer came quickly. "It is he, the one who tried again and again to kill his own child, the blessed Prahlad. It is he who created this possibility, this thought form. He must be destroyed before these thought forms enter the minds of men, and such behavior takes over the earth, before the abuse of women, the abuse of children, becomes common behavior."

Soma opened her eyes. Seeing the look of horror on our faces, she hurried to say, "I do not mean to frighten you, but to show you what torture Mata had to endure."

"Was all this due to Ravana, all these illusions?" asked my mother in a hoarse voice. Soma nodded and continued.

Through his actions Ravana was embedding in the collective mind a type of behavior that did not yet exist. Someone had to stop these terrible thought forms from manifesting. He was setting a course for humanity that would lead to disaster, self-destruction, and the destruction of all life. Because of his power, he was very dangerous. Only Shakti herself could contain him, and that was why Mata had been born on earth. When Mata saw the thought forms emerging in his mind, she felt helpless. The suffering seemed too great, and at that moment she thought to shed her form and merge with the infinite. Maybe it was time for her to return to her celestial home. As this thought emerged, she fell onto the ground and felt herself leaving her body, which became limp as life was leaving it.

Just then she heard the gentle voice of her beloved Ram say, "No force in the universe can overpower you, Sita, for it is your love that sustains not only me but also all of the universes." She looked up and saw the form of Shri Ram. As she uttered his name, the calm of his eyes took away all the agony she had experienced. His name entered her body and spirit and, from that moment on, his name never left her. Every atom in her body began to reverberate with *Ram Ram Ram.*

Her resolve returned and her strength revived. She began lifting the dead children around her and repairing their limbs. As she did so, the scene disappeared, evaporating like a dreamed mist, and she found herself standing in vast open space amid the planets of the solar system, with the earth in the distance. She saw Ravana take a large meteor in his hands. Staring at her in a fit of fury, he threw the meteor toward earth and burst into laughter. "I will destroy all of this!" His voice resounded throughout the ethers.

Quickly Mata moved so that her body was between him and the earth and she absorbed the force of the meteor's impact into her body. Ravana went from planet to planet shooting meteors directly at them, but she took the meteors that were racing toward the planets into herself. "I will protect all that you seek to destroy," she called out to him.

Ravana approached the sun and said, "I will blacken this ball of light."

"And I will ignite Surya Dev again," she replied fiercely. Gazing at him steadily she said, "The love that gave birth to this universe and sustains it cannot be overcome by all the hatred and anger you have created. These negative thoughts will be transformed."

He disappeared and called out to her from a distant solar system, "You cannot reach me here." But she appeared before him and proceeded to pursue him from galaxy to galaxy. She could not lose sight of him or his destructive powers would yield untold horrors on the universe.

What was the force behind him? What gave birth to such ugliness, anger, and hatred? Suddenly Mata stopped her pursuit of Ravana. She whispered, "Ravana has the memory of his previous birth, when he was the Maharaja (named Hiranyakashipu) who tried to kill his own son, Prahlad, for worshipping Lord Narayan. What pain must be buried deep inside! How can I release his pain?"

Soma grew quiet and then asked. "Do you understand what I am describing?"

My mother and I both shook our heads, but the chorus of ascetics spoke softly, "Yes, Soma, we are following you. We understand what Mata had come to do."

Soma continued.

You see, Mata had to enter Ravana's mind, but he was very clever. Now he knew that she could see his thoughts, so he tried to intimidate her by creating all kinds of illusions to demoralize her. He almost succeeded, as she was beginning to feel overwhelmed and would have given up her body had not Shri Ram prevented this. This was the second time Shri Ram held her on earth. The first time was when she was young and had entered a very high state of meditation in the forest. Neither Janak Baba nor all the sages gathered could bring her back to earth. She was in such a state of bliss that her body would have dissolved had not Shri Ram appeared to her, and that was before she had met his physical form. This time, in Lanka, she nearly dissolved her form due to the suffering of the world. She had taken in so much suffering that she thought to return to her original nature. It was Shri Ram again who prevented this.

"I must pause before I tell the rest of this narrative, as it is a very important part of the story. It is what led to the birth of Ravana."

My mother and I were glad for a break as our hearts were very burdened by all we had heard.

"You did not take the morning meal, did you?" asked Soma. We shook our heads. "Then let me fix you something, and let us go greet Surya Dev, who by now must be midway through his daily journey. And let us greet all the forest creatures. We have been inside for too long and our hearts are weighed down. Let us lighten them before continuing. Mata would want that."

THE CURSE THAT CREATED RAVANA

"Now, where was I in the story?"

We were back inside Soma's hut. It had been too hot for us to eat outside. She had insisted on preparing food for us, but we managed to convince her that some fruits and water were enough in this heat. We quickly took our refreshment and retreated again to her small room, which surprisingly always seemed to have a gentle breeze passing through it.

"Oh yes," she continued, "I was describing the memory that Mata recalled."

It was a memory of an event that took place ages ago when she was in the form of Narayani, walking by the side of the celestial form of Shri Ram, Narayan. Waves of bliss flowed unhindered between them as they walked in silence in Vaikuntha, their heavenly abode, exchanging thoughts about the beauty of the flowers. Each morning showed a new variety and today's assortment was of striking colors. As they were walking, Narayan said to her, "The Four Kumaras (the mind-manifested sons of Lord Brahma) came today."

"Why have they not come to see us?" she asked.

"They did, but they were turned away by Jaya (an attendant)."

"Turned away?" She was surprised.

Narayan continued, 'The Kumaras came in the form of children, and Jaya didn't want to disturb us, or so he said, but in truth, he was envious of their love for us and did not want them to meet us. I will speak with him in time."

Looking out into the distance, Narayan spotted the Kumara sages. Nodding in their direction with a beaming face, he said, "Let us go to them. They have much to share with us."

"What a joy to meet them again," she replied. They walked toward the four sages, filled with happiness.

One of the sages looked down and began to say, "Forgive us, Narayan, for not coming to meet you." Narayan and Narayani simply smiled and the sages understood that they were aware of what had taken place.

"I am sorry for the misbehavior of our attendant," Narayani said.

"It is nothing," he replied. "We are with you now, *Prabhu* (Lord) and Mata, and so we rejoice. We have come to share news of the unfolding events on earth."

After the Kumaras took their leave, Narayan and Narayani went to find Jaya, their devoted attendant. He saw them coming and tried to hide, but there is no hiding from Narayan. He saw the seeds of pride and jealousy taking root, seeds that had been there long ago when Narayan had allowed Jaya to live in that high celestial realm in the hopes that in time these seeds would dissolve. But he saw that seeds, which had rested dormant for so long, were now beginning to grow, and he was concerned for his servant. "You turned the Kumaras away, who had come to see us after a long absence. In this abode, Jaya, no one is turned away, let alone such great sages."

"Prabhu, what I did was not wrong. They were rude children and spoke to me in such a disrespectful manner. I did not think you would want to see them in that state of mind, and so I told them to go and calm themselves."

Narayan saw that he was speaking untruth and realized the seeds of deception were also taking root in his mind. "Jaya, what you are saying is not true. You should know that you cannot deceive me. You must retreat into meditation at once. Root out these seeds of dishonesty and pride that are taking hold of you. You will not be able to remain here long unless you free yourself from these illusions." He gave instructions on where Jaya should go and the type of meditation in which he should engage. Narayani looked on as this scene unfolded.

Instead of retreating as Narayan had advised him, Jaya went to the Kumaras and upbraided them. "Why did you go to the lord and trouble him with your complaints?" Jaya asked in an angry tone.

The sages looked at him in amazement. They knew what had just taken place, that the lord had advised him to retreat into meditation. Ignoring his remark, one of the sages offered to guide him in meditation practices, but this only made Jaya angrier. The sages looked at one another, realizing what lay ahead. There was no possibility of anger or pride in this realm. All negative emotions cease to exist when one enters the higher celestial or causal planes, and if even the shadow of a negative emotion arises, one would of necessity need to withdraw so as not to disturb the higher vibrations emanating from there that sustain the denser worlds. If these subtle vibrations were to be disrupted, negative ripples would echo throughout the universe.

Narayan appeared and calmly spoke to Jaya. "I have already advised you on what to do, Jaya, and will now advise you for a second time. Withdraw yourself immediately into meditation and remain there until every negative impulse is dissolved. I will come for you at that time."

Jaya apologized to Narayan and took his leave, saying to himself, "It was not necessary for the lord to chastise me in front of the others. He has humiliated me." The seed of self-pity took root. "I will find a way to make those sages pay for the disruption they have caused in my relationship with my lord."

He did not withdraw himself into meditation as Narayan had advised, but instead began to scheme. As he was sitting alone he saw a celestial woman carrying a basket of fruits. Thinking they were for the sages, he approached her. She was beautiful and gracious. "Let me carry these fruits to the sages for you," he said. But Jaya had no intention of bringing the fruit to the ones who were the cause of his humiliation; she saw this and hesitated. In that moment, lust arose in him. She shrank back, shocked by the intensity of his desire, a rarity indeed in this realm.

Devi Narayani manifested in front of him and in a stern voice called out, "There is no place for lust here, Jaya. You are seeding negative thoughts everywhere and creating a tormented course for yourself. If you don't immediately retreat into meditation, you will be forced to withdraw from this realm."

"But Mata," he struggled inside to find some excuse, but it was too late.

A booming voice rang out from one of the sages, "Jaya, you have crossed all limits. We have tolerated your insults to us, but cannot tolerate the insult to this woman sage, a woman honored throughout the three worlds. Your emotions are more fit for the human world; thus, I curse you to be born seven times in the material realm, where you will have to squash the seeds of your negative emotions. Beware, for they will multiply a thousand-fold and you will see the damage you have inflicted. If you do not purify yourself, only the lord will be able to release you."

Narayan manifested himself and Jaya fell at his feet, crying out, "Lord, save me from this curse. I will withdraw myself into meditation now."

"It is too late, Jaya," Narayan replied sorrowfully. "I tried to counsel you, as did Narayani, but you took no heed. This is the result of your thoughts and deeds. No being can escape his own mind. It is that which determines his future. You are aware of this law and yet did not consider it." Jaya continued to plead his case, but Narayan said,

"The curse of a sage cannot be undone, but it can be ameliorated. The time will be condensed and you will need only three births on earth to work through these illusions of yours, but your own deeds will determine whether you can return here or not. If you enter into deep tapasya, over time you will be able to free yourself of anger, pride, and lust and return here. But if you allow them to grow and cause harm to the natural realm, your return will not be possible."

Jaya turned to Mata and cried out, "Mata, do not abandon me. You can prevent this. Tell me what I should do."

Looking at him with great compassion, she replied, "You have already caused much harm. Your negative thoughts are already filtering into the denser realms, creating instability. You have great powers, Jaya, and can reverse this damage. But if you do not heed Narayan's warning, you will sow great conflict, conflict such as earth has not seen, and then he and I both will need to come redeem you. It will be a brutal battle, so I plead with you to seclude yourself on earth and go into deep meditation. Meditate on Mahadev. He will guide you on your tapasya."

"Mata!" he cried, but his form was already dissolving, preparing to take birth on earth.

A song spontaneously arose in Mata as she recalled this history of Jaya. She remembered Prahlad, the son Jaya had tried to kill when he took his first birth on earth. At every opportunity Prahlad used to play his heavenly instruments and sing the chant he had heard in the celestial realms, a chant that Jaya once also sang—a beautiful song of love and devotion to Narayan and Narayani.

As the song filled the ethers, Ravana stopped in his tracks. That brief respite allowed her to reach into his mind—that twisted and perverted mind—and awaken the memory of the celestial song of praise to Narayan that Prahlad used to sing. As it reverberated through the universe, Mata whispered into Ravana's ear, "Remember, this was Jaya's song before his first birth on earth as Prahlad's father; it is your song of love and longing."

He was startled as the memory stirred. His body shrank and shrank in size, and she heard him utter in a pitiful voice, "Why did you desert me, Mata? Why?"

"We never deserted you, dear Jaya. Your Lord will be here soon to release you from this birth. Your own deeds led you here and you can only return through your deeds. You must dissolve your anger, your pride and your lust. Why have you so degraded yourself, you who are capable of so much good?" she asked in an anguished voice as she reached out in vain to catch him as he started to fall.

With a confused look, he murmured, "My son, I killed my son. I killed many sons."

"But you didn't kill Prahlad," she replied. "Narayan came to save him and to spare you that agony." She reached out to him again as he was falling, falling through the pathway of the planets and the gallery of stars, until he was less than a speck in the vast universe before he fully disappeared from her sight. The scene evaporated like a dispersing mist.

The celestial realm disappeared, and the memory of it began to fade. Mata found herself in a sea of light. From every corner she heard sweet voices chanting, *Jai Shri Narayani. Jai Shri Narayani.*

Slowly the forms of women sages emerged from the light, hundreds of them, young and old, women Mata had known on earth and also from the celestial realms. She looked around in amazement. "Sage Anasuya," she whispered. Anasuya nodded, and Mata remembered how she had offered her the fruits of her tapasya when she and Shri Ram had left Sage Atri's and her ashram. There was Sage Ahilya and Sage Gargi, whom she had known from childhood, standing with those Shri Ram and she had met during their journey through the forests, and others who came from the celestial realms. The great sage Devahuti, who had attained the highest realization, was there with her nine saintly daughters. These women had great powers; they could create and sustain entire solar systems as well as mending individual broken hearts. Mata's heart was filled with such deep appreciation.

One by one they offered their love and gratitude for her sacrifice.

As the sages faded away, the form of Parvati Ma became visible. Sita found herself again in the garden of Ravana, in the dark of the night, seated before Parvati Ma. Mata was confused. So much had taken place, she had witnessed so much. Was she really back on earth?

"Where am I?" she asked Parvati Ma, after pranamming to her.

"You are back in physical form, in Ravana's garden."

"What has happened?"

"You have remembered the long ago cause behind all that is taking place now. You and Narayan had cautioned Jaya about the course of action he should take when he was forced to leave Vaikuntha. Instead of heeding your words, his arrogance and pride, anger and lust have grown a hundred-fold, as the sages had foretold. The damage he has done to life on earth will take a long time to heal, but the time for his release from this birth is approaching. Shri Ram will soon come to free the earth from Ravana's damage."

"Shri Ram," Mata whispered. "He is safe?"

Parvati Ma nodded and smiled. "He is gathering an army and will arrive before too long."

"I cannot feel him at all. The link has been broken. Can you re-establish it, Mata, so he will know that I have survived?" Sita pleaded with the goddess. "I can withstand any test as long as I feel that link within me."

Parvati replied, "Mahadev has sent his energy into the form of Hanuman, who will assist Shri Ram and will soon appear to you. He will re-establish that link, but Sita, you have already done so. Can you not hear every atom in your body humming his name? That will see you through. But I must caution you, until Shri Ram arrives, you must not eat or drink anything from this land. Ravana had tainted all the food and water that will be served to you to trap you in his illusionary worlds. You had a taste of his mental manipulations through the water you took when you first arrived. It was necessary for you to know the depth of his depravation.

Through that experience you have healed and released many of the women he assaulted. That is why the women sages came from all corners of the universe to sit before you, to acknowledge what you have achieved in your short time here, and to give you strength. You have also seen the future: that Ravana's thoughts can multiply here if this world is not freed from him. But that is Shri Ram's work. He will work from the outer field while you work from the inner."

Parvati continued, "You must remain in meditation most of the time, but in your meditation do not lose consciousness of the outer world. You will be sustained by *amrita,* the nectar of immortality, so you can do without drink or food. You must also forfeit sleep for the duration of your stay here so you can ever be on guard. Ravana is very clever and has many illusionary powers, as you have seen. He does not recall the cause, as you do, of what is happening now, but he has great anger toward you and Narayan for allowing his fall. His arrogance and lust are uncontrolled. Together, Shri Ram and you must contain them if he is to be transformed.

"This is his second birth in the earth realm after many thousands of earth years. His first birth was as the asura king Hiranyakashipu. His anger toward Narayan was such that he sought to rid the earth of his worship. The great devotee Prahlad was born as his son to try to awaken him, but to no avail; Narayan had to take the form of Narasimha to rid the world of his terror. After this birth as Ravana, one more birth will be needed for him to be fully freed of the curse. But he will not be able to return to the subtle causal realms for quite some time, until there is no shadow of ego left. We have seen the damage that even the buds of his negative thoughts and emotions can do."

"Mata took this all in. The memories of the celestial realm had grown distant, but were not submerged. She recalled her true nature and that of Shri Ram and remembered now why they had taken birth. It was not only for Ravana, but also to help in the turning of the cycles, to set new patterns of human behavior that would guide the future. Ravana was inhibiting their ability to set the course for human civilization to thrive. Having taken birth from a human father and asura mother, he was seeking to turn the earth into a demonic realm, subduing it and holding humanity captive through fear. That could not be. That was why she had agreed to enter his kingdom so that Shri Ram could accomplish what needed to be done.

"I must take my leave now," said Parvati Ma. "Daybreak will soon arrive. I will not be far. Now and then I will come in a form you will know." Mata sought to express her gratitude, but Parvati Ma stopped her, whispering, "You shared my pain, and so I will always be with you in yours."

Mata remembered how she had been present when Parvati's son Ganesh had been decapitated. It was she who had caught Parvati Ma when she sank to the ground in her agony. It was she who accompanied her through the subtle worlds, seeking her son's spirit, so that he would return to his bodily form. She had loved the little Ganesh and had felt Parvati's pain as if it were her own. Remembering this time when a deep bond had formed between them, Mata smiled and nodded. Then she watched as Parvati Ma turned into a small white bird and flew to a perch on a high branch of the Ashoka tree under which Mata was seated.

"This tree will always be blessed because of your presence," Mata whispered as she looked up at the bird. Just then the guards, who had fallen asleep, began to stir. Mata had no idea how much time had passed since her arrival. This was the first time she had opened her eyes since that day when she sought refuge under the tree.

"Sita, you have returned to the world," said the woman guard who had offered her food and water when she arrived. "We thought, dear, that you would never recover from your state of shock."

"How long have I been here?" Mata asked.

"Several weeks. You have been in meditation or a stupor. Ravana has been here every day to see you, but he said you had entered a state of shock due to your captivity. I have been bringing food and water every day but you have touched nothing. I was so afraid you would die from lack of nourishment. It seems that only I can approach you. There is some force surrounding you that prevents anyone else from approaching. You must be very hungry, dear. I will bring some fruit and water."

Mata shook her head. "I have no need to eat. But I want to thank you for your kindness. What is your name again?"

"Trijata."

"Trijata. I will remember you when this is over."

"I want to warn you, Sita, do not test Ravana's patience. All of Lanka knows it is best to do whatever it takes to prevent him from getting angry."

Mata didn't need to be reminded of his anger. She remembered vividly the scenes she had experienced in his dark world.

Ravana arrived a short time later and began to mock her. "I am glad to see you have survived the shock of your captivity. But I hear you are still not taking food. Do you seek to starve yourself to death, Sita? Because if it is death you want, I can accommodate you right now." He raised his sword.

Mata turned her eyes away. She would not look at him, but replied in a quiet tone. "I have no intention of dying, Ravana. As I have already told you, I am not your captive. Whatever is taking place is for your liberation, to help free you from your arrogance, pride, and lust."

He broke into a sharp laugh. "My liberation! You had better be more concerned about your freedom, Sita, and whether or not you will get out of here alive."

Closing her eyes, Mata slipped back into meditation without responding.

Each time Ravana approached Mata, her heart started pounding as she remembered what Parvati Ma had said about his illusionary powers. Day after day he came to taunt her, telling her that her husband's death was not far off. He tried all sorts of illusionary tricks, and when his frustration and anger grew great, he tried to harm her physically but would always be rebuffed. There was a mysterious protective energy around her that would not allow any weapon to come in contact with her body.

As the days passed and Ravana saw that her strength and stamina were not diminished by a lack of food or drink or sleep, he grew envious and even more furious. Who was she that she could hold herself so calm and steady in the face of his fury? How could she go without any sustenance day after day after day? He considered himself to be the most disciplined yogi, having given decades to deep meditation. How was a mere woman able to hold her own against him? He became obsessed with breaking her will. But Mata had another thought in mind. She was set on awakening in him remorse for his sexual assaults and abuses, for his thirst for power.

From time immemorial there have always been men who could not contain their lust and thus abused women, but these incidents were once the exception and were dealt with harshly. Ravana had established a new pattern of behavior that allowed him to dominate women for the sake of power. He relished this power, which led to more and more abuse, with no possibility of justice for the women. Allowing this pattern of behavior to enter the world would lead to the diminishment of women over time, which troubled Mata greatly.

One night as she was deep in meditation, the vistas of the future opened before her; Mata saw the gradual oppression of women that would take place. She heard a gentle voice say "One day, far into the future, mothers will kill their unborn daughters thinking they are of no value. Husbands will confine their wives to home and assign them the most menial work. Women will have no access to education or wealth. They will lose confidence and begin to feel inferior. They will be valued for their physical beauty alone, not for their wisdom or attainment. They will be denied spiritual training and be seen as unfit to reach the highest goal of life. My daughters, highly advanced seers who have created and sustained solar systems, will be all but forgotten, known only as the wives of the rishis. Their attainments will be lost in the annals of time."

Hearing these words, Mata's heart grew heavy when suddenly the wonderous Maharishi Devahuti appeared. Mata had recognized her voice and the sadness her words had brought were countered now by her joy in meeting the sage once again.

"*Dadi!* (grandmother)," she exclaimed. "Is it you?" It had been long indeed since Mata last set eyes on the great Devahuti, who was sitting mid-air in meditation. She now drifted down to seat herself in front of Mata, her long white braid winding down her chest to reach her knees, her skin as clear and radiant as sparkling snow. With glowing eyes she took Mata's hands in hers and began to converse through an exchange of thoughts. No words were needed, but her meaning was clear. She had come to awaken another memory in Mata, a memory that would foretell the future.

"It is all but certain in the turning of the cycles that we women will retreat into the shadows of life. Women hold the memory of the inner worlds and, with the downward arc in the cycle of time, knowledge of these worlds will decrease. It is necessary for the outward development of the planet, for civilization to proceed. Then, after a long period of time, the upward arc will begin again and women will bring back the knowledge. You must plant the seeds for the time when women will come forward and reclaim what they have to offer. Women will lead this upward movement, reclaiming the memory of the inner worlds. You who are my mother, my child, my grandchild, this is the reason for your birth in the human realm. Your work is not only for the present moment but also for the millennia that lie ahead."

Soma stopped to ask us if we were growing tired. Far from it. We were hanging on her every word. She offered us a drink that she said would keep our minds clear and alert, as she was about to tell us of an even earlier time when Narayani had descended to earth. Soma continued her story.

As Devahuti's thoughts were being transmitted to her, Mata remembered a far distant past, when the role of women had been more prominent. Maharishi Devahuti's father, the great *Manu* (enlightened ruler of earth of this age), had searched the world for an appropriate husband for his daughter, a greatly advanced yogi. He found a suitable sage, Kardama Muni, doing intense tapasya deep in a forest, and approached him about a marriage. Kardama Muni's greatest desire was for union with *parabrahman* (ultimate reality), yet he could not refuse the great Manu. So he agreed to the marriage on one condition: that after conceiving children he could depart to the forest to continue his tapasya. Devahuti consented to the match her father had arranged.

Before he left to take up again the ascetic life, Kardama and Devahuti enjoyed many years of marital happiness, and she bore him nine daughters—Kala, Anasuya, Sraddha, Havirbhu, Gita, Kriya, Khyati, Arundhati, and Shanti—each of whom became an advanced yogi. Then she bore a son, Maharishi Kapila, who was a manifestation of Narayan. Seeing the birth of the boy, Narayani could not help but come hold her beloved in a young boy's form. Just as Kardama Muni was leaving for the forest, Narayani appeared to Devahuti to console and guide her as she sought to raise and train her ten children in yogic ways. And when the time came for the marriage of her daughters, it was Narayani who helped facilitate their unions.

One of Devahuti's daughters, Sage Khyati, had a gentle and kind disposition, and her vision was fully open to the inner worlds.

Narayani had deep affection for her and guided her on how to enter the higher, subtler realms. After Sage Khyati's marriage to Rishi Bhrigu, they appeared in the celestial realm of Vaikuntha to seek Narayani's assistance in bringing certain knowledge to the human realm. During their discourse, Sage Khyati was as taken with the wisdom of Narayani as Sage Bhrigu was with her beauty. The desire to have Narayani be born as her daughter entered Khyati's mind , but she was far too modest to ever suggest such a thing.

Sensing his wife's desire, Bhrigu entreated the devi to be born to them for the good of the human world. She agreed, but only after Narayan assured her that he would bring her back to Vaikuntha at the right moment. And so Narayani, also known as Shri or Maha Lakshmi, was born as the wise and beautiful Bhargavi. In her descent into the human world, she retained much knowledge that she later shared with Sage Bhrigu, guiding her father in understanding how the stellar bodies impact all beings in the physical realm. Later he was able to develop the system of predictive astrology based on this knowledge.

Sage Bhrigu had a second wife named Usana, who was the mother of Shukracharya, a learned sage and guru to the asuras. During that time there was a great battle between the devas and the asuras over control of the physical realm. Many of the asuras had been destroyed, but a brutal band of them sought refuge with Usana. Seeing her son's disciples in such disarray, she granted them refuge. The devas soon came to her and asked her to allow them entry, but she refused, saying she had given her word to her son's disciples to protect them. As Narayan was on his way to bring Narayani back to the celestial realm, he heard the argument between the devas and Usana; he appeared and cautioned her to let the battle take place, come what may. He said, "Those who uphold dharma will succeed, as it should be. Do not stand in the way." But Usana refused, saying she had given her word.

"To go against one's word is unfortunate, but to go against dharma is a far greater misdeed. One must weigh the outcomes of these two, and use discrimination." Narayan advised Usana in a calm voice. "I urge you to allow the devas to fulfil their function. It is for the protection of the human world."

Usana was adamant, which placed Narayan in a difficult position. Bhargavi arrived just then. Seeing the plight, she went to Usana and pleaded, "Ma, you will lose your life if you don't retreat. I will release you from the pledge you have given to these asuras, who have brutally killed many people. You should not stand in the way of justice being fulfilled."

Seeing that there was no way out of her plight, Usana looked at Narayan and pleaded, "Prahbu, it is my time to leave this physical form, and it is my desire to leave by your hands. Please help me out of this difficult position. I cannot go against my word, and I do not wish to impede dharma from being fulfilled. I surrender myself to you."

At that moment Narayan reached down and gently lifted her spirit from her body, freeing her from the pain of inaction. Narayan then stepped back and allowed the devas to slaughter the asuras. When the massacre was done and the devas had fled, Sage Bhrigu came out of meditation. Arriving at the scene and seeing his dead wife, he broke down and sobbed, calling out to the skies, "Whoever has done this, I curse him that he too will know the pain of separation from his beloved." The sky cracked open at the sound of this curse, so intense was the voice in which the words were spoken, as Sage Bhrigu had just returned from meditation and his spiritual powers had been heightened through his tapasya.

Narayan stepped out of the shadows and, feeling Sage Bhrigu's suffering, said, "I take your pain onto myself and accept your curse, sage." Realizing what he had done, he fell at Narayan's feet and cried "No, No. I did not realize it was you, Prahbu. Please, help me revoke this curse."

Gently lifting him, Narayan said, "I will ease your pain and take it into my own heart at some future time when Narayani and I are both in human form." Bhargavi, distraught over her father's agony, looked gratefully at Narayan. Gladly would she take from her father the suffering that had fallen upon him.

Brought out of her meditations by the curse that had reverberated through the three worlds, Sage Khyati, Bhrigu's first wife, hurried to the spot where they were gathered. Realizing what had just taken place, she chastised her husband and said, "In cursing Narayan, you have also cursed your daughter. What father would do this?" It then hit Sage Bhrigu that Narayan's separation from his wife would mean equal pain for his daughter. Taking her in his arms, he begged forgiveness and again asked that the curse be retracted.

"A sage's curse cannot be undone," replied Narayan gently.

"But it can be softened," said Sage Khyati. "Let it be a partial separation, and let it manifest at a time of your choosing when it will benefit the world."

"When the time is right, as you have spoken, it will come to pass," replied Narayan. Then turning to Bhargavi he motioned to her, "Come, it is time for our return."

Bhargavi knelt at the feet of Sage Bhrigu and Sage Khyati. Her mother lifted her and privately counseled her, "There was a time when a rishi's curse was needed to help carry out the law of cause and effect. It is no longer so. The time for such denunciations is passing. May you one day take away this power, lest in the declining ages it be misused." Gazing into her mother's eyes, Bhargavi nodded and then assumed her true form as she and Narayan departed.

Mata sat in silence for a long time as these memories returned to her. "So this is the cause of my separation from Ram?" she finally asked Sage Devahuti.

The great sage shook her head. "This current situation was designed by the two of you for the release of Ravana. The separation that was predicted still lies ahead, but do not think about that now. It is in the future. A great battle lies before you. When that time comes, you will know what to do, and it will be for the benefit of the world, just as my daughter Khyati had spoken. I want to show you something now, my child, something that will help you realize the work that lies ahead when these events have passed. Take my hand."

Mata took her hand and in their light bodies they flew to the Sarayu River in Ayodhya. As they approached, Mata heard the most beautiful chanting. It was just before dawn, and the first hint of sunlight was beginning to creep across the horizon. As the night sky lightened, so did the sound of the chanting *Jai Mata Sita, Jai Ma.* Quietly their voices blanketed the river. A wave of joy and surprise swept over Mata. Dozens of women were gathered and chanting her name, invoking the deities for her protection.

"This is what has created the protective shield around you. Every day since your departure from Ayodhya, these women have come to the river to chant and pray for your safety. At first there was only one, that woman over there who is absorbed within." Devahuti pointed to a woman standing knee deep in the water, her eyes closed, her hands in prayer position. "Then others came. When word of the captivity reached Ayodhya, dozens and dozens joined them, every morning, no matter the season. Rain, thunder, winds, nothing deters them. This is the power of these women. Even Ravana cannot penetrate what has been created through their devotion. Therein lies your work, Sita, the seeds you are sowing for the future when the power of women will need to be awakened. The purpose of your life is not only for now, but also for all who will come in the years ahead, for the women, Sita, who will follow the path you set."

"I have felt their devotion," replied Mata quietly, "but I didn't know from where it came. I have sensed a great love coming from Ayodhya, but I assumed it was for their rajah, Shri Ram. I did not think the women of Ayodhya would feel this for me, as I was still a foreigner in this land when I had to leave it."

"These women do not know the power they have created. They are praying for your well-being without realizing the protective energy with which they have surrounded you. Take solace, Sita, in the love and devotion of these women." The sight before Mata began to fade. The women, the Sarayu River, the sunrise all faded from view and, before she knew what was happening, she found herself back under the Ashoka tree.

The light form of Sage Devahuti also began to fade away. "Dadi, don't leave," Mata called in a faint voice, as her heart burst with love for Maharishi Devahuti and all that she had gifted humankind.

Vibrating in the ether for a moment longer, the sage said by way of parting, "Ram will fulfil the outer needs of this battle; you must fulfil the inner ones. Work from the inside, Sita, as you have been doing, from inside Ravana's mind. That is where the real battle is taking place."

Dawn was quickly approaching. Mata tried to hold on to the scene of Ayodhya, but the reality of Lanka again took hold of her. The guards approached with offerings of food and drink, trying to whet her appetite and entice her into Ravana's distorted universe. When Mata refused all food, they retreated, keeping their guard at a distance, and Mata drifted into meditation.

A short time later, she heard a gentle woman's voice softly address her. Opening her eyes she found Mandodari standing before her with a platter of food. Mandodari was Ravana's queen; she was devoted to her husband and was a pious woman who had continually pleaded with Ravana to release Sita. Every day Mandodari had been cooking food for Mata and leaving it before her meditation seat. And every evening she came to reclaim the untouched food.

"Sita, I have cooked this food with my own hands, my best dishes, loved by all the household. I beg you to eat."

Mata was silent as she gazed at Mandodari, a dignified woman but one whose beauty was cloaked in a dress of sadness. Finally she said, "Mandodari, I am not unaware of your kindness and the purity of your heart, but I cannot eat or drink until Ram arrives. I am sorry not to be able to accept your offer, truly I am." Seeing the pain on Mandodari's face, great compassion arose in Mata's heart.

"How will you survive, Sita? It could be months."

"Do not worry about me, Mandodari. I am being sustained, but I promise you that the first food I take will be from your hands."

"I wish I could do something for you, Sita."

"You can." Mandodari looked at her expectantly. Her pain over Mata's condition was evident on her face. "You can make peace with yourself." Mandodari looked at her with confusion, but Sita said no more. She had retreated again into meditation.

SITA'S TEACHINGS TO MANDODARI

Soma had been speaking for a long time. "Are you tired, Soma?" asked my mother.

"My rest will come soon enough," Soma replied. She took a deep breath and continued her story.

A few days after speaking with Sita, Mandodari had a terrible dream. She remembered the time when she was a young woman and her parents had refused Ravana's offer of marriage. His anger disturbed the whole household and she grew fearful. Then in the night he abducted her. Her fear of him gradually led to her surrender, and finally she had no choice but to marry him. Eventually that fear turned into love and devotion and he became the center of her life. All of her actions and thoughts were devoted to his well-being, and she gave no consideration to her own needs. He had become her god. In the dream she saw his demonic form and once again fear came over her. She awoke in a great sweat.

Quickly dressing she hurried to the garden where Mata sat in meditation. Not wanting to disturb her, Mandodari sat down quietly and tried to calm herself. She didn't know why she had sought out Sita, but she had nowhere else to turn. She feared that her dream was a bad omen, and that something terrible was about to happen to Ravana, her beloved husband.

Gradually Mata opened her eyes and found Mandodari seated in front her. Fear was etched across her face, and gazing at her with compassion, Mata took hold of her hand. As soon as she touched her, Mandodari dissolved into tears.

"Just as he abducted you, Mandodari, how many others has he abducted? You, he married. The others he cast aside. He is instilling new norms in the human mind, and this is very dangerous for society. Others will follow his lead. Women will be seen as objects of pleasure and then tossed aside. No, Mandodari, this cannot be. He must be stopped."

Mandodari was quiet. Wiping her face of all remnants of tears she then asked Mata, "What have I done in the past that I have grown so attached, so devoted to one who is causing such disruption to the world? Why, Mata, why? What have I done in the past to be in this position?"

"Close your eyes, Mandodari, and see the past." Mata gently tapped her on the forehead and scenes from a previous birth came before Mandodari's inner eye. She saw that her parents would not agree to any marriage. They could find no one suitable for their beautiful daughter, and so she remained unmarried. Yet her heart longed to find a husband to whom she could devote herself. She vowed again and again that if she could marry, she would be the ideal wife, sacrificing her needs to those of her husband. This longing remained with her throughout her life, and on her death bed her last thought was that if she were so fortunate to find herself a husband in her next life, she would sacrifice everything for him.

"In order to fulfil this past desire, you sacrificed yourself," said Mata gently. "Your mistake was in placing this desire of yours over the good of society, and what was truly best for you. One's first responsibility is to one's dignity, Mandodari. That comes even before devotion to one's husband. You have succeeded in one area and have been the perfect wife, but you have not succeeded in maintaining your dignity as a woman. But then, can you be an ideal wife if you have not maintained your dignity as a woman? You have sacrificed dharma for the sake of your husband, and this is a course that leads to pain and suffering. You have known about his treatment of other woman and remained silent. You have seen his quest for power, his arrogance and hatred, and did nothing to oppose him."

Mata continued. "Not only did Ravana capture your body, but he also captured your mind. You must free yourself from that captivity. You must, Mandodari, not just for your own sake, but for the sake of Lanka. You are the real captive here, not I, so do not feel sorry for me. Ravana holds no sway over me. Freedom is in the mind, Mandodari. Free your mind."

"What could I have done, Sita? Ravana has grown so powerful. What could I, a woman, have done?"

Mata laughed. "Are you not powerful as well, Mandodari? Do you not realize that had you left Ravana, half of his power would have fled as well?"

"Leave him?" That thought had never entered Mandodari's mind and it made her shudder now.

"Is it really love that keeps you here, or fear, or a vow taken long ago under very different circumstances? Love is not born out of fear or out of selfish desire. Love is born of freedom. Are you free, Mandodari?"

She didn't answer. Then she said, "I see the terrible consequence of his actions. I see it coming, Sita. But will my children also have to pay the price for his misdeeds?"

"Nobody is made to suffer for another's misdeeds. They will only reap the consequence of their own actions. There is still time for them to disavow their father's behavior, but will they do it? I am afraid, Mandodari, that many on both sides will die. That is the real tragedy of this whole affair. It could have been prevented, and perhaps still can be if we could somehow shatter Ravana's arrogance and pride, free him of his lust and greed."

"What can I do, Sita?" Her tears had ceased, and she looked at Mata with the glimmer of hope in her eyes.

"You have a choice, Mandodari. You can leave and return to your maternal home, or you can stay. But then you must fortify yourself for what will come. Seek the guidance of Parvati Ma. She will give you the strength you need."

Mandodari was quiet for some time, reflecting on Mata's words. Then she said, "I must bear responsibility for what will come to pass. I must be the witness of what happens when women's voices are muted. And so I will stay in the hope that I can repair what damage will be done." Suddenly the image of her sons came before Mandodari, and the tears began to flow again. "You are not a mother, Sita. You don't know a mother's sorrow."

"You are wrong, Mandodari. All that you see, these are my children, and I suffer with them. I am your tears flowing for the death of your sons. They are my sons as well." Mata paused and then began again. "You are not of this clan, Mandodari. Their ways are not your ways. Separate yourself in your mind so that your healing power will grow stronger. It will be needed."

"Sita, I have seen you be firm as a rock and soft as a gently flowing river. How is it possible to be both? If one is soft, one can be crushed; if one is firm, it is difficult for love to flow. Ravana has used all of his illusionary powers to break you, to no avail. He has tormented you, threatened and imposed the worst of his magical illusions on you, and still I have seen you speak with compassion, with no anger or hatred toward him. How is this possible?"

"Anger and hatred are for the weak of mind. One must rise above these harmful emotions. If I were to succumb to anger or hatred, that would be Ravana's victory over me. The love that sustains this universe is far greater than any human emotion, and that love is both gentle and firm, personal and impersonal. There is no contradiction here, Mandodari. That is one secret that Ravana has yet to learn. His heart appears to be devoid of love."

Mata turned her eyes from Mandodari and gazed off into the distance. "But that is not the truth. No one is without love, but it can be deeply hidden. Pain can overshadow it and one must learn to erase this pain, to rise about it, so that the hidden love can be released." Turning back to Mandodari, she added, "All that you have done for him, Mandodari, all that you have sacrificed, has not served to awaken the love that is buried deep in his heart. Something else is needed."

Mata was quiet for a few minutes and then said, "It is most important, Mandodari, that you make peace with yourself and free your mind from Ravana's clutches. You must leave it to others to awaken him to his true nature." Internally, Mata whispered, "You must leave that to Ram; that is the reason for my presence here."

The sun was just peeking above the horizon and Mandodari made a motion to rise. As she did, Mata suddenly touched her arm and asked, "You have a daughter, don't you?" Mandodari nodded in surprise. Nobody in the palace spoke of her daughter, as she had been gone a long time. "She is with her husband's family. I have not seen her for a number of years."

"Call her to you."

"Call my daughter?" Mandodari could not conceal her surprise.

Again Mata nodded. "She is wiser than you know. She will be of assistance to you now."

Thanking Mata for her counsel, Mandodari took her leave.

It was not long afterwards that Hanuman arrived and found Mata. When he appeared before her, Mata recognized immediately that he was the manifestation of Mahadev of whom Parvati Ma had spoken, and she rose and sought to touch his feet.

"Nay, Mata," he said, stopping her. "I am your devotee."

Mata shook her head. "How can that be, Prabhu?"

"I have come to serve Shri Ram and you."

"I cannot see you as my devotee, Hanuman, but I can see you as my son." Hanuman smiled. That suited him just fine. From that moment on she called him *Putra* (son) Hanuman. "But how did you find me? Lanka is such a maze and Ravana has hidden this garden so that none can enter without his permission."

"I heard the sacred name of Ram humming through the ether, and I followed the humming to its source. Every atom in your body, Mata, is reverberating with *Ram Ram Ram*. My body, mind, and spirit also resonate with the name of Ram."

Mata smiled. "Your appearance here has brought me much joy in this loathsome place." Mata took his hands and held them to her cheek. How happy she was that he had found her. It made her feel that Shri Ram was not far away. Then Hanuman took out the ring Shri Ram had given him to bring and handed it to her. When she saw Ram's very own ring, a cry of joy escaped her lips. Placing the ring on her finger, her bond, her link with Shri Ram was re-established. "After so much time, I can hear his heart beating again," she whispered. "My Ram is alive and well. No one knows the agony this separation has caused, not knowing what his condition has been."

Mata then took out her hair ornament, the only ornament, aside from her mother's pendant, that she had been wearing on that fateful day she allowed Ravana to capture her, and handed it to Hanuman. "Give this to Ram and let him know of my condition. It will help him to feel my proximity."

Hanuman nodded. Sensing the austerities she had endured, Hanuman was concerned. "Mata, you have not eaten in so long. Let me bring you some mangoes from the garden."

She shook her head and told him that she was unable to eat or drink until Shri Ram's arrival. "Putra Hanuman, you eat on my behalf. What you eat will nourish me."

Mata looked up and saw the small white bird perched on an upper branch. She smiled at it, and the bird hopped about in response. Seeing the interaction between Mata and the bird, Hanuman smiled and replied, "I understand. I see the one who has been your companion during this captivity."

"How much time has passed since that day?" Spending most of her time in meditation, Sita had completely lost track of the time.

"Over nine months, Mata. Shri Ram has been gathering an army and will be here soon."

"A war will cause such devastation," Mata said mournfully. "Putra Hanuman, your compassion is unrivaled. You are the heart of the world. Please talk to Ravana and seek to awaken him to his true nature."

Hanuman said, "I will try. If he is unable or refuses to relinquish his arrogance, the destruction of Lanka will begin. I will be the first to light that flame. That will be an act of compassion to all who live captive in this land."

"Before you leave, let me gaze on you a little longer, putra. You have so lightened my spirit." Mata took in his radiant form, which emitted a gentle golden hue, his long flowing abundant hair, his shining eyes that glowed with such love. Finally she directed him to the garden where he could fill himself with fruits. Sure enough, he ate his fill and then allowed himself to be taken captive and brought before Ravana.

Despite Hanuman's attempt to penetrate Ravana's locked heart, Ravana's blinding arrogance made him strike out against Hanuman. Hanuman was wearing a simple cloth tied around his waist, falling just below his knees. Ravana instructed the guards to set fire to the cloth he was wearing, but Agni Dev would not appear and so the fire did not light. In a fit of anger, Ravana's eldest son, Indrajit, grabbed the torch, and mocking Hanuman, calling him an animal and a monkey man, he tried to light the cloth and then he tried to lift it.

"Let's see if this monkey man has a tail," he exclaimed as the guards who were gathered around broke into wild laughter. Still Agni Dev would not come until Hanuman beckoned him. "Agni

Dev," he whispered, "let the purification of Lanka begin." And so the rear of Hanuman was set on fire, but through his mental powers he transferred Agni Dev to the administrative buildings of Lanka and they burst into flames as the fire on Hanuman subsided. Everyone scattered to put out the burning buildings and Hanuman was able to escape.

When Sita realized what had happened, she shook her head sadly. "Ravana's son did not know that he was dealing with the Lord himself. That fire is the seed of his destruction, and his death is now sealed."

The meeting with Hanuman renewed Mata's strength, for she knew that Mahadev's presence was now with Ram, and she began to let down her guard. As she did, Ravana's mental assaults increased.

One day as she was seated in meditation, Mata saw a terrible scene unfold before her—a massacre taking place in Mithila. As her parents lay dying, her father called out her name in an agonized voice. With her emotions in turmoil, Mata's eyes flew open and she jumped up. She had to reach them. Realizing where she was, she sank back into meditation, inwardly calling out to her father to feel his presence, but again the horrible scene arose before her. Hours passed as she struggled with her emotions.

Toward the end of the day Ravana arrived and, in a sympathetic voice, said, "Sita, I am so sorry to have to bear this news. There has been an attack on Mithila and your parents have both been killed." When Mata didn't respond, he repeated the news as if she hadn't heard him.

"How do you know this to be true?" she asked in a cold tone.

"My spies have just returned and have reported the news to me." Mata didn't respond. She wouldn't let Ravana see the emotions that were smoldering within her.

"Cold-hearted daughter! You don't even respond to the death of your parents." Mata shut her eyes and withdrew into meditation. "Now there is only the death of Ram to await, and then you will have no one left but me. You know that after Ram dies you will never be accepted back to Ayodhya, and now that Mithila is finished, where will you go? Who will rescue you?"

The thought then entered Mata's mind that he had arranged for her parents to be killed. Mata kept her eyes closed and held her emotions in check until night arrived, when she could let go the floodgate of tears. Her agony released, she called out to her father again and again. In the middle of the night, as she was gaining control of her pain, she saw a ball of light emerge from the sky and approach her. It took the form of Sage Anasuya, who then settled on the ground before her.

"Sita, Ravana has created the illusion of your parent's death. He has managed to trap you again in his illusionary world. See for yourself, your parents are alive and well. Mithila is safe." Mata closed her eyes. In a vision she saw her father deep in meditation at a forest hermitage and her mother safe in the palace. Opening her eyes, Mata touched the feet of Sage Anasuya with her hands and thanked her for revealing the truth.

Sage Anasuya saw that Ravana's mental manipulations were wearing Sita down. Taking Mata's hands in her own, she said, "Draw from me whatever strength you need for this battle, Sita. You are entering a new phase in the effort to awaken him, and the mental battle that must now begin in not for your survival but for his release. You have been on the defensive, resisting his mental attacks, now you must strike out in the same manner. As Ram performs the outer work, so you must do the inner."

She told Mata that Ram was approaching and would soon be there, and as he came closer, Ravana would grow more desperate and would stop at nothing to defend himself. "He will not harm you physically," she said. "He is unable to do that. But he will assault you mentally, and so you must now engage with him." Mata looked at her questioningly. "You must bring before his mind all the damage he has done, the suffering he has incurred. Enter his dream world, Sita. That is the only way to reach him now. He has closed off every other access point. Unlike you, he is unable to do without sleep, and so you can reach him when he is asleep and his guard is down. I will show you how to enter his mind in this way."

For a long time they sat together in meditation. When Mata opened her eyes again, Sage Anasuya was gone. The first rays of dawn were just beginning to reveal themselves.

As soon as the sun mounted its way across the morning sky, Ravana arrived, expecting to find a distraught Sita mourning her parents' death, but instead he found her calm, unmoving. It was a rare occurrence for her to look directly at him, but this day her eyes met his and she said, "You must know, Ravana, that deceit brings its own return. No longer will I be subjected to your illusions."

Her words evoked thunderous laughter from him. "Sita, you are trapped in my world, a world from which there is no escape."

Fire rose within her spine. "It is not my duty to end your illusions of power. That duty belongs to Ram. I have told you before and I will tell you again that no power of yours could keep me here if I did not will it. I am here only to help Ram release you from your illusions."

After more laughter and taunts, Ravana left and she spent the day meditating on Sage Anasuya's words. That night she did enter Ravana's dreams, not as herself but as one of the celestial woman he had abused. In the dream the woman berated him and called out for justice. An army of devis responded and surrounded him; they threw weapons at him from all sides.

Ravana did not appear before Mata the next morning. And that night, another of the abused woman appeared in his dreams and called out for justice. And so it went night after night as the women he had violated came to claim justice. One night they all appeared together and their voices rang out so loud that even the great Ravana shook. And it was not just the women. All of his atrocities were laid bare before him, with voices echoing from everywhere as they called for justice.

Mandodari came before Mata one morning and told her that Ravana was now afraid to sleep. "He is haunted by dreams and refuses to even lie down," she said in a worried tone. "He keeps himself occupied all through the night so that he won't sleep. But his lack of rest is unnerving him and affecting his mind." She asked Mata what potion could help him, but Mata only replied, "Let the work be done, Mandodari. Do not stand in the way of justice."

Two weeks passed and Ravana had not come before Mata. The dreams that tormented him were appearing to him even in daytime. Finally, one morning he appeared before Mata in a livid mood and blamed her for bewitching him.

"Why blame me?" she asked. "It is your own deeds you are seeing."

But he blamed her presence, her tapasya, and could not accept that anyone could have such power over him. He decided to kill her, thinking that would relieve him of his tormented nights, but Mandodari ran to him before he could raise his sword and stood between the two of them.

"You will bring your own downfall!" she shouted at him. "I will not let you destroy yourself."

"Move away, Mandodari," he cried. "This woman has bewitched me, and for that she must die."

Mata sat calmly in meditation, with eyes closed as if not even hearing the commotion around her. The protective shield created by the women of Ayodhya still hugged her form, and not even Ravana's rage could break through. When Mandodari refused to move and broke down in tears, Mata opened her eyes and said gently, "Mandodari, I have told you his fate lies in his own hands. He cannot bear to see the effects of his past deeds, and thus he hides himself in a shroud of anger. He cannot face himself. Neither you nor I can save him. Only he can do that."

Then turning to Ravana she said, "You call yourself the master of the three worlds, but you are not even the master of yourself. The dreams you see are but a reflection of what you have become. It is not too late to change, Ravana. There is no deed that is beyond forgiveness."

Mata's words infuriated Ravana and he departed in a fit. That night, despite his best efforts to stay awake, he drifted to sleep.

Instead of being haunted by the past, he found himself standing before Narayani, who said, "Your deeds have taken you very far away from Vaikuntha. So far that it will be difficult for you to find your way back. But it is not beyond your means if you allow the remembrance of who you are and where you came from. Let go of your anger, your lust, your jealousy, your thirst for power and revenge. Uproot those seeds that have dug themselves deep into your being and let love flow again in your heart, as it once did." Ravana awoke with a start. It was still night.

Disturbed by the dream, he made his way to his mother, the powerful Kaikesi.

"Sita is no ordinary woman, Ravana," she mused after hearing about his series of dreams. "She has managed to enter your mind and is seeking to mold you to her will from within. She is powerful. Stop fighting and marry her. You will gain even more power through her. But how to reach her? I sense some protective shield around her. I will find a way to break it. Sit with me and I will transfer to you some of my power through the sacred mantra I use when nothing else will work." They sat together for some time as Kaikesi repeated the mantra.

Ravana's approach to Mata changed after this as he sought to court her. This presented an even greater danger, so Mata had to withdraw deeper into meditation, hardly ever opening her eyes. The more she withdrew, the greater grew Ravana's desire, until one day he lurched at her, seeking to break the protective shield around her with his sword. For the first time, Mata was in physical danger. His power was such that he would have broken through had not another power come to protect Mata.

As Mata saw him lurch toward her, before she could even respond, she saw the light form of Sage Lopamudra emerge from the ethers. The sage transformed herself into many, and with strokes as quick as streaks of lightning, her many hands encased him and threw him backward. He reeled all the way across the garden and landed on his back, seemingly unconscious. The guards rushed to his aid and carried him off. The many forms of Sage Lopamudra merged into one and she stood before Mata, shining more brilliantly than the light of day. Mata folded her hands in gratitude, her eyes betraying the deep appreciation for all the women sages who had come to her aid, guarding and protecting her.

"You have done your part, Sita; the rest belongs to Shri Ram. Do not be deceived by Ravana's outer behavior. You have stirred the seeds of his shame. He is now rattled by discontent, which will not subside, and this will open the way for Shri Ram's victory. Now you must turn your attention to the outer battle that lies ahead. The balance of the worlds depends on this battle, and it will be fiercely fought. You must nurture the regenerative powers for Shri Ram's army so they will not suffer defeat. We will all be present to assist." Her light form faded into a faint outline.

Through the rays of the sun, Mata could perceive the light forms of the many women sages who had visited her since her arrival in Lanka. Parvati Ma sat at the front with lines of women seated beside and behind her in meditation. "We are the invisible army," they said. "We guarantee Shri Ram's success."

THE INNER BATTLE

Soma continued uninterrupted.

It was in the days before the great battle that Ravana approached Mata in a state of fury. When his efforts to woe and charm her failed, he once more resorted to threats, worn down by sleepless nights and burning with anger as a result of what he called her "witchcraft." The very thought that a woman could outwit him was beyond what he could bear. All of his efforts to trap and confine her in mental illusions no longer had any effect. Mata was on constant guard, for by now she knew how subtle were his ways. He approached one morning determined to weaken her by creating in her mind the illusion of Shri Ram's death. Laughing and taunting her, he projected an image of Shri Ram lying fatally wounded on the battlefield. "This is the future; your husband is but days away from his death," he laughed in that raucous voice of his.

Mata had been seated in meditation. The image of Shri Ram lying lifeless was before her, but this was not the first time Ravana had projected such images into her mind. She showed no outer emotion, but inwardly her heart trembled at the sight of her beloved lying there, even though she knew it to be an illusion. She opened her eyes and with a steady gaze slowly rose to her feet. Shaking her head slightly, allowing the shadow of a compassionate smile to cross her lips, she spoke to him: "Your decades of tapasya, Ravana, have been for naught. Your years of meditation, supplication, and invocation have taught you nothing. You have wasted so many precious years, years that could have steered you toward your goal. This is not the reason for which you were born—to torment people by creating false worlds, worlds without substance and no bearing in reality."

"Reality?" he laughed. "I create reality. I can enter any mind and insert any thought, any image. What is reality, Sita, but my own creation?"

She shook her head. "You are mistaken. You have mastered the illusionary arts, but all you have created is falsity, with no semblance to reality. It can all be destroyed in a moment. There is a reality, Ravana, beyond the world of illusions, but this reality is far from your reach. You know nothing of the Self. You know nothing of who you truly are. You think you are Ravana, lord of the three worlds, but that is not the truth. That is not who you are."

Ravana seemed shocked that she would speak such words. He thundered, "Have you not seen how I control this world? I create streaks of lightning to crash down on the earth, unleash the rains, stop the movement of the planets—they are all under my control. Shall I show you?"

"All illusions," she persisted. "You have created the illusion that you can do these things, and many believe you. But I have seen through your mask, Ravana, and know that you are locked in a torturous web of lies, all lies."

"Sita!" he yelled. "I can take your life at any time."

"You cannot take my life," she replied, shaking her head. "You may take this body, but this body is not who I am. Have you not realized this yet? Have my words all these months had so little effect? I am not trying to spare your life, for it is too late for that. But I am trying to spare you from what will come after, from millennia of wandering far from the place to which you seek to return, the place that was once your home. That is what I am trying to remind you of. Awaken, Ravana, to who you truly are." Her words rang out from all directions, not from her lips alone.

He stood speechless before her. She thought she caught a glimmer of remembrance in his eyes and so she took advantage of the moment. "You were born with great potential and could have achieved much for humanity. That was the purpose of your birth, to use your gifts. Your years of tapasya, your scholarship, the boons you received—what were they all for if not to benefit society? Instead, you created a warped world for yourself which you thought you could control. But the one truly caught in illusion is you, Ravana, not the many you have destroyed."

The glimmer of remembrance faded away, and once more anger shook his being. His face grew red, and his eyes nearly popped out of his head. He sputtered some words and with a threatening glare stalked off.

Mata knew that she had created an opening in him, and it was for Shri Ram to do the rest.

Mata had begun transmitting to Shri Ram whatever knowledge she could uncover about Ravana's military strength and strategy. She also conveyed to him her distress over the death and destruction that a war would incur. And so when Ram arrived in Lanka, after overcoming the many obstacles Ravana had placed in his way, he sought to prevent the conflict, but it could not be avoided. Ravana defied his efforts, taunting him to try the strength of his army against the army of Lanka, and so Mata braced herself for what was to come.

Through her inner eye, she saw Shri Ram standing on Lanka's shore, looking sorrowfully over the kingdom that was soon to be destroyed. Both armies had access to highly advanced weaponry, weapons that could cause massive destruction to all living creatures. Innocent plants and animals would suffer; they too would be destroyed. A deep sigh escaped both of their lips as they took in what lay ahead. The pain in his heart was her pain. His was the outer role, hers the inner one. For this battle, they had to work in harmony. She had to be attentive to every detail so that she could assist from her station inside the mental framework of the demon kingdom.

The day the fighting began, dark clouds hung like thick wet tresses clinging to the land, divided only by the plethora of arrows that shattered the air. For hours it continued, exploding the earth, leaving the stench of death. Day after day it went on until many of Ravana's top generals were killed, including his son and heir. The pain was unbearable for Mata. She could not distinguish one death from another. It no longer mattered to which army they belonged. When she felt bodies being torn to pieces, it was all part of the same life, life that also belonged to the earth, the trees, the land.

One day just as the sun was setting, the demon guard Trijata came running to tell her that Lakshman had been killed. Mata shook her head in disbelief and whispered, "It is not possible." But Trijata had become her friend and guardian and would not lie.

"It is true, Sita. I heard it directly from the battlefield. He has been hit with a poisonous arrow, for which there is no antidote, at least not anywhere nearby. I am so sorry. It will be a great loss for your husband to lose his brother."

Mata slipped immediately into meditation and through her spiritual eye she saw Lakshman writhing in pain. The words of Surpanakha returned to her, condemning her beloved brother-in-law to a painful death. Shri Ram was seated beside him wiping his twisted face with a wet cloth soaked in medicinal herbs, trying to calm his agony. She saw a physician there instructing Hanuman to go in search of the sacred *sanjivani* plant, the only medicine that could counteract the poison. But he had to return within a few hours, the physician said, or the plant would be of no avail. Time was of the essence as the poison was entering his blood stream.

Only once before had anger arisen in Mata, when Ravana had grabbed her by the wrist, but now that anger rose again. Riding a wave of fire that shot up through her spine, she found herself exiting her body and standing before Lakshman. She wanted to reach out to him, but she was not in physical form and could not be seen or heard. She could not touch him or do much to assist. As she stood thus wondering how she could help keep him in his body until Hanuman returned, she saw a shadowy figure approach. She immediately recognized Yama Dev, the Lord of Death, coming to lift Lakshman's spirit from his body. Pushing aside the great winds that flew in the wake of Yama's approach, tossing away the dark clouds that had begun to engulf Lakshman's body, she placed herself between Lakshman and Yama Dev, and stretching her arms out wide in a protective stance. She cried out, "You will not touch him!"

"It is his time, Mata. Please stand aside," replied Yama. When she refused, he pleaded, "I do not want to fight you, Mata. Please let me do my work. This is his karmic return for having disfigured a woman who was no threat to him, and for all the killing of the asuras. Ram too must make a sacrifice in this great battle."

"But what he did was in my defense," she cried.

"Every action brings a reaction. This is his due. His allotted time is up, and I must take him."

"You will have to take me before you take him." And so their battle began, Mata against the Lord of Death. Throughout the night they fought. Yama tried to approach Lakshman from every angle, but Mata was too quick, leaping from one side to another, and managed to keep him at bay. Again and again she cried that he would have to take her first, and again and again he replied that it was not her time. Finally, he said to her, "I will leave him, but you will have to give me something in return."

She was by now exhausted from the battle, and so agreed. "I will take some years from your life and extend his," Yama said. She nodded. As soon as she gave her consent, she saw him fade away into the distance and the dark clouds around him dispersed. Realizing that Hanuman would soon be back with the sacred herbs, Mata also withdrew. She awoke some time later to find herself lying on the grass beneath the Ashoka tree. It was just after dawn and Trijata was standing beside her, trying to revive her, telling her that Lakshman had survived the wound.

Soma said, "When Mata told Hanuman that story, she said she did not know whether the battle that she had with Yama was a dream or reality. It didn't matter. Lakshman survived and that was all she cared about. But Hanuman told me that when he returned with the sanjivani plant, and when Lakshman opened his eyes, his first words to Shri Ram were, 'Where is Sita?' When Shri Ram told him that she was still captive in Ravana's palace, Lakshman shook his head and said, 'No, that is not possible. I saw her here. I saw her standing before me.' That is how I came to know that Mata's battle with Yama Dev really did take place.

This was a turning point for Mata. Her energy was depleted, but the battle was almost over. Nobody knew about this incident with Yama Dev, aside from Hanuman. Mata never spoke of it. It was only in the year before she left this world that Parvati Ma told Shri Ram what had taken place. When I questioned her about the incident, she was reticent to speak of it and said only that she did what any mother would do for her child. Lakshman was indeed like a son to her."

Soma stopped her storytelling, as her tears prevented her from speaking. When she could speak again, she said, "There is so much about Mata that nobody knows. Her work was unseen, hidden from the world, and she was content to keep it that way. She told me repeatedly that the true work to preserve this world takes place away from the eyes and ears of humankind."

The day had slipped into early evening. We had been transported to another time and place, and as I came back to my normal consciousness, I looked around and saw that Soma's small hut was now filled with ascetics, some seated, some standing, some leaning in from the small window. They had come for nourishment of their bodies but instead had received nourishment for their souls.

"Perhaps we should let you rest now. You have spoken all day, Soma, and we are so very moved by what you have narrated," said my mother.

Soma shook her head. "We are almost at the end. I will finish this part of the story, of Mata's sacrifice."

Both armies suffered great losses, and the damage to the wildlife and trees, the ocean life and all living creatures, had been great. It was now time for Shri Ram to face Ravana. Mata had not communicated to Shri Ram what she had seen about the true identity of Ravana for fear it would impede the battle. But Shri Ram intuitively knew. This made his task all the more difficult but also more urgent; he desperately needed to free his devotee from the great delusion that had overtaken him.

During her time in Lanka, Mata had done her best to penetrate the deep recesses of Ravana's mind to try to awaken him. His mental ability, his acuity and discernment had weakened from many months of lack of sleep. Now it was Shri Ram's role to complete the process. In the end, it was Shri Ram's love that undid Ravana. As they battled through the day and night, Shri Ram saw the work Mata had done to unravel the intricate web of deception he had built.

Mata described it like this: she was seated in meditation when she felt a tremendous burst of love rush over her in unending streams, like gushing fountains of the most refreshing waters. She sat there in great bliss. Eventually she opened her eyes and saw waves of love rushing over everything, the trees, the plants, the guards around her. Then she realized it was coming from Shri Ram. Before he shot the final arrow, he stood for a moment peering into Ravana's spirit and freeing him from his delusions. He sent that flood of love, of which he is the source, and then unleashed the final blow, cutting the roots of the ten deadly traits that had held Ravana captive in illusion.

As Ravana lay dying, the two of them spoke. Deeply humbled, Ravana asked Shri Ram if he could now return to his true home. Shri Ram sadly shook his head and said that although he had destroyed much of the karma Ravana had accrued, one more birth was needed for him to free himself fully, to ensure that his lust and pride were completely uprooted, his ego dissolved. That last effort had to be his to make. As Mata had foreseen, he would wander for millennia before that last birth. It would be a long time before he could gain acceptance back into the higher realms.

Mata knew the moment the battle was over. At that exact time, the amrita that had sustained her stopped flowing. As she began to emerge from meditation, the waves of love were replaced by a great fire that engulfed her body, the heat from her tapasya bursting into flames. It was thus that Shri Ram and the others found her, seated in a bowl of fire. Lakshman called out in panic, thinking that she was being burnt alive. He started to run toward her, but Shri Ram stopped him. In amazement he gazed at the sight and said, "She is consuming all the impurities of this place and the effects of the war. This fire is the heat of her tapasya; let it burn." The fire then withdrew back into her body and subsided.

"At that moment, the fire she had lit in Ayodhya went out," Soma said. "I had been guarding it when it burst into a bright flame and then extinguished itself. After fourteen years of burning incessantly, Mata's flame went out. I knew then that it was either victory or death." She continued:

"In Lanka, after the flames had been absorbed into Mata's body, she felt the presence of Shri Ram and opened her eyes to behold him. In a moment of overwhelming joy she rose to greet him. But she had not stood on her feet for days, and with the amrita gone, her body suddenly experienced weakness from lack of food and water. As she tried to rise, the world began to spin around her, and Mata fell to the ground unconscious.

"Although Shri Ram also needed to be treated for his wounds and was depleted from the battle, he carried her into the palace and for days sat by her side, pouring drops of water into her mouth. Finally she came to, and just as promised, she took her first food from Mandodari's hand, telling her that now she had to heal the land by feeding the people. Before leaving Lanka, Mata and Mandodari cooked and arranged a feast for all the people of Lanka. Feeding people was Mata's way of expressing her love. And then, of course, as you may already know, her last act on Lanka was to go to the sacred Ashoka tree that had sheltered her and to touch her forehead to its roots, paying homage to the great being who had been her companion and witness during that difficult year."

Soma fell silent. Then after a few minutes, she looked around and for the first time noticed all the ascetics gathered. She looked surprised. "So many of you have come, and I have not fed you," she said quietly. "Please forgive me. I will get your food ready."

She started to rise, but one of the ascetics stopped her and said, "Not tonight, Soma. Our bodies are satisfied, for you have fed our souls."

My mother and I quietly took our leave, saying that we would return in the morning.

THE RETURN TO AYODHYA

My mother and I walked back to our cottage in silence. Neither of us wanted to eat and so we decided to skip the evening refreshments offered by the hermitage. Exhausted by the emotions aroused by Soma's narrative, my mother went right to sleep. After turning and tossing for a few hours, I stepped outside to take in the night sky. So many questions had awakened in me during the day, and I thought perhaps the stars would guide me to the answers I sought.

A crescent moon shone down, leaving enough darkness for the stars to display their brilliance. There seemed to be an infinite number of bright stars and faint ones, those in clusters and solitary ones. Did those star beings so far from earth know of our Maharani? Did they witness her austerities, her struggles and triumphs? Did they come to support her or were they silent observers? Did they love her as I did? As I gazed at them, I wondered who they were.

My mind wandered to the women sages of whom Soma had spoken. Where were they now? Perhaps they were overseeing some of the stars and planets, relieving some distress far away. After all, their concern could not be for our earth alone. Perhaps our Maharani was with them, tending to some important matter in another part of the universe. If that were so, how could my prayers reach her?

For as long as I could remember, my heart had always been filled with love for Maharani Sita, but meeting Soma opened in me a far

222

deeper quality of love. Hidden in my heart was the desire to stay with Soma, to learn from her, to serve her, but I dared not mention this to her or to my mother as I was destined for marriage, a destiny I now would accept. Listening to Soma had mysteriously broken some block in me, a resistance that arose from a source I couldn't identify. It didn't seem to matter what path my life took; as long as the path brought me closer to Maharani Sita, I would be content. This was the only measurement that mattered to me now.

Eventually I laid my head down on the soft ground outside our cottage. I must have fallen asleep because I did not notice the dawn rays approaching. It was my mother's voice that awakened me. "Anasuya," she called gently. I opened my eyes to find her seated beside me. "Tomorrow we must begin our journey home. We have not had a chance yet to speak with Soma about your situation."

"It is not necessary, Ma," I hurried to inform her. "I will do whatever Pitaji thinks is best."

"Such a change of heart," she replied with a smile. "Soma's magic has already worked. I am glad. Now we must let her finish her narrative."

After taking a small meal at the hermitage we headed to Soma's hut, where she was resting upright in the same spot where we left her the evening before. My mother explained to her that we had to leave the next morning, and she nodded. "What more can I tell you?" she asked, turning to me.

All of my questions of the previous night vanished and I replied shyly, "Can you share with us how it was when Maharani Sita returned to Ayodhya? How did she come to live in this place so far from the city?"

"Ah," replied Soma with a smile. "That is quite a long story and a complex one. It is difficult to convey what Mata's role was in the world since so much of what she did lay hidden, even to this day. But I will begin." Soma was quiet for what seemed like a long time. With closed eyes, she began to rock back and forth ever so slightly and a slight hum, sounding like an *Om*, emerged from her throat.

I rested my back against the wall as I sat by Soma's side and closed my eyes as I listened to her narrative, seeing the images emerge in my mind's eye as she spoke.

After Shri Ram and Mata left Lanka, their first stop was to offer prayers to Mahadev at the spot where Shri Ram had done puja to Mahadev and the army had built the bridge to Lanka. Then they went back to Panchavati, where Mata and Shri Ram visited Sage Chandrika. Mata had promised that she would visit again, but she had been unable to do so because of the kidnapping. Now she kept her word. She was pleased to see Chandrika steady in her meditation and in a much better situation than when she had first met her. She was still living as a hermit in the same broken down hut, spending all of her time in austerities. Mata told her that in a few years a son would come to her.

"How is that possible, Mata?" she asked in amazement.

"You will find a small boy wandering in the forest. The one who abandoned you will now find himself abandoned by his mother. Take him in and raise him like a son. He will become your student and learn from you, and grow very attached to you. There is much love in your heart that needs to find fulfillment. Shower it on him, as only your love can heal him of his past deeds." Chandrika's eyes filled with tears at these words.

"I will find him again?" she asked in a gentle tone.

Mata nodded. "Only this time he will be much better behaved. You will set him on a course from which he will not stray."

Shri Ram stood by and watched this interaction. When they were finished speaking, Shri Ram said, "Chandrika, your prayers were a source of strength to Sita when she was in Lanka. For that I am ever grateful."

"Prabhu . . ." she began to protest modestly, but Shri Ram and Mata smiled at her.

Mata whispered to her, "The recovery of your husband in the form of a son is the blessing of Ram. It was he who performed the last rites for your husband when he found him dead in the river, and it is he who is guiding him back to you."

"Raise your son to be the sage he was meant to be," said Shri Ram. After blessing her, they took their leave.

There was great celebration when they returned to Ayodhya. I have no words to describe the joy I felt in seeing Mata and Shri Ram again, but I also saw the toll the long journey and her tapasya had taken on her. Her beauty was as striking as before, unchanged except perhaps it was a more mature beauty, but I felt a weakening in her life energy. Nobody else seemed aware of it, but I could not help but notice and in my joy there was also sadness. Her sacrifice had taken a toll. The same may have been true for Shri Ram, but I was not close to him and so I could not tell. I knew Mata so well that I could see it in the steps she took, the pace with which she walked, the way in which she spoke.

One thing everyone noticed is that the youthful couple that had left Ayodhya fourteen years earlier was now a mature and accomplished pair, more deeply bonded to each other, more open with their love and complete dedication to one another.

I did not ask Mata any questions about her long journey, but she pressed me about the other servants who had come from Mithila and who didn't survive to see her return, about the maharanis and all the others. Her first thought upon arriving was for her sister Urmila, who had been doing intense meditation during their long journey. That was a happy reunion. You can imagine the joy everyone felt. The coronation of Shri Ram as king took place and Rani Mata settled back into palace life.

Many changes had come to Ayodhya during the fourteen years. The city had grown, trade had increased, new lands had been acquired, and many foreign traders and visitors now flooded the streets and markets, making the streets less safe than they once had been. It was considered unwise for women to wander the streets alone. We were all confined to the palace much more than previously. This was a reality Mata had difficulty accepting, especially after years of wandering at will through the forests.

One day Mata and Shri Ram were driving in their chariot when suddenly, as they approached the market, Mata asked the charioteer to stop. She quickly stepped down and hurried toward a stall selling plant medicines. A man was there seeking some remedy for his ill mother. "You will not find what you need here," she hurried to inform him. "Follow me." The man recognized her and, greatly surprised that she would stop for him, didn't know what to do. But she urged him again, and he followed her down to the river. The guards who had been accompanying the chariot did their best to keep up with her. Once they reached the river, she pointed to the other side. "You will find there the plant to treat your mother's ailment." She then described the plant in great detail and told him how to prepare it for his mother. "When she has recovered, please ask her to come see me," Mata requested with a smile. Then seeing the guards approaching, Mata turned before he could even thank her and hurried back.

Shri Ram had stepped down from the chariot and was calmly waiting for her, but the guards were beside themselves with fear that something could have happened to her. He put their concerns to rest. "If all the demons of Lanka could not harm her, do not worry about the people of Ayodhya, or the foreigners," he assured them. Word spread through the palace, and the chief of the guards came to Shri Ram, pleading with him to restrain Mata's movements.

Some weeks later, I was outside by the palace gate when I saw a woman being turned away. I recognized her at once as the woman who had gone down to the river every day to pray for Mata during the exile.

"What did that woman want?" I asked the guard.

"This is the second time she has come requesting to meet the

Maharani. I told her to go to the public audience where anyone can approach her and the Maharaja. But she has refused, saying it is a private matter."

That evening I told Mata what had happened. Mata was thoughtful. "It was her son who was seeking medicine for her. I saw him in the market. After directing him to the right herbs, I asked him to tell her to come see me when she had recovered. I am so sorry she was turned away."

Shri Ram entered at that moment and, seeing the disturbed look on Mata's face, said quietly, "Sita, do what you need to do." Mata nodded. She told me to come get her before dawn with trays of flowers and incense, as if preparing for a river puja. "And bring me some of your clothes, Soma."

The next morning I came to Mata's room and helped her dress in my clothes. The two of us quietly prepared to leave the palace. As one of the guards stopped us, I replied that the Maharani had asked us to go to the river for a special puja. He nodded and let us pass. First we did go to the river and offer our prayers. Mata so enjoyed meeting again her beloved Sarayu Devi, but as dawn was approaching we could not stay long. Mata seemed to know how to find the woman's house. We arrived there just after dawn. Her son opened the door and was shocked to see the Maharani standing there in servant's clothing. Falling to her feet, he exclaimed, "Maharani, I could not thank you before. What you have done for my family . . . my mother was so ill and you brought her back to life."

"It was not I but the medicine," Mata replied with a smile. "There are wonderful medicinal plants growing by the side of Sarayu Devi about which our physicians seem to know nothing. I am so glad she has recovered. May I meet your mother?"

"Please come in," he rushed to say. Sitting in the corner was an older woman whose body was still frail after her illness. She slowly rose to meet Mata.

"Please remain seated," Mata said gently, placing her hand on her shoulder. "You have still not fully recovered. I have come to apologize for the guards. I had asked to meet you and they turned you away. Please tell me your name."

"Abhitha," she replied in a faint voice.

"Abhitha," Mata repeated quietly. Tears came into Mata's eyes as if she was recalling something, and for some time she was so overcome by emotion that she couldn't speak. Finally she said, "Abhitha, from far away in Lanka, I heard your chants, your prayers for me. I saw you at the river, the sacred Sarayu in the pre-dawn hours, you and the other women of Ayodhya. When the rest of Ayodhya was asleep, you and the others were praying, in the rain, the cold, the dark. You were my protection. Your prayers created a shield around me that prevented any ill from reaching me. I am ever grateful and will remember you always."

"Maharani," she replied tearfully, moved by Mata's words. "I am nobody. I was only doing my duty. I am your servant . . . and my only wish is for your well-being."

"We are all servants here," replied Mata, smiling at her, "serving each other in various ways."

Abhitha's son, who was standing nearby as a silent witness to this all, asked if he could offer Mata food or water. But Mata shook her head. "I must be getting back to the palace before I am missed. You see how I had to dress to escape the guards," she said with a smile. Then turning once more to Abhitha she said quietly, "You must regain your strength, for you will have a grandson and you will have much to offer him. He will love you dearly and will carry forward the love that is in your heart." Then taking her hands in her own, Mata squeezed them and, with a broad smile, stood up to leave.

As she was approaching the door, Mata suddenly turned back. I saw her touching the silver pendant that hung around her neck, the one given to her by Sunaina Ma when she left Mithila. She had been wearing it when she went into exile, as she rarely took it off. But I saw her slowly remove it and hand it to Abhitha. "I want you to have this. My mother gave it to me before I left Mithila. I can think of no one I would rather give it to than you," said Mata in a most moving voice. "Someday you will give it to your grandson. It will make me very happy to know that he will have this."

"Maharani, this is too great an honor . . . ." Abhitha lowered her head, hesitant to accept it, but Mata pressed it into her hands.

Something had occurred in the exchange with Abhitha that touched Mata deeply, but I didn't understand it. I could see that she was distracted as we left their home. It was broad daylight by now and so we rushed as fast as we could back to the palace. The streets were already filled with people.

At one point Mata stopped as if she had been overcome by the crowds. "Are you all right?" I asked her. "We can stop and rest a few minutes." She shook her head and we started again. Right at that moment a man carrying a huge load rammed right into her and Mata fell to the ground. As her head cover blocked most of her face, he couldn't see who she was. He yelled at us, "You servants should stay out of the way." He made a motion as to kick her, but with all my weight I pushed him aside. I lifted Mata to her feet and for a moment her head covering fell away. A few people had gathered around and one of them seemed to recognize the Maharani. She quickly covered her head again, as I shouted, "Make way for the servants of the Maharani," and we made our way back to the palace as quickly as possible.

Once back in her room, I helped her bathe and change into her clothes. Then I expressed my dismay that a citizen of Ayodhya would have attempted to kick her. "He made no apology, Mata, after knocking you down." I was incensed.

"What is dismaying is that a citizen of Ayodhya would even consider to kick a woman," she replied sadly. "No matter who it is."

"But to raise his foot to you of all women, Mata," I replied sorrowfully.

"It doesn't matter that it was me, Soma. It is the same if it is me or any other. I would rather take the hit myself than to see it fall upon another. We have seen today the best and worst of Ayodhya: a woman who has put aside all thought of self in order to serve, and a man who puts himself before all others, no matter who he steps on. Let us remember Abhitha and hope that she is the future of Ayodhya." At the remembrance of Abhitha, a smile crossed Mata's face.

"Mata, what was it about Abhitha that made you give her your precious pendant?" I ventured to ask. "I know all that she had done, but the pendant?"

"There is more to the story, Soma. In a previous birth, she was a very pious woman from a prominent family in Mithila. Her husband misbehaved and was cursed by a powerful sage. They lost everything and suffered greatly. The husband died, and she was left alone to raise her son, her only surviving child. The others had died due to the curse. The Janak family felt keenly for her and took in her and her son as servants. She was immensely grateful and vowed to dedicate her life to my family in her future births. She served in the household faithfully but died when she was still quite young. She took a subsequent birth in Mithila and served in the household. Then she was born in Ayodhya, but her devotion to my family never ceased. She has no memory of any of this, and yet that vow she took has remained with her through all these years and births, and somewhere deep inside she knew me to be the descendent of that family. That is what led her to the river to pray for me. What took place was long ago, but her devotion did not die. This is the power of love, Soma. It is carried from one generation to another, from one birth to the next."

I was stunned by what I heard. "Was she . . . was she the ancestor of Meenakshi?" I asked in disbelief.

Mata nodded and replied, "Indeed she was. You know that Meenakshi's great, great-grandmother had to suffer her husband's curse although she had done no wrong. It touched me deeply to see her devotion through all these years and births, devotion that has not died. That is why I gave her my most precious possession. Love is not a stream that flows one way. It must flow in both directions to flourish.

The love she gave to the Janak family and that we returned to her and her descendants continued to flow through her prayers by the river, and I came to meet her to acknowledge and return this love. This is the cycle of love that sustains us, and this is how the universe works."

I was still absorbing this information when Shri Ram came to get Mata; they had a public audience that morning. During the audience, someone from the public mentioned that a rumor was circulating that earlier in the morning the Maharani had been seen in the street dressed as a servant.

"The Maharani dressed as a servant?" inquired Shri Ram with a sly smile. "How can that be?" The man shrugged his shoulders. "It is just a rumor, Maharaja, but I hope you can put it to rest. It is not proper for such talk to circulate."

"It is not proper to be disrespectful of women," replied Shri Ram. "I have heard that one of the merchants knocked down a resident of this household, and did not help her up. Did any one of our citizens who witnessed this come to her aid? It is not proper to treat a woman in this fashion. And it is not proper to question the actions of the Maharani," he added quietly. Mata did not speak during this exchange but sat there smiling at the group.

The months passed. Mata did not leave the palace much after this episode. I knew that she felt confined, but she never spoke of it. Her only wish was to support Shri Ram. I didn't spend much time with Mata during that time, only to help in the morning and evening, because most of her time was with Shri Ram. The love that had blossomed between them in the forest was now evident to everyone. It didn't matter whether they were alone or among the whole household, one could feel the intensity of their love and appreciation for each other. Their joy was infectious and the whole palace seemed to sing with a bubbling happiness.

Soon news spread that Mata was with child and the joy increased even more. Every face in the palace and in the city wore a smile. It seemed that the sorrow of the past fourteen years was now fully behind us, and there was so much to look forward to. The household would soon be bursting with the youthful energy of the heir to the throne, Mata's child. What greater joy could there be? So we all thought. But this joy was not to last long. One night Mata had a dream that ended it all.

Soma stopped her narrative here. Opening her eyes she took in a deep breath and turned her eyes to us. When we had begun, there had been only my mother and me. By now a few more had gathered. Some nodded to each one of us, and then turning to me, she saw that I had a question. "What is it, child?" she asked. "You may ask anything." When I didn't respond, she encouraged me again.

"Soma," I began. "You said that Abhitha was the ancestor of Meenakshi." I paused.

She nodded and said, "That is right. This is what Mata had said."

"But who is Meenakshi?" I asked in a curious voice.

Soma smiled, keeping her gaze fixed on me. "It is not important, child. She was also from Mithila. She was someone who loved Mata very much. That is all you need to know."

Suddenly my mother seemed very tired. "Perhaps we should let you rest, Soma. I also need to take some respite as the heat today is very strong. Hopefully the rains will come soon. We can return in a few hours." Soma nodded, and although I was hesitant to leave her, I followed my mother back to our cottage and within minutes of lying down was fast asleep.

RETREAT TO THE FOREST

It was not long after we returned to Soma's hut that we heard the sky crack open and release rushing streams of water, pounding the dirt outside as the rains came thundering down in a ferocious outpour. The sky had quickly darkened, and we could barely see the outline of Soma's form. An eerie feeling pervaded the small hut, which now held just the three of us, and I could not help but shiver although I was not cold. The air that hugged me was still warm and humid, but the crackling thunder had created a sense of foreboding, as if some inauspicious event were about to unfold. I inched closer to Soma. When she closed her eyes, I did as well, hoping to dispel the unease that had overtaken me.

She picked up the story where she had left off.

Mata knew early on that she was carrying two sons. She told me that she felt two heartbeats, not one. It made her happy to know she was giving birth to brothers, as she so much enjoyed the closeness Ram had with his brothers. Despite the difficulty of the pregnancy, she was experiencing much joy, much happiness. We all felt it.

One night, many months into her pregnancy, Mata had a vision during the pre-dawn hours in which she saw Rishi Bhrigu mourning the death of his second wife, Usana. She saw him raise a fist and curse the one who had caused her death. Issuing words that could not be retracted, he cried, "Whoever is responsible for this, I curse you! You, too, will know the pain of separation from your beloved."

Mata saw her beloved Narayan step out of the shadows. It was he who had taken Usana's spirit at her request to spare her from having to reveal the whereabouts of Shukracharya's demon students, who were causing such chaos on the earth. With a calm demeanor, Narayan accepted the curse for the sake of taking onto himself the pain of Rishi Bhrigu. Mata saw herself standing by in her human form as Bhargavi, the daughter of Bhrigu, but she also saw herself in her eternal form as Narayani, the wife of Narayan. She had been an innocent witness to the death of Usana, and yet she, too, would have to accept this curse. She saw Narayan glance at her, and she saw herself nodding her head in response, accepting the curse. The vision was the same as she had seen when she had been visited by Maharishi Devahuti in Lanka. As Mata was having this vision, a strange restlessness caused me to awaken, and urged by some mysterious force, I hurried to check on Mata. I found her standing alone outside her room on the portico, staring at the still dark sky. She was visibly shaken, but when I asked what was wrong, she simply asked me to arrange for a chariot immediately.

"Where are we going?" I was distressed to see her like this.

"To Sage Arundhati," she replied quietly. "She will guide me on what I must do."

There was an urgency in her voice. Without further question I hurried to arrange for a chariot and a few guards to accompany us. After gathering a few things for her, and some fruit and water for the journey, we left the palace. Shri Ram was not yet awake. She was eager to leave before he rose so that he would not see the disturbance on her face.

Sage Arundhati, the wife of Sage Vasishta, the guru of Shri Ram's family, was standing at the gate to their hermitage to receive us, as if she were expecting our visit. Another woman stood beside her. When Mata saw this woman, a cry escaped her lips and she quickly descended from the chariot and ran to her. The woman gathered Mata in her arms and held her there for quite some time. I still did not understand what was going on. It was not until much later that I came to understand all that was taking place. I learned that the woman with Sage Arundhati was her sister, Sage Khyati, also a daughter of the great Maharishi Devahuti and the first wife of Rishi Bhrigu. As she embraced Mata, I heard her say, "Do you remember, I weakened the curse, my dear. It will only be a partial separation."

Mata ran her hand across her protruding stomach, and Sage Khyati seemed to know what was on her mind. "Did you not say recently that you wanted to raise your children as you were raised, with the freedom to roam the forests, to know the animals and plants as their family?" It is true Mata had spoken those very words to me a few weeks earlier, but I wondered how this woman could have known that.

Mata said, "Must it be so soon? We have just returned from a separation. Must it be now?"

"I am afraid so," the sage replied. "The timing was set by the stars long ago. They are now in the right conjunction. It is what you and Narayan planned before you took these human forms."

Later Mata told me that at that moment she realized how much these two women had sacrificed for the sake of humanity. Sage Arundhati had sacrificed her sons so that Rishi Vishwamitra could attain liberation and bring benefit to humanity. Sage Khyati had lost many children in the battle between the devas and asuras to bring stability to the celestial world, which then provided stability to the material world. When she saw the love and compassion on their faces, she could ask nothing for herself. Could she not also make this sacrifice?

"It is not just the result of a curse," said Sage Khyati, "it is also in service to humanity. You must steer the education of your children so that the values you instill in them will be the foundation of the future. You must help stabilize the earth for changes that are to come as a result of the destructive war, which has unsettled so much. You must support the forest life so it is not destroyed as human society expands. You cannot do any of this from the confines of the palace. You must be free to do the tasks you have come to do, Sita. And . . ." she paused, as if she was staring into the future. After several minutes of silence, she continued in a firm but quiet voice, still staring off into the distance, "And you must fulfil the vow you took so long ago, the vow to end the power of the curse. To achieve this you must experience its effects for yourself."

Sage Arundhati then spoke, "How many sages have I seen now issue curses out of anger, not wisdom. There was a purpose in earlier times when the sages had to establish the forward path for humanity, ensuring that the concept of justice was implanted in the human mind. That work is done. Ram will now set up the institutions to ensure justice and will establish the laws to guide human society. Curses are no longer needed. They have become a hindrance . . . ."

As these two great women spoke their minds, Mata heard again the curse of Rishi Bhrigu, dictating this separation between her and Shri Ram. The separation in Lanka was by her choice; this one was not. She and Shri Ram would now have to undergo the pain of parting, more difficult now that there were children involved.

"And Ram?" she asked in a faint voice. "How am I to tell him this?"

"Vasishtha is with him now," replied Sage Arundhati compassionately. "He left before dawn this morning. He will revive Ram's memory of the incident that took place so many millennia ago."

The two women sages laid out for Mata much of the work that needed to be done in the forest. I remember Sage Arundhati's words: "From now and well into the future the forests will be under threat. One day they could even disappear completely, and this earth could become a barren place, like so many other planets, stripped of all life. This is what the asuras have tried to do, take the resources for their own use while disregarding the needs of other life forms. We must secure in human hearts love for the forests, love for the rivers and the mountains, a protective instinct that will ensure their survival. In freeing Ravana, Ram released a quality of love previously unknown on earth. You must take this love now and embed it in the human heart, so that life on this planet will be protected. We must peer far into the future, Sita, and the protection of Mother Earth is of utmost importance for the whole of the universe. Her fate in the future will lie in the hands of humanity. You know her better than the rest of us. You can instill in the minds of many love for her. Once implanted, that love will never die and will ensure her future."

As she spoke these words, the expression on Mata's face transformed. Where there had been despair was now understanding and acknowledgement, a willingness to assume the responsibilities before her. Over the years I had learned to discern Mata's expressions and thoughts, and I saw her concern for Shri Ram, as it would be he who would be the most affected, deprived of her presence and that of their children. It was not until he arrived some hours later that I saw her face fully relax.

By the time Shri Ram stepped down from the chariot with Rishi Vasishtha, his memory had been fully revived, and he knew they had to face now the effects of a cause set in motion long ago. When he saw Mata, he drew her to his chest and said gently, "Sita, in Lanka the bond that kept us as one was broken. This will not be the case now. No being now has the power to break our unity. I will never leave you, and you will never leave me."

"This is the truth, Ram. But in the human realm difficulties can arise. This human body will want to feel your touch and see the love flowing from your eyes, your eyes that always bring me back to my true self."

"You will feel my touch," he promised. "Do you not remember how the great Khyati weakened the curse?" His eyes turned to Sage Khyati. "How grateful I am that you were present then. It was through the power of your tapasya that you were able to give us this blessing."

"She was my daughter, Prabhu, and will always be," whispered

Sage Khyati, her eyes filling with tears. "No father should cause pain to his daughter. Even now, I have not fully forgiven him."

"I had some responsibility in that event, Ma," Sita said. "I stood by and did nothing to prevent Usana Ma's death. I did not intervene or protest. I bear some responsibility for his suffering."

Shri Ram looked at Sage Khyati caringly and said, "When Sita and I first left for the exile, we rested at the small hermitage of Rishi Bhrigu. You were not there at that time, and so we were not able to meet. We spent many wonderful days with him, and he was especially tender with Sita. Of course, neither of us had any memory of this curse. But he told us that in his very long life, there was only one act he regretted, an action taken long ago in anger. After that, he vowed that he would never again let even the hint of anger enter his being, and he said it never has." Shri Ram then added quietly, "he said that until that unfortunate act of his was fulfilled, he could not be fully liberated. His guilt was great, and it weighed on him constantly. Now Sita and I have the opportunity to help liberate Rishi Bhrigu. The very thought gives me the greatest joy."

A look of joy also crossed Mata's face. "Yes, we must bring this event to completion. I had not remembered his words to us then, and of course at that time we could not have understood them."

"And now is the time for your forgiveness," he said gently to Sage Khyati. "For he will not find liberation without that. In the end it will be you who gives your husband the final freedom. As long as you hold any ill feelings, his spirit will not be able to merge into Brahman." We could perceive the struggle in Sage Khyati. Ram touched her on the forehead. "You have turned what could have been a disastrous outcome into one of benefit, for you decreed that this curse be for the benefit of humanity. And so it shall be. But to bring this incident to completion, you must release the remnants of accusation against Rishi Bhrigu, who only seeks the good of the universe. His one fault has been corrected; his attachment to Usana long ago dissolved. There is no shadow of anger in his being. He is ready for liberation."

Tears were streaming down Khyati Ma's face, and Mata took her hands in her own and pressed them to her cheek. Then Khyati Ma said, "I will withdraw myself into solitary meditation, Prahbu, until I am free of the last vestige of ill will. I know that you will release me of the remnant of what I held against him for his anger and his curse, and in doing so, you will free us both." With those words, Khyati Ma's form began to fade away and she was gone.

"You have done a great deed, Ram," said Rishi Vasishtha with a beaming face. "The curse is the means for the liberation of both Khyati Ma and Rishi Bhrigu, and this will bring great benefit to the whole universe. Within a short time, they will both achieve union with Brahman. Come, let us go within to express our gratitude for what is taking place."

Rishi Vasishtha, Sage Arundhati, Mata and Shri Ram sat in meditation, while I went to help the hermitage students prepare food. After some hours of meditation, they ate in silence, but before leaving there was a brief conversation about practical matters: where Mata would go, what would be told to the household and the kingdom, and other such matters. Toward the end of the day we began the journey back to the palace. Mata and Shri Ram rode in one chariot, and I and Shri Ram's attendant in the other. On the whole ride to Ayodhya I was pondering what I would do after Mata retreated to the forest. I had come to the conclusion that if I were to be separated from her again, death was the only course for me. During her exile the purpose of my life had been waiting for her return. Now that she was to depart again, what purpose would my life have?

I could not hide my glum expression. Back in her room, Mata exclaimed, "Soma, why are you contemplating death!" I could hide nothing from her.

"Because there is no purpose to my life, Mata, aside from serving you. If we are to be separated . . . ."

"Who said we are to be separated?" she exclaimed. "The separation indicated is only between Ram and me."

"Mata? I am coming?"

She nodded with a smile. "I would not ask you to endure more than you already have, Soma. You have been put through much suffering for my sake, and I would not have you undertake any more."

A cry of joy escaped my lips. I could not have asked for anything greater. Living in the forest with Mata would be far superior to living in the palace, where I could see her only at particular times and had to comply with all the formalities of the household.

And that was how it was decided that Mata would retreat to a hermitage, which offered her a cottage. Shri Ram selected one not too far and not too near, in a beautiful forest full of the natural wonders that would bring her joy, and close to her beloved River Ganga. But no timetable was set, so we continued at the palace while the babies grew within her.

One evening I was seated with Mata on the balcony massaging her feet, which had become swollen due to the pregnancy. Shri Ram came to sit by her and I was about to withdraw when she indicated that I should stay and continue with the massage. As they began to speak, I noticed that they were finishing each other's sentences, expressing each other's thoughts. It came so naturally that they took no note of it. They began to laugh about one matter or another, and such joy flowed between them that I began to wonder if anything could disrupt this joy. Then suddenly the laughter ceased and they both fell quiet.

"It must be soon," Mata said. "Before the babies." Shri Ram nodded. A shiver ran through me.

"I think it best that Lakshman take us," said Mata in a quiet voice, "early tomorrow morning, before the household awakes."

"Are you prepared, Sita?" he asked, taking hold of her hand.

She nodded. "And you?"

"We must remember why this is coming to be, what will be achieved. Rishi Bhrigu's liberation will bring great joy to the universe, as will Sage Khyati's. I have come to see there are many reasons for this. It is for us to display to the world that no separation is possible, that where Ram is, there is Sita, and where Sita is, there is Ram. This will be our message to the world. It is easy to declare this while we are living together in the palace, but all will come to know this despite the semblance of separation. The love we have brought into this material realm must now be dispensed to all. One day, when we are no longer here, others will need to overcome the semblance of separation."

Mata then nodded at me to withdraw. I do not know what exchange took place between them after that. I am not sure what the household was told, or the kingdom for that matter. Perhaps they were told it was her health, her need for the quiet of the forest, for rest. I never thought to inquire. A new chapter was opening for me and for Mata, and I was more than ready to embrace it.

LIFE IN THE FOREST

S oma stopped her tale long enough to bring us each a drink of
water. Refreshed, she continued.

The first person to visit us after our arrival in the forest was Shanta,
Shri Ram's elder sister. Mata was standing in the doorway of our
cottage one day when she saw a woman with the dress and bearing
of an ascetic walk up the path. An expression of joy escaped Mata's
lips as she ran to greet her. Mata had only met Shanta once before,
after her wedding.

Well before Ram and his brothers were born, Maharani Kausalya
had given birth to a daughter, Shanta, who had been married off to
the great sage Rishiyasringa, but not of her own volition; she had
to abandon palace life for the austere life of an ascetic. Living far
from Ayodhya, she rarely had the opportunity to meet her family,
and they rarely spoke of her. It seemed they had all but forgotten
her, except for her mother, Maharani Kausalya, who continued to
long for her. During Ram's youth, Shanta was an idealized figure
for him. She often appeared to him in dreams when he was a child,
and so he bonded with her from an early age.

When Shanta heard of Shri Ram and Mata's return from the exile, she made plans to meet them but then was delayed. After she heard of Mata's retreat to the forest, she hurried to see what the situation was. She embraced Mata, then withdrew with a frown on her face. She asked, "Why, Sita, why are you here and not in the palace in your condition?"

"Come, Shanta, you have had a long journey. Let me feed you and then we will speak," Mata replied with a glowing face. Upon Mata's insistence Shanta allowed herself to be ushered into the cottage and served. When they had finished the meal, Mata took her hands and said in a serious tone, "Let me show you the past, the cause for the present situation." They went into meditation. Later Mata told me that she showed Shanta the scene in which Rishi Bhrigu had cursed Narayan and all that followed. Upon seeing this, tears came into Shanta's eyes and she said quietly, "So you, too, accepted the curse."

Mata responded, "Didn't you accept the ascetic life of your husband and leave the comforts of the palace? But there are other reasons for my being here, Shanta, reasons that will reveal themselves in time. My children will grow up as I did, with the freedom to roam the forests, unhindered by palace regulations. I want to give them their early training, and this would not be possible in Ayodhya, you know that. I want them to learn humility and service and love for the natural world. There will be plenty of time for them to know the power of their position later."

"The world will benefit from your sacrifice, Sita. But it saddens me that Ayodhya does not honor its women."

Mata immediately put her hand over Shanta's lips and exclaimed, "Do not say so." Then speaking in a soft tone, she said, "There is nobody, Shanta, nobody that Ram respects more than you. During our long journey, he spoke often of his brothers with such love and tenderness, but when he spoke of you, his whole tone and demeanor would change. He said that you prepared the way for us to lead an ascetic life during those fourteen years. You made it possible through your efforts. He thought of you often as we made our way through the difficult journey, sometimes going without food and shelter. You are an ideal to him, an ideal of what a woman can be. He told me that I reminded him of you." With a gentle smile, Mata turned to face Shanta and added, "And I replied that this was the greatest compliment he could pay me."

Shanta now placed her hand over Mata's mouth and said softly, "Do not say so."

Mata removed Shanta's hand and continued in a halting voice, "He once told me that his brothers and he did the visible work, in the open for all to see, but you and I did what needed to be done in the unseen world, unnoticed, quietly. Isn't that what we desire, Shanta, to do what needs to be done in the shadows, benefitting the world without any acclaim? Isn't that the path we have chosen?" Shanta nodded her head in agreement. "He told me how you used to come to him in dreams when he was a child, and that is how he came to know his elder sister."

A broad smile settled on Shanta's face. "We came to each other in dreams. This little boy would come and give me teachings. A great love developed between us although we rarely met in person."

"I know that during the last days of Maharaja Dasaratha's life, you were there by his side. All of his sons were gone, but you came to sit by him, to hold his hand and comfort him so that he could leave this world in peace, despite the great pain in his heart from the breakup of his family. When Ram told me this, he said he would be ever grateful that you performed this function, which he could not do, that you gave your father peace in his last hours. And I know you traveled a great distance to be there, enduring many hardships. Shanta, your sacrifices are not unknown to Ram or to me."

Struggling with emotion, she asked, "You knew this?"

Mata nodded. 'This is what gave Ram peace after his father's passing, knowing that you had been there." Mata paused. "Your modesty will not allow me to speak of your spiritual accomplishments, but Shanta, after I arrived in Lanka and during the worst of my ordeal, I saw you with the other great women sages who had come to comfort me. You were there behind them all, in the back. Your modesty would not let you come forward, but I saw you, and you do not know the comfort I took from your presence. It was as if Ram was reaching out to me through you. I am ever grateful for that." Tears flowed from Mata's eyes as she remembered that time in Lanka.

"I was there, Sita," she replied firmly with great emotion, settling her eyes on Mata. "I was in meditation when I heard the call from Parvati Ma. That call of hers rang throughout the universe. I felt my spirit rise from my body and before I knew it I was seated with those great women sages. I did not deserve to be there with those women of such great spiritual attainment, but my heart drew me. My heart followed you and Ram through all the fourteen years of your exile, and there was not a day during your exile and captivity when I did not pray for you and offer for your protection all the fruits of my meditation. What you endured in Lanka was for all of us, Sita. That is why the women gathered around you, coming from so many parts of the universe, the seen and unseen world, to acknowledge the benefit you were bringing to the world. You and Ram together cleared the darkness so that a new light could shine through, the light of love."

Mata didn't respond. Silence pervaded the hut for quite some time, and then Mata cheerfully said, "That time has passed. Now I have these two children to plan for."

'Two?'

Mata nodded.

"Let me stay with you, Sita, for the delivery."

"Shanta, there is nobody I would rather have with me during this time. Please stay and help me receive Ram's children into the world."

And so Shanta stayed with us through the labor and delivery. She was the first to hold the children after they were born. During this time I came to know how dear she was to Mata. Mata saw her as both an elder sister and a sage. During their fourteen-year exile,

Mata had spent much time with women sages, and she missed that in her life now. Having Shanta with her brought those memories back. They would spend much time together in meditation and in discussions of spiritual matters. Sometimes hours would pass, and they would be fully absorbed in their discussions.

After the birth, Mata's sister Urmila came from Ayodhya to be with her, and Shanta felt it was time to depart. She and Mata embraced, and Mata tried to express her gratitude and love. Shaking her head, she said with deep feeling, "Shanta, I have no words. I am blessed to have you as my sister and my friend."

Shanta quietly replied, "And this world is blessed to have you. One day the world will know who you are."

I was overcome by the tenderness of the moment as they stood together, unwilling to part. Finally, casting one last look at Mata, Shanta turned and began her long journey home. We watched as she made her way down the path leading into the forest until we could no longer see her slender figure. Mata was to see her only once more, just before her departure from this world.

Later that night Mata said to me, "The world will forget Shanta. The deeds of her brothers will be long remembered, but her greatness will slip from sight. Yet I will always remember and cherish her. What she has brought to this family with her spiritual wisdom will never be known, but it will yield many blessings well into the future."

Later I asked Mata if Shanta would be safe traveling such a long distance alone on foot. Mata simply smiled and said, "She has many mystical powers. After all, she is Ram's sister."

It was not long after that Shri Ram came to meet his children. I think the joy he felt as he held them in his arms spread through the three worlds. One could almost hear rejoicing in the many realms.

Soma stopped speaking and the hut filled with silence. After a few minutes, she opened her eyes and looked around the hut. It seemed she was returning gradually to the present time. I noticed that several ascetics had entered and were quietly listening to Soma's narrative. I had been so absorbed in Soma's story that I had not heard them enter. Seeing them, she slowly rose from her seat and said, "I must prepare food for you all, then I will continue."

My mother protested, saying that we didn't want to trouble her any further.

'Trouble?" Soma asked with a laugh. "I am doing only as Mata has commanded me. She used to say to me, and to Hanuman, you must feed whomever comes to you. That is how they will know our love, by nourishing both their bodies and their spirits. So I cannot do otherwise. Come, I will make a most delicious meal."

We followed her outside to the kitchen area. The rain had stopped and the refreshing scent of wet earth filled the air. It was beginning to get dark. We realized that the hermitage would now be serving the evening meal, but we had no desire to return as it seemed Soma had more stories to share, so we helped her prepare the food. Several other ascetics appeared and Soma seemed to know them well because she smiled when they approached. One of them said to my mother, "We heard Soma had visitors and was telling stories of Mata Sita, so we could not resist a visit."

As I began to eat, I suddenly became aware that I always felt relaxed and peaceful after eating Soma's food. "Your food is different from other food. It has a very soothing effect," I said to Soma in a curious tone.

She smiled. "Mata taught me that food is to nourish the spirit as well as the body. She said that different types of food have varying effects on the nervous system and also affect the mind and emotions. Vasundhara Ma, who is sustaining us through the food, has designed it this way so all our needs are met. If we are conscious of this when we prepare the food and perform our preparation work with gratitude to Vasundhara Ma, we are able to awaken the special qualities of each plant."

When we finished eating and cleared away the eating area, we moved inside to the cushions where we had sat previously and waited. Soma seemed in no hurry to resume her narrative. She chatted with my mother about the gurukula, asking many questions about the students and teachers, as I impatiently sat waiting for her to dive back into the past. Finally Soma closed her eyes and entered the meditative state. After some time she began to speak.

It took me many years to understand why Mata had been called again to the forest, why she had to undergo tapasya yet again. But for all she had to endure, it was that much more difficult for Shri Ram. He felt the separation far more keenly, and Mata knew this and suffered on his behalf. How she yearned to prepare the right foods for him to ensure his health and peace of mind, and to serve him, to discuss with him the decisions he had to make for the kingdom, and to comfort him when there were difficult times.

After Mata recovered from the birth of the boys, Luv and Kush, she began to spend much time wandering in the forests as she used to do when she was a child in Mithila. Sometimes I would accompany her with the babies. I would find her stooping down to see a creature. On occasion she would say to me, with a touch of sadness in her voice, "In the future this species will be gone. But look how precious it is." A glow of joy would brighten her face. All manner of creatures would come to our cottage and Mata welcomed them all, taking such delight in their various forms and colors and the sounds they emitted—everything about them brought her joy. She loved to look into the eyes of the larger creatures, and I knew she was communing with them through unspoken means. She once told me it was through a visual exchange. She could see the pictures in their minds and send them pictures, and in this way they communicated.

One day as we were walking through the forest, I watched her stop to observe and speak to this one and that. In astonishment I exclaimed, "Mata, you are imbuing the natural world with such love, such love . . . I have never felt this intensity of love before." And then it dawned on me: this was her purpose for being here.

She smiled and said, "Why does that surprise you, Soma? These animals, these trees are a manifestation of love. For no other reason have they come into being. They are a reflection of the love that sustains and upholds the universe." Then she added sorrowfully, "Humanity once knew this, but all too quickly they are forgetting it. And when they block the channels of love that flow between them and the rest of the natural world . . . ." She shook her head. "It is my greatest desire to prevent this from happening, and so we must saturate the world with more love, Soma. That is our sole task."

"So that is why you have been called back to the forests?" I asked.

She laughed. "You know the reasons, Soma. Why must you keep deliberating over this matter?" After a few minutes of silence she asked, "Would you prefer to be in the palace, with all its comforts?"

I shook my head. "I am happy to be wherever you are, Mata. I would follow you into the darkest corners of the universe, if you would permit me."

She smiled. "You have followed me. Wherever I have gone, you have been there, Soma, and it will always be that way."

Soma paused in her narrative. "I cannot describe what happiness flooded over me as she spoke those words. It is something I had known, but to hear it affirmed by her . . . I never expected to hear those words with these human ears." Soma's voice drifted off and she became quiet, a faint smile brushed across her face as the memory returned to her.

After a short pause she continued.

Mata explained to me that it was not only the power exercised by Ravana over the natural world that had unsettled the earth, it was also the weapons used by both sides during the great war. Some of the celestial weapons gifted to Ram had not been used before in the material realm, and their effects were far reaching. Had they been in the wrong hands, they could have destroyed life on earth. That is why Ram tried every means to avoid the war until there was no other way to subdue Ravana. He had to use these weapons, but he did so with extreme caution. Vasundhara Ma is still reeling under their effects and will do so for a very long time to come.

Mata told me that she could not counter the effects of these weapons, but she could soothe the pain inflicted on Vasundhara Ma with her love and hope to moderate the imbalances that could result, some of which might not manifest until well into the future. When Mata spoke like this, a distant look would come into her eyes as if she were seeing far ahead into a time not yet imagined. It was then that I understood the gravity of the situation. Such a war does not occur without leaving a deep mark, deep imprints on humanity and the planet. It was Shri Ram's role to plant the seeds for the flourishing of a new civilization. It was Mata's work to heal the damage that had been done before and during the war.

THE EDUCATION OF LUV AND KUSH

For the first few years after the birth of her children, Mata fully immersed herself in caring for them. Shri Ram came from time to time to visit, and these were very happy years. As soon as the children could crawl, they started exploring the forest floor, picking up little creatures to examine them and touching all the plants. She wanted them to feel part of and to love the natural world. She also wanted them to develop courage and strength, so she would allow them to encounter the larger forest creatures while in her presence, to climb the boulders and trees, and to embark on all kinds of adventures. I would often be fearful of the possible dangers, but she would calm me and say, "They are Ram's children. They must come to know their potential." This was the education she gave them in their early years.

Our idyllic life changed as people began to visit Mata with their problems and questions. One day a sage turned up from a faraway village. He was very knowledgeable about the plant medicines and wanted to alert Mata to the fact that some of the plants that had been used for ages to heal certain imbalances in the body were becoming scarce. He mentioned one in particular.

"That plant grows in abundance here," Mata told him. "Let us go in search of it, and you can take some of its seeds back home." So they went into the forest. When they didn't return after several hours, I became worried. Just before sunset they returned, with

Mata's basket full of plants.

"You found what you were looking for," I said with a sigh of relief.

Mata shook her head. "He is right. That plant has completely disappeared. It was nowhere to be found. Very strange. But I found its relative, which should have the same beneficial qualities."

Later I asked her why the plant they were looking for had disappeared. She said, 'The conditions of all these forests are changing. Many species will disappear, but new ones will arise. That is the beauty of Vasundhara Ma. Her world is one of infinite variety and surprise, ever changing to suit the changing times. When I was searching for that particular plant, I heard Vasundhara Ma tell me that its potency had begun to weaken, and so she allowed it to die off. A new branch of its family could now flourish—one that effectively could treat the bodily imbalances that are becoming more common. We now have a new variety to befriend and come to know."

The sage returned to his village, greatly relieved that he could continue to treat the people in need.

After we had been in the forest for a number of years, the sage Chandrika came to visit with her young son. Mata was overcome with joy to see her and very touched that she had undertaken the long journey on her own with the child.

"How could I not come, Mata, when you have given me the great blessing of a son?"

Mata gazed at the young one and smiled. "He was a good man, Chandrika, but had the weakness of pride. What Surpanakha did was to bring out that weakness. He has learned his lesson, but there will be a karmic test when he grows older. He will be tempted again, but this time he will resist. He will not abandon you but will follow the ascetic path until the end of his life. And he will achieve the realization that evaded him in his past birth."

Pranamming before Mata, Chandrika replied, "I can never express the gratitude I feel for you, that you have given him a chance to return to the path of dharma, and for giving me the opportunity to support him through my love."

"It gives me joy to see the steadiness and clarity of your love, which is not shadowed by personal desire but is pure and unconditional. You are a model of forgiveness arising out of true compassion, and you never lost your dignity, Chandrika. It is your love that has earned him this opportunity to make amends, and it is a testament to the fact that love can moderate karmic conditions. Never falter on your path, Chandrika, for by your example you will bring much benefit to the world."

Chandrika stayed with us for several days. Mata could see that there was something else on her mind and requested that she speak freely.

"I am saddened, Mata, by your separation from Shri Ram," she said hesitantly. "People are saying that it was Shri Ram who sent you away. Why must you suffer further, you who are the essence of purity and goodness?"

This was the first we heard of such talk and it shocked me, but Mata seemed unperturbed. I began to protest, but Mata gave me a glance indicating I should not respond. She replied softly, "There is no separation, Chandrika. Those who see one do not see the truth. Were Ram and I not one, this would not have come to be. He is as much in me, and I in him, as if we were living side by side. We must show the world that separation is only in the mind. We must not make separation from *Parabrahman,* the One Supreme God, and separation from the natural world a reality. If we do, then begins the downfall of humankind. And people who say such things, they do not know Ram; it is not possible for him to depart from dharma, even in the slightest manner. A husband who sends his wife away is not living the life of dharma, so how can this be? Ram is the essence of love. There is no dharma without love. Ignore such talk, Chandrika. It is not worthy of a response."

Mata fell silent as she looked off into the distance. She continued in a strange voice, "People will also say that Sita was a helpless victim, kidnapped by Ravana. Those who will say this do not know

Sita, for I am neither helpless nor a victim. What took place in Panchavati was by my own choosing. Had I not gone voluntarily into the demon realm, the great war could not have taken place, the world would still be under threat, and Ravana would not have been freed from his demon life. No, Chandrika, there is much that people do not know, and it is better that way. For such things are difficult to understand, even for the sages."

A great relief came over Chandrika's face. "Mata, you have lifted the last burden from my mind."

Mata embraced her and said, "Go, Chandrika, and be an example to the world of what a woman, abandoned by her husband and society, can achieve. Show the world how you brought him back to the path of dharma so that he never abandons a woman again. This is what Ram and I ask of you."

Some days later I found Mata alone sitting outside when I brought her the evening drink. It was after nightfall and the children were asleep. Mata was gazing at the night sky. Through the dim light I could see an expression of longing on her face, something I hadn't seen before. "What are you thinking, Mata?" I asked her. She didn't answer. I sat quietly beside her, wondering whether I should leave her alone or stay by her side.

"My mind is on him," she suddenly spoke in a barely audible voice. "The words I spoke to Chandrika are true. Sita lives in the heart of Ram, and Ram lives in the heart of Sita. There is no separation between us, and yet we have come into this human world to experience both its joys and pains. Though they are but illusions, at times they seem real, for we are also under the spell of maya, as is all material creation. We have human bodies and human minds and human feelings, and sometimes longing arises. I feel his longing now as he rests alone in the palace. I have the children, the forest, the animals, the plants, but he is there with so much responsibility, so many duties, so many things to look after. Who is there to care for him, to comfort the human part of him?"

I ventured to say, "Lakshman, Bharat, Shatrughna, their wives, including your sister, and the queen mothers."

"Yes," her face softened. "I need not worry. He is surrounded by love and devotion. But still, as his human body longs for me, this human body longs for him. We cannot shake the human part of us, Soma, and are not meant to as long as we inhabit these forms. I experience this human body, and then retreat into reality." With those words Mata withdrew into meditation, and I knew to take my leave.

We had two small cottages, one for Mata and another for the children and me. When they were very young, the children slept with her, but when they grew older, I took them so that Mata could have time alone. She didn't sleep much but spent most of the night in meditation.

When the boys were around six years of age, Mata developed the habit of having them meditate for a few minutes before bed and then telling them a story. They loved to hear tales of the sages. One night after meditation, Mata asked them what story they wanted to hear. They both said the story of Sage Anasuya and the river. Mata smiled. She had told them that story so many times, and each time it was as if they were hearing it for the first time.

Since they had requested it yet again she began: "When Sage Anasuya and her husband Sage Atri were looking for a quiet isolated place to build their hermitage, they entered a desolate forest. The trees were dying for lack of water. Many of the animals had fled, and there were no humans in sight. Sage Atri thought this would be a perfect place to meditate, as there would be no disturbances, but the lack of life made Sage Anasuya very sad. One day as she was walking in the forest she came across a tiger, who was thin and faint for lack of food. She found him digging with his paws into the earth in search of water. Her compassion was awakened. 'What happened to this forest?' she asked him.

'This forest has been cursed and there has been no rain for ten years,' he said sadly. 'Please, Mata, help us. My family has lived in this forest for many generations, and it is not right that we should have to flee.' Anasuya made a commitment then and there to bring water and life back to the forest. That night in meditation she traveled to the celestial world in search of help."

Luv began to get fidgety. "Where is the celestial world, Ma? Is it above the clouds?"

Mata smiled and shook her head. How many times had she explained this to him? "Close your eyes," she instructed. Tapping them gently on their chests, she said to the boys, "The celestial world is inside you. See how beautiful it is!"

She continued the story. "Sage Anasuya saw all the beauty and life in that celestial world and wanted to manifest this beauty on earth. She came to a river and called out to the beautiful river goddess, Mandakini Devi. The goddess arose from the river and the sage addressed her. 'Please help me restore life to the forest. Come with me to earth.'

But the river goddess shook her head. 'You are asking me to come to that desolate place and leave this beautiful world? Why?'

Sage Anasuya could not restrain herself. 'Out of love,' she replied, with urgency in her voice. 'Out of love for the trees, for the animals who have no water, for the humans who depend on the plants and animals for food. Come out of love.'

"The goddess was moved by the extent of the sage's devotion. 'For you I will come,' she said, 'if you can replicate the beauty that is here. If you can bring life back to the forest, I will come nourish it.'

"Sage Anasuya returned to her physical form and engaged in intense tapasya. I have told you what tapasya is.'

The vision of the celestial world vanished and both boys now opened their eyes. "It is long meditation," said Kush.

"And sacrifice. Giving up food and sleep," added Luv.

Mata nodded. "It can take many forms, but all of these disciplines are for one purpose only. Do you remember what that is?"

"To strengthen the will?"' Luv asked.

Again Mata nodded. "There is more power contained in the human will than all the power of Surya Dev, the brilliant sun, but we don't know how to use that power. It is locked inside of us. Tapasya unlocks the power of the will. You must remember that always." Their eyes were now wide open. "And it also strengthens devotion."

"You mean even we have that power?" asked Kush.

Mata nodded. "That was the gift to human beings, but it is a gift of which most humans are ignorant. It takes much practice and training to awaken the will. Only the sages know the secret of this. Sage Anasuya had tremendous power of will, which she awakened through many years of dedicated meditation. There was a huge boulder behind her hermitage, a mountain that no ordinary person could climb. But Anasuya climbed to the top of that huge rock through the power of her will and sat in meditation without food or sleep. The years passed and she did not move. The devas were in awe and tried all sorts of tricks to disturb her meditation."

"Why would they do that?" asked Kush. "Why would they want to disturb her meditation when she was only trying to help the world?"

"They were testing her will power. They saw her as only a human being and were sure she could not withstand the test of the devas. But she did. Through the sheer power of her will, she made the trees bloom. With life returning to the trees, the animals also returned. Still there was no water, but Sage Anasuya had created on earth the scene that she had experienced in the celestial realm. And so she returned to Mandakini Devi and asked, 'Now will you come to earth so that the plants and animals that have been revived will have water to sustain them?'

"So many years had passed that Mandakini Devi had forgotten her promise. When she saw what the sage had created, she bowed before her. 'Oh great sage, for you I will come, whose love is such that you have sacrificed greatly for the welfare of the world.'"

Sita added, "Your father and I visited her and Sage Atri at their hermitage, and what she created there truly looks like a celestial world. The river is as clear as crystal and is abundant with fish, turtles, and frogs croaking their evening songs. Beautiful swans grace the waters, and peacocks run freely through the forests. There is an abundance of plant and animal life, and now it is a settlement again for humans. All of this was accomplished through the power of will, and love. Never forget the love that Sage Anasuya showers upon the world."

"Will we meet her one day?" asked Kush.

"I hope so." Mata added quietly, "It is my wish, Anasuya Ma, to meet you again before I leave this earth."

After Mata had spoken these words, a gentle breeze carried the reply, faint yet so audible that even I could hear it: "And so you will."

The next night when it was time for the evening story, the boys asked to hear about Sage Anasuya and the river again. Mata laughed and replied, "I told you that story last night. Don't you want to hear a new tale?" They both nodded. "Then I will tell you about Sages Arundhati and Vasishtha. Do you remember meeting them?"

They shook their heads no. "They visited you, but you were too young to remember. Sage Arundhati and Rishi Vashishtha, both very wise and powerful rishis, were married. Rishi Vasishtha had brought forth mantras that could repel any weapon and Sage Arundhati had the power of bounty. She could feed any number of people. One day a maharaja named Kaushika heard about their powers and came unannounced to visit them with his vast army. Sage Arundhati fed them all. When the army was ready to leave, the maharaja asked for her secret. How could she produce so much food with no notice, no time to prepare?

"Sage Arundhati was very modest and replied it was all due to the blessings of the lord. Some of the maharaja's soldiers said they had heard that Rishi Vasishtha had a sacred cow, called Kamadhenu, that produced endless amounts of milk. They assumed this cow was the secret to their plentitude and so asked the sage to gift the king that cow. Rishi Vasishtha apologized and said that Kamdhenu was very attached to his wife and would only produce for her. The cow would be of no use to them. This refusal made the maharaja very angry. No one ever refused to give him a gift that he requested, and he told his soldiers to go take the cow.

"Sage Vasishtha glanced at his wife and, since they were of one mind, she knew what to do. She stood in front of the cow and said, 'I beg you, maharaja, do not seek to separate this cow from me as I am like her mother, and it is a great injustice to separate a child from her mother. It is against the laws of dharma.'"

"The maharaja was incensed by this, and eventually a battle took place between him and Rishi Vasishtha. When the maharaja saw that the sage could repel all of his powerful weapons through the use of mantras, he became even angrier. He realized that the power obtained through tapasya was greater than physical might. He decided to abandon his position as maharaja and engage in deep meditation so that he could also acquire powers.

"And he did. He became a powerful sage in his own right, but when he saw that nothing he did could match the powers of Rishi Vasishtha, in a fit of anger, he said to the two sages, 'Since you refused to gift me your cow, who you see as your daughter, I curse you both that all your sons will die.' Through his meditation he had gained the power to curse.

Mata paused as she saw the horror in her sons' faces.

"Did they all die?" asked Kush in a quiet voice.

"Indeed they did. Sages Arundhati and Vasishtha watched their many sons die; they were helpless to prevent it because a sage's curse cannot be revoked. The maharaja could not defeat them, but he could strike at their hearts. But the curse did not touch their daughters, and when their daughters saw the grief of their parents, they gathered round and asked themselves what they could do to relieve their parents of their suffering.

"One of the daughters went to her mother and said, 'Ma, I plead with you to create a world where there are no curses, no senseless killings, no grief for parents.'

"Sage Arundhati saw the hope in her daughter's eyes and said,

'Yes, that is what I will do. I will create such a world.' She asked her daughters to help her.

"Now her daughters were very wise and accomplished in meditation. With all her daughters by her side, she went into deep meditation for a long time with the intention of creating such an ideal world. And do you know what the result was?" The boys shook their heads. "Come with me outside and I will show you," said Mata, taking each one by a hand.

"They stepped into the night and Mata scanned the star-strewn heavens. 'There,' she exclaimed, pointing at a faint star. 'That is the world created by Sage Arundhati and her daughters to show the human world what is possible, a world free of curses and grief. And next to it is the world created by Rishi Vasishtha, to protect that ideal world. Do you see how bright it is? He stands there guarding the world created by his wife and daughters, and it is a symbol of their love. Those two stars always remain close to one another, reminding us of how we need to guard and protect, support and nurture one another. The creation of these worlds brought hope and light back into their life. Sage Arundhati's daughters now govern that world, and it is a beautiful one. Would you like me to take you there?' she asked with a smile.

"No, no!" exclaimed Kush, clinging to her. "I want to stay here."

"Have you really gone there, Ma?" asked Luv.

"Indeed I have. It is a beautiful world. I wanted to pay tribute to Sage Arundhati's daughters, who healed their parents of so much grief."

"Ma?' began Luv. Mata turned to face him. "Is that why we hold cows so dear?"

"In part," she replied. "When I see a cow I always think of Kamadhenu and the love and loyalty between her and Sage Arundhati. The maharaja would have misused Kamadhenu's gifts and made her life a misery. To protect her daughter, who had given them so much over the years, from this fate, Arundhati had to sacrifice her sons, who were so dear to her. She was upholding dharma at a great personal price." Then Mata smiled and added, "You should look at all female animals as your daughters."

"And all male animals as our sons?" Kush asked.

Mata nodded. "You must protect them the best you can. Come let us go back inside. There is a chill in the air."

Once they were settled back in the hut, Kush asked, "What happened to that wicked maharaja who cursed their sons to die?"

"Oh, he became a great rishi. You know him as Vishwamitra!" The eyes of the boys opened wide. "Yes, after many, many years of tapasya he became a great, great rishi, and was overcome by tremendous grief as a result of what his uncontrolled anger had led him to do. After many long years of meditation, he was able to bring forth one of the greatest mantras, the Gayatri Manta. You recite that every morning, don't you?" The boys nodded. "It was Sage Vishwamitra who was able to hear this mantra in the celestial world and bring the words into the human realm so that our ears could hear it. You know there are many beautiful and powerful celestial sounds our human ears cannot hear, but through his meditation he was able to make this powerful mantra audible to human ears.

"Rishi Vasishtha was in meditation one day when he heard the Gayatri Mantra being chanted. He bowed and said, 'I pay homage to the one who has given us this mantra.' Just then he realized who had brought the mantra into the world, and his heart opened in forgiveness. Soon after, Rishi Vishwamitra came to Rishi Vasishtha and asked for forgiveness. The sage forgave him, but said he had to gain the forgiveness of his wife, who mourned deeply the loss of her sons.

"Sage Arundhati's heart is as big as the sky. She is unable to hold any anger in her, and so when the rishi approached her, she had already forgiven him. She kindly said, 'Look how much good has come from such a painful situation. You have become a powerful force for good in the universe and will bring benefit to so many, and my daughters have created a world free of suffering that will set an example for humankind in the ages to come.'

The boys were thoughtful, and Mata asked, "What have you learned from this story?"

Luv was the first to answer. "That even the most terrible deed can be forgiven and good can come of it."

"That is a most important lesson. Our hearts must be large enough to forgive even the worst of deeds, but the doer of such a deed must come to understand the wrong that was done. Only then is forgiveness possible," replied Mata. She turned to Kush. "And what did you learn, Kush?"

He didn't respond right away. Finally he said, "I am thinking of Sage Arundhati's daughters and what a great thing they did for their parents, but . . . ." He fell silent.

"But what, Kush?" she asked gently.

"But you don't have any daughters. If something were to happen to us, who would help you get over your grief?" he asked in a concerned tone.

She smiled. "You are right, I don't have daughters. But I will have granddaughters. Each of you will give me one. And nothing will happen to you, I assure you."

"I wish . . . I wish . . . there would be a world with no more curses," he replied with a yawn.

Seeing how tired they were, Mata and I took them inside. They insisted on sleeping with her that night as they were still concerned that something might happen to them. As Luv was drifting off to sleep, he asked, "Ma, how did you get to that world? It is so far away."

She began to explain, "While you sleep, I walk among the stars, making sure that love and peace prevails . . . ."

"How can you walk with no earth beneath you?" asked Kush in the dreamiest of tones.

"There are many ways of walking, sons, and many ways of traveling. This earth is not the only place in need. There is life all over this universe that needs care."

The boys drifted off to sleep, and Mata slipped out and sat gazing at the night sky. I found her thus when I went to take my leave for the night.

"I won't be in this world to see my granddaughters, or even the wives of Luv and Kush." She spoke in a quiet voice as she stared at Arundhati's star. "But you will be, Soma. You will know my granddaughters, and I will have to hold them through your arms and look at them through your eyes. I will want them to have all the freedom I had in Mithila. You must see to it. You must promise me that."

"Mata, why do you say this? You are still young and in good health." I was alarmed, and a trembling came over me. She didn't respond to my question but insisted that I make her this promise. Finally, I said, "Mata, you know that whatever you ask will be done by me. But please do not speak of departing from this world. That I will not be able to bear."

This was the first time such a subject had come up between us, and it was the first indication that Mata would not be long with us.

Some days later as I was putting Mata's sons to bed, Luv said to Kush, "The stories Ma tells us are so different from the ones we hear at the hermitage. She must be a very great sage, greater even than Guruji."

"I think she is the greatest sage that ever lived, even greater than the rishis," replied Kush with a yawn. I smiled and thought to myself, if only they knew who their mother truly was.

Mata continued to tell stories to the children over the years of their growing up. One night they asked her to tell the story of Lady Ahilya and Sage Gautama. "How do you know about them?" she inquired. She had never told them that story, thinking they were not old enough to understand.

Kush replied that one of the boys at the hermitage had said that Sage Gautama had cursed his wife for being unfaithful to him, and this was a lesson for all woman. "What does that mean, Ma?" asked Kush. Mata was quiet, and I suspect she was debating whether to speak to them of that matter. In the end she decided to tell the story.

"I will tell the story of what happened, because I knew them."

she began. "When I was a child, the son of Sage Gautama and Sage Ahilya was our family priest. I was fond of him, but there was a sadness about him that I couldn't penetrate. Whenever I asked him why he seemed sad, he replied there had been a family tragedy many years ago that had never been resolved. I went to my father and asked what could be done, but Pitaji just shook his head and said we must wait until the right moment. Nobody would me tell me what this tragedy was.

"Then one day I met Sage Gautama. He was among the many sages who came to speak with my father, your grandfather. I saw the same sadness in him as in his son and so approached him. He replied that he had once committed a terrible deed and was suffering the consequences. So I went to my father and asked him, 'Sage Gautama is so wise. How could he have committed a terrible deed?'

"Pitaji replied that no one knew for sure what had happened as Sage Gautama refused to talk about. But it was said that Gautama's wisdom and his wife's beauty were so great that even Indra Dev (chief among the deities) envied the couple. Out of jealously, Indra came to Lady Gautama in the guise of her husband when Sage Gautama was away and caused her to be unfaithful. She thought he was truly her husband. When Sage Gautama returned and saw what had happened, he cursed her and she became like a stone. She remains like that to this day. This is what my father explained to me. Is this the story you have heard?" They nodded. "Then I will explain what truly happened. I did not believe that Indra Dev could deceive such a pure and knowledgeable woman as Sage Ahilya. I cried about this and finally determined that I would approach him and ask Indra Dev himself, and so I did."

"You saw Indra Dev?" asked Kush in amazement. Mata nodded.

"You went to Swarga Loka, Mata?" I asked in amazement, as she had never told me this story.

She nodded and replied, "Indeed I did. It was before you arrived at the household, Soma. It was in dream. One night I found myself in

Swarga Loka standing before Indra Dev. He looked at me lovingly and said, 'Child, ask your question. You may ask of me anything you wish.'

"Why did you deceive Sage Ahilya?" I asked, with tears streaming down my face.

He replied, "It is the role of the devas and devis to test all the sages to help bring out whatever imperfections remain. This is necessary before they are permitted to enter this heavenly realm. So I took the guise of her husband and went to Sage Ahilya to test her powers of perception. As soon as I entered the cottage, she saw through my disguise and challenged me. 'Indra Dev, why have you come in the guise of my husband?' I told her that I had come only to test her perception, to see whether she could perceive truth, and I took my leave. Just then Sage Gautama was returning from his meditation. He saw me leave his cottage, still disguised as him, and assumed his wife had misbehaved with me. A great anger arose in him. He started to curse me, but Sage Ahilya ran out to prevent this deed, which would have had terrible consequences for the natural world. She stood between her husband and Indra Dev and received the curse herself. She immediately turned into a stone-like form, silent as a boulder.

Indra went on to say, "I turned to him and said with great sorrow, 'See, great sage, what your anger has wrought on an innocent woman, who has done no wrong. I only came to test you both. Sage Ahilya saw through my disguise and did not err, but you were not free from anger and doubt.' Then I gave Sage Ahilya the choice of coming with me to Swarga Loka or remaining in that stone-like body until her husband freed himself of anger. She chose to remain so that they could enter the celestial realm together."

"Is there no remedy for this?' I asked Indra Dev in a pleading voice.

"A remedy will come very soon, my dear." I awoke after hearing those words and my heart was at peace.

Mata fell silent and glanced over at Luv and Kush, who were looking at her in amazement. After a few minutes she asked them what they had learned from the story. Kush replied that anger was the cause of so much suffering. One must conquer anger. She nodded and turned to Luv. He was quiet for a long time. She pressed him, "What else is there to learn, Luv?"

Finally he replied, "Sage Gautama did not trust Sage Ahilya even though she was a great lady. This was his true fault."

Mata said, "You both are right. Without trust, there is no love. Without love, there is no goodness, no dharma. Love is the basis of all. Sage Ahilya knew that if Indra Dev received the curse, the whole of the natural world would be disturbed. Without even considering herself, she intervened out of love for the world, and then she chose to remain in that stone-like form out of love for her husband. Sage Gautama had great knowledge, but Sage Ahalya had great love. Knowledge without love is not wisdom.

"When Sage Gautama saw what he had done to his wife, he was terribly distraught and vowed to undergo intense tapasya to atone for his mistake. In the process, he left his helpless wife alone, who could not speak or move, and this was another great error. He chose tapasya over care for the one who had sacrificed so much. It was the devis who kept her alive during this time. It took him many years to acquire love and free himself from the last vestiges of anger and doubt."

Mata smiled and added, "So often the sages turn to tapasya for their advancement, but if only they would open their hearts to the love that is inborn in every particle of creation, their progress would be so much quicker. I am not saying that tapasya is not good and necessary, but if it does not open the heart to love, it is of no avail. It grants power but not wisdom, and power without wisdom has caused so many to fall." Mata fell silent as if reflecting on her own words.

"But Ma, you have not finished the story," urged Kush. "Wasn't it Pita... I mean Maharaja Ram, who freed her from the curse?'"

"You are right. It was Maharaja Ram who freed them both. He freed Sage Gautama from his anger and doubt and opened his heart to love, and freed Sage Ahilya from her stone-like life. After he touched her feet, she could move and speak once again. Her beauty returned and she came back to human life." Mata then hurried the boys off to bed.

When I came to bring her the nighttime drink, I found her seated outside, withdrawn. I handed her the drink and then sat nearby. Mata said, "I used to wonder why Sage Ahilya had to suffer the indignities that she did. But I have come to realize that she underwent that great test out of love for her husband so that he could overcome his anger and doubt and enter Swarga Loka with her. To this day the world deems her guilty, and no one knows of her great sacrifice. As a result of the suffering he had caused her, Sage Gautama underwent very difficult meditations, but this did not open his heart. It was only when Ram's love freed Sage Ahilya that his heart opened. Do you remember, Soma, when we heard this story about Ram before his arrival in Mithila?' I nodded. "It was then that I recognized he was the one who had brought me back to my earthly body that day in the forest. Do you remember that day, Soma, so many years ago?" Again I nodded. "When I met Ram, my first words to him were ones of gratitude for having freed an innocent woman from the suffering she had taken on. Do you know what he replied?"

"What did he say, Mata?" My voice trembled. I was so moved by this story, which had made me silently shed tears.

She looked at me with glowing eyes. "He replied that when he saw her suffering thus, he had no notion of innocence or guilt. There was no thought of judgement. He saw only the great love that was locked inside her stone-like form, and he knew that he had to unlock that love so that it could once again flow to the world. That is why he has come to this earth, Soma, to release the love that resides in all. That is who he is. That is the purpose of his being."

"But why must women suffer so, Mata?" I had seen for myself how my Mata, a great devi among women, had undergone so much.

Knowing the train of my thoughts, she said with great love, "Soma, I have not come into this world to be a maharani, that you know."

"But Mata, you are a maharani!" I exclaimed, wiping my tears.

"That I am, but that is not why I have come. When I took birth, I chose to first know the arms of Vasundhara Ma. I chose to take birth in her womb so that I would truly know her as a mother. This was to set an example for the world, so that all would know her as their mother, as was known in the distant past. But that knowledge is fast fading."

She turned her eyes from me and looked off into the distance. "I will come again and again into this world, Soma, sometimes seen and sometimes unseen, doing my work quietly to bring that knowledge back, that love for Mother Earth and all that lives. This is why I have come."

SITA'S UNSEEN WORK

One day not long after this a very strange incident took place. As soon as I came into her cottage that morning, I sensed a rare uneasiness in Mata that overshadowed the joy that normally exuded from her being. She seemed disturbed by something, but I couldn't identify any cause. Luv and Kush were fine. Our food was plentiful. Mata seemed perfectly healthy. Nothing seemed amiss. I watched her during the day. At one point I asked if anything was wrong.

She looked at me and nodded, but only replied, "It will reveal itself."

The day passed. Periodically she would look out the door and glance toward the forest, as if she were expecting someone. I thought perhaps she was missing Shri Ram and was silently hoping for his arrival. But it was another arrival she was awaiting.

The next morning found a tigress lying at the gate to our cottage. As soon as she saw Mata by the doorway, the great beast lifted her head and let out an agonizing cry, which frightened the children. Mata looked at her for a few minutes and, shaking her head, she slowly closed the door. All day and all night the tigress lay there, periodically emitting a cry. Finally, I could not stand it.

"Perhaps she is wounded," I suggested, knowing full well that if that were the case Mata would have certainly attended to her.

"She is wounded, but in the heart, not in the body," Mata replied.

"Do you know what the problem is?"

Mata nodded. "I will go to her, but not just yet. She must realize her grave mistake." The second day and night passed and still the tigress did not move. On the third morning, Mata went to her.

I watched from the doorway as Mata knelt in front of her and I saw the tigress place her head on Mata's lap. Mata stroked her head and began to speak to her. "What you did was wrong," said Mata, lifting the tigress's head and looking directly into her eyes. "Now take your cubs and go deep into the forest and stay away from human habitats. They will hunt you now, so go quickly deep into the forest."

As Mata spoke these words, three cubs emerged from the edge of the forest, where they had been hiding behind some trees. They approached Mata and she blessed them that they would be safe. When they were gone, I asked Mata to explain.

She sighed and said, "A hunter killed the eldest of her cubs and, in a fit of anger, she went into a village and killed a little boy. Now the villagers are hunting for her. Thus begins the war between man and nature," she said sadly. Then added. "I must go find that family, Soma. Let us cook." She went to kitchen area and began to prepare a large pot of food. All the while, she kept repeating the words, "I must have Hanuman with me. I must have Hanuman . . . and the chariot."

Throughout the morning, as we prepared food, she repeated that refrain. By early afternoon, I saw the chariot drive up and out stepped Hanuman. He greeted us as if nothing were out of the ordinary, but Mata exclaimed, "Thank goodness you have come. Now let me dress and we will go."

"I heard your call, Mata, but where are we going?" he asked.

"We will see." She rushed into the cottage and I saw her dig out her royal clothes from a wooden chest in her room. Helping her dress, I asked what this was about. "It will be more meaningful to them if they see their Rani."

"More meaningful to whom?" I was perplexed, wondering if she was going to Ayodhya. She didn't answer but rather directed me to load the food onto the chariot. She told me to stay with the children, and she and Hanuman took off. The rest of the story I heard from Hanuman after their return.

They had ridden from one village to the next until Mata finally said, "I think this is the one." When they got down from the chariot, they found a village in mourning. She asked Hanuman to bring the food and they went from hut to hut until she found the weeping mother. Mata whispered to Hanuman, "A hunter had killed the cub of a tigress and in her anger the tigress killed that woman's child. Now the village men are hunting the tigress. I must stop them."

Mata stood at the doorway of the hut, waiting to be invited in. Hanuman described to me the pain on Mata's face as she saw the agony of the mother, who was calling out to her small son who had been killed. When her husband saw that it was the Maharani who was standing at their door, he quickly touched Mata's feet and begged her forgiveness. "We have just lost our young son," he said. "Please forgive us for not being able to receive you properly, Maharani."

"I heard about the incident and have brought you some food," she replied. "Please let me tend to your wife." He invited her and Hanuman to enter. Hanuman brought the food to Mata, who laid it out before the weeping mother. When she realized it was the Maharani who stood before her, she wiped her tears and exclaimed, "Forgive me for not receiving you as I should."

Mata looked at her with compassion and quietly spoke to her. "Nothing I can say can ease your pain. I am also a mother, and so I know the deep wound in your heart. But please let me offer you this food that I have cooked with my own hands. It will bring you some relief." Mata had put special herbs into the food to calm the emotions. She laid out the food and the woman ate; as Mata watched, she saw the woman was weary from lack of sleep. After finishing her meal, she lay down beside Mata and fell asleep.

"I don't know what you have done, but I am ever grateful," said her husband. "She has not eaten or slept at all since he was killed four days ago. He was the youngest of our three children and the only son. He was most dear to her." Mata shook her head in sorrow when she heard those words. Then he asked, "Where will you spend the night, Maharani?"

Mata hadn't thought of that. They were far from the hermitage and night had fallen. She looked at Hanuman to see whether they could manage to get home, but he shook his head. "It is better we wait until daybreak," he whispered in answer to the question she did not voice.

"With your permission, I will make arrangements for your stay with the village chief," the man hurried to say.

"We have only come to comfort you," replied Mata in a gentle voice. "No need to worry about our accommodations. But I hesitate to leave your wife in her condition. Yes, we will spend the night so I can speak with her when she awakes." Mata glanced at the door and saw that the villagers were peering in. They had all come to see the Maharani. She walked out the door and the villagers scrambled to allow her to pass. One by one they bowed and touched her feet. "How gentle and respectful they are," whispered Mata to Hanuman.

"We will find that tigress and kill her!" shouted a man from behind, thinking perhaps that this would please the Maharani. Mata stopped and turned to see who had spoken. She saw standing amid the crowd a man who looked like one of the village elders. She shook her head and said, "If you do, more violence will follow. You must end this killing now."

The crowd fell silent. "But Maharani, if we do not kill that vicious animal, she will kill again."

"I met the tigress," Mata said. "A hunter had killed her cub and in anger she retaliated, but in that process she killed an innocent boy. I have sent her deep into the forest. She will not kill again. Let her be. You both have suffered."

The man did not respond, and Mata and Hanuman proceeded to find a place to spend the night. At daybreak Mata roused herself from her semi-sleep and stepped outside, where she saw the village elders led by the man who had spoken out the night before. They were ready to go in search of the tigress. Mata approached them and once more pleaded with them to abandon their hunt, but the men insisted.

"Please forgive us, Maharani, but you know what we have suffered. We cannot risk losing another child in this village." As Mata stood there wondering what more she could say, she saw the village women emerge from their huts and encircle the men.

"What is this?" asked one of the elders.

"Our Maharani has come all this way to comfort us; we will not allow you to disregard her pleas. We will not let you leave here."

Neither side would move, neither the men nor the women. Suddenly Mata saw the mother of the deceased boy emerge from her hut. She walked as if in a dream until she reached Mata and fell at her feet. Mata gently lifted her and asked in a whisper, "You have seen him, have you not? Your son came to you last night in a dream, did he not?" She nodded. "What did he say? Tell all the village what your beautiful son said to you."

"He asked me not to cry any more . . . and he asked me not to kill the tigress. He said she, too, has lost her child." Tears filled her eyes as she spoke. No one said a word. Finally she turned to the elders and pleaded, "Please do not disobey the Maharani. It is for the sake of my son that I ask this."

The group slowly disbanded, returning to their own huts. But as they left, Mata said to the hunters, "To keep peace in this forest, take no more than is needed for your sustenance."

"It is not we who are transgressing, Maharani," said the village chief to her. "It is the people from the city, from Ayodhya, who are coming into the forests now, hunting not for food but for pleasure. And we are reaping the results. We do not know how to stop them."

A look of surprise and concern crossed Mata's face. This was a new development, one that she had not heard before. "I will see what can be done," she said.

Before taking her leave, Mata embraced the mother and said to her, "In a few years you will have another son. He cannot replace the one you have lost because each child is an irreplaceable treasure, but he will bring joy back into your life. The son you have lost must now continue his journey to a new birth. Your tears will hold him back, but your love will help him proceed. Send him love unceasingly. That is the role of the mother, to help the child along his or her journey." The woman nodded, and profusely thanked Mata. Then Mata and Hanuman took their leave.

Before getting into the chariot, Hanuman asked Mata, "You found that boy in the celestial world, didn't you?"

"He was lost, unable to return to life and unable to move forward, held back by his mother's tears. I asked him to go to her and ease her pain, then he would be free to proceed. I also asked him if he would protect the tigress who had killed him. He agreed. He is a wise soul who will have a good birth."

There was an air of silence around Mata when she returned, so I knew not to ask any questions. There was an uneasy feeling in the air that evening as she fed the children and asked me to take them to bed. There would be no story that night. She seemed preoccupied. When I awoke in the morning, I went to her cottage to find her gone. Hanuman was seated by the gate. I hurried to him and asked if he has seen Mata. He pointed to the forest, where I saw her seated by a tree in meditation.

"When did she come out?" I asked.

"In the middle of the night. I was sleeping outside when I saw her leave her cottage and walk into the forest. I decided to stay up and keep watch over her."

"What happened yesterday, Hanuman? She seemed so preoccupied when she returned."

That is when Hanuman told me what had passed. "She hardly spoke on the way home, only to say that she saw what lay ahead," he said, after he had recounted the events of the previous day. "She said the separation between man and the rest of the natural world would increase to such an extent that many life forms would be endangered. She saw this. She saw destruction and pain ahead." He added, "Take care of what you need to, Soma. I will stay here and keep watch until she emerges from meditation."

Mata stayed in meditation for days. I began to feel concerned and finally asked Hanuman if he should go to Ayodhya to let Shri Ram know her state.

"He is already with her," he replied simply.

"What do you mean? Has he come?" I glanced around for a sign of Shri Ram.

Hanuman smiled. "I saw him come the first night, not long after she went into meditation. I don't know whether it was he who called out to her, or she who called to him. But I saw him walk up to her and take her hand and lift her out of her body. I saw them both walk into the forest. When I went to follow, Mata turned and asked me to stay. I knew then where they were going. They are traveling the earth together, blessing every part of it, journeying through the lands they walked together during the exile as well as foreign ones in distant parts of the earth. There is not a field or forest, valley or river, ocean or mountain on earth that will not have the blessing of knowing the footprints of Shri Ram and Mata Sita. They are embedding their love into every particle of the earth. That is the gift they are leaving. I believe it is because Mata sees what lies ahead." A look of such great love and devotion came over Hanuman's eyes as he spoke. "And I know that when they leave this earth, I will follow those footsteps wherever they will take me. I will bow down before each and every imprint they are leaving on the body of Vasundhara Ma."

"But I don't understand, Hanuman," I murmured. "Mata is seated there. How can she be circling the earth?"

He smiled. "In Ayodhya, Shri Ram is locked away in his room in meditation, and yet I saw them both, in their physical bodies, take their leave. That is the mystery of Shri Ram and Mata Sita. They are not confined to their physical forms. They can assume multiple forms at once if need be."

As Hanuman spoke I looked up at the darkening sky, which threatened a downpour. The dry season was still upon us, and we were awaiting the rains as the land was parched. Hanuman saw the advent of rain and I heard him mutter, "No, Lord Indra, you will not harm the body of Mata." Almost immediately the clouds dispersed.

"Hanuman, the animals and plants have been waiting long for this water. Mata would not like us to delay it. What should we do?" I asked.

He nodded, "You are right, Soma. She would not want any interference with the course of nature. I will take care of it." Soon the rains came in a great downpour, but to my amazement Mata and the ground around her remained completely dry. No water touched her body. It was then that I came to know the great powers of Hanuman.

I don't remember how many days passed before Mata returned to waking consciousness, but when she finally did a beautiful glow graced her form. Each day I had been placing water and a basket of fruits before her, and every evening I saw the animals come and enjoy the offering. I smiled to think how pleased Mata would be, but I also was worried for her health. When she finally rose from her meditation spot and walked toward the hut, I saw that her body exuded great strength, as if she had been eating and drinking all along. She did not seem weakened in the slightest by her days of abstinence.

"Mata!" I exclaimed when I saw her. "Let me prepare some food for you."

She smiled. "I have eaten well." When she saw the confused expression on my face, she added, "Wherever we have gone, people have offered food, such interesting, exotic dishes. We have tasted food from all parts of the world. Such generosity and good will, and such care for the forests, for the animals and plant life. Now I know there will always be those who have unbounded love for the earth, who will always care for and protect the life here." She didn't bother to explain. Perhaps she knew that Hanuman had already told me about their excursions. She asked about the children and soon everything was back to normal after Mata's journey around the earth.

Some weeks later Shri Ram arrived. Over the evening meal, he expressed his gratitude to Mata for visiting the family of the little boy who was killed by the tigress. Word had spread throughout the kingdom. "Every citizen must feel that he or she is cared for, that their concerns are our concerns, and you set this example, Sita. You gave a wonderful gift to that mother, and there could be no better service than helping to heal a mother who has lost a child."

"But something must be done," replied Sita thoughtfully. "It was a hunter from Ayodhya who set this whole series of events in motion, senselessly killing a young tiger cub. First he tried to capture it and, when he couldn't, he killed the poor cub. The killing was not for food, but for pleasure, to assert power over the animal kingdom. That is not the way to maintain harmony between man and nature."

"You are right," he mused. "As a result of Ayodhya's growing power, some people are beginning to overstep their bounds, and disregard the laws of nature. Hunting will now be restricted to the forest communities who know to take only what is needed. Every village will need to keep a part of the forest that is for the animals only, where humans cannot enter. We must now establish regulations to balance man's needs with the needs of the other life forms."

Another incident occurred a year or so after that which made Mata's presence here known to the people of Ayodhya. Luv and Kush were now spending more time studying at the hermitage, which freed up our time considerably. One afternoon, as Mata returned from gathering medicinal plants from the forest, one of the teachers from the hermitage came running up the path to our cottage, out of breath, with a look of fright on his face. He explained that a chariot carrying the wife and daughter of a family very close to the guru had been on its way to the hermitage to seek the guru's blessing for the upcoming marriage of the daughter. The chariot had been waylaid by robbers, who killed the guards and harmed the daughter. Mother and daughter both had taken a bad fall and were unconscious.

"Guruji will be furious when he returns and discovers this," the teacher exclaimed.

"Where are they? Bring them to me right away," insisted Mata. Mother and daughter were soon carried into our cottage. The daughter's clothing was ripped and she was bleeding badly. Her breathing was shallow and irregular, leading me to fear she might not live.

Once we were alone, Mata examined them both and said, "The mother is all right, but the daughter is badly wounded. She has been violated multiple times." Mata shook her head. "Bring me the basket of medicines. Fortunately I gathered today just what I need."

I proceeded to clean the girl while Mata prepared the herbal mixture. For hours she rubbed the herbs on her womb area, while I tried to get some of the liquid into her mouth. That night Mata sent me off to care for the children while she sat watch over the daughter. After I had put them to bed, I returned and found her seated by the girl's side in meditation, uttering mantras in a barely audible voice. This went on for hours. I continued to rub the girl's womb with the herbal remedies. I must have fallen asleep but I was called back to the world by a commotion outside. It was early morning. I found Mata bending over the girl, checking her breathing.

"She is coming back to life," Mata remarked with a slight smile. "Her breathing has returned to normal." The commotion outside grew louder. Mata looked up with a strange expression on her face and then she shouted a resounding, "Nay!" Before I knew what was happening, she was gone. Like a streak of lighting, like the shadow of the wind, she was one moment seated beside the girl in our cottage and the next moment outside. I ran to the door and saw her standing in front of two men who had been thrown to the ground, as if shielding them. Guruji stood before her with raised hand, about to utter a curse.

I heard Mata's voice, but it did not seem to come from her physical body. The voice seemed to come from the sky, the earth, the trees, from every living being. It shouted, "NAY, NAY! This is the end of the time of curses!"

I saw Guruji standing there, frozen as if paralyzed. And I saw that Shri Ram was just arriving. After a few moments Guruji lowered his arm. Before I knew it, Mata was back in the cottage standing by the widow, with her back toward me. Her whole body was trembling, vibrating with great force. I could not even approach her, such was the power emanating from her body. About thirty minutes later, Shri Ram approached the cottage. I didn't know whether to leave or stay, as I didn't understand what was happening, but I felt I needed to continue to tend to the young girl, so I stayed by her side. Shri Ram stood for a few minutes in the doorway. Mata didn't look up. She didn't greet him. Whatever had just occurred disturbed her terribly. Her body was still trembling as if currents of lightning were passing through her. It was the shakti she had invoked.

"How are the mother and daughter?" Shri Ram asked in a sober tone.

"The mother is unharmed, just a bruise on her head. The daughter was badly wounded but will recover," I replied.

He went over to Mata and placed his hand on her shoulder. As soon as he touched her, the trembling ceased. "Those two men have been banished for killing the guards and for theft. No mention has been made of the violence against the young girl." Mata turned to look at him. I could see the struggle on her face. He continued. "What you did was right. Early on, curses were necessary for the enactment of the law of cause and effect, for the sake of justice. But you are right, Sita, the time for curses has passed. Too many have been issued out of anger, not for the sake of justice.'"

"The girl has been violated multiple times," Sita said quietly. "But she will have no memory of it, and her body will bear no signs. Her mother also will have no memory. They will be completely healed. No one must know what truly took place, so that her marriage can proceed."

Shri Ram nodded. Mata continued in a sorrowful tone, "A girl is violated through no fault of her own, then society rejects her and her life is destroyed. This is not justice."

"It is ignorance, Sita, that makes it so. Dispelling ignorance is the only remedy."

"Such misdeeds have taken place since the beginning of human society, but in the past it was due to lust, to a lack of control of one's passions." Sita sighed. "This was different. It was for revenge. Those two had a grudge against the family and did this terrible deed out of hatred. They wanted to ruin the daughter to get back at the father. What is this new form of abuse?" She was quiet for a few minutes and then continued. "I saw that both of those men had young daughters. Guruji was about to curse their families and the curse would have extended to them as well. The men should receive their due punishment, but the families should be spared. Why should a daughter suffer for the actions of her father?"

Shri Ram replied in a grave tone, "We could not prevent Ravana from setting many new thought patterns that are now spreading through society. Just as man is learning to dominate nature, he will seek to dominate women, and that is the character of the darkened ages that are to come. But that, too, will pass. We must insert the thought patterns that will secure this world until time moves through the approaching cycles and begins to bring back access to the knowledge that is being lost."

Shri Ram continued, "It is not just women who will suffer, Sita, when Shakti withdraws herself. It is the whole of the natural world. In the times to come, the separation between mankind and nature will prevent them from seeing the devas and devis who animate this world. They will forget that the rivers and mountains are alive, and even the rivers will forget who they are. So much knowledge will be lost. Men will forget that women are the bearers of shakti, the force of life, but women will forget this as well. Shakti will patiently wait for the time when she can restore the world. It is for this we have come, Sita, to imbue this remembrance into humanity. When the time is right in the turning of the cycles, this knowledge will reemerge. We will come again into this world, you and I, to reawaken the realm of matter." He turned and smiled at her.

The mother who was lying on Mata's bed began to stir. Her eyes flickered open and she uttered a sound. Mata went to her. After a few minutes, she was able to focus her eyes on Mata and asked in a weak voice, "Where am I?"

"You are here at the hermitage," Sita replied. "There was an accident with the chariot, and you were thrown to the ground."

"My daughter?" She tried to rise from the bed.

"She is right here, not yet recovered. But she will be fine." Shri Ram took his leave so that Mata could devote herself to the wounded pair.

That night, Guruji came to check on the condition of mother and daughter. Mata began to apologize for her intervention, but he prevented her. "What you did was right," he humbly replied. "It is up to our Maharaja to set the punishment. I am ever grateful for your care of the mother and daughter. Her father is a close disciple and is distraught at what has happened. Without your help, I don't know what would have become of this child."

"Give them a few more days and they will be ready to go home. And let marriage planning proceed."

"Can I move them to the hermitage?" he asked. Mata nodded. I think she realized that the wound she had healed in the young girl's body was about to manifest in her own body. Later that day, Mata was overcome with pain in her womb area and began to bleed. In the evening Shri Ram came to check on her. When I saw him approach the cottage, I stepped outside and said to him, "Prahbu, please excuse me for saying this, but Mata has asked that you not see her in her present condition."

He replied solemnly, "Soma, this is one time I must override her wishes. I will not permit her to endure this alone. I must be by her side." For a moment I wondered what to do. I had never disobeyed Mata before, but when I looked up at Shri Ram and felt the love pouring out of him, I realized he would bring comfort and healing to her. I stepped aside and let him enter, saying that I would leave food and water by the door in case she should want it.

Shri Ram did not emerge from the cottage until the next morning. All night I had rested outside by the cottage in the event that they would need me. As soon as I heard the door open, I asked him if I could bring food or drink to Mata and to him.

"She is sleeping, but I would welcome some food, Soma," he replied with a slight smile.

"How is she?" I asked.

"The effects have passed through her body. She will now begin to recover."

As I served the food to Shri Ram, I asked, "Prabhu, she took on herself this pain to save the life of that young woman, and this is not the first time she has done this. How much can she endure?"

"For Sita, every life is precious. How many times she would have given up her body to save another. How many times I have had to intervene to keep her here. One day I will not be able to do so."

A look of pain crossed my face as he continued, "Soma, even I do not know the extent of what she sacrificed in Lanka. That is her wish, to serve quietly out of public view. The world will never know what she has given to preserve life on this earth." He was quiet for a few minutes and then added, "When she stood in front of the two accused men with her arms outstretched, she set a new precedent of compassion, extending even to those who have committed the most vile of offenses. At that moment, I saw her drawing in many of the negative thought forms from all parts of the earth. They entered her body to be consumed and destroyed. I could not stop her. That is my pain, that I cannot take from her the burden of the world that she has assumed."

It took several days before Mata could rise from her bed and walk without pain. Shri Ram stayed throughout this time, but when she was able to function normally he left to return to Ayodhya. Before he departed I heard her say to him, "I am no longer able to bear children."

He replied, "All life on earth are our children. What more do we need?"

Some days later as I was serving her first full meal, I repeated what Shri Ram had said about her sacrifice. She smiled and replied, "Whatever I have done is only a fraction of what he has undertaken. I am but a reflection of his love for this world, and indeed all worlds that hold life."

This is how they spoke of one another. They saw in each other the perfection that was there. Their love was as pure and sacred . . . there really are no words to describe it. We all should aspire to manifest even a small portion of the love they brought to earth.

A few weeks after this incident, I had gone to the forest to collect some wood for the kitchen fire. Upon returning I found Mata deep in conversation with two women I did not recognize. I had not been gone long and wondered how they could have appeared so suddenly. They were seated in the garden surrounded by flowers. I couldn't help but stop to look at the beautiful sight. Both women seemed older than Mata, in their mature years, and yet a youthful beauty graced their faces. They were dressed as ascetics, yet something about them indicated otherwise. I went behind the hut to begin the fire for cooking.

When it came time for the noon meal and Mata still did not appear, I went around to where they were seated and found them still deeply engaged in conversation. For a few minutes I debated whether to offer them a meal or not, but I heard Mata's voice inside asking me to please prepare a proper meal for them. I gathered the various vegetables we had picked from the garden in the early morning and mixed them with some herbs we had retrieved from the forest the day before. The scent of the cooking must have drawn them because as soon as the food was ready they appeared, with broad smiles on their faces.

I saw from Mata's face that she wanted to serve them and so I began to busy myself in another part of the kitchen area. Over the years I had learned to read Mata's every expression. A glance of her eye, a nod of her head was enough to indicate to me her desire. After they had finished, they retreated again to the garden area. They sat there until dark and then I saw Mata walk into the forest with them, and the two women disappeared.

I could not help but inquire about these mysterious women who had suddenly appeared at our hut and then disappeared again into the forest.

"They were the sages Arundhati and Khyati Ma," she replied in a surprised tone. "Didn't you recognize them? I wondered why you didn't greet them by name. They had come to remind me of a vow I took long ago, and to express their pleasure that I had fulfilled that vow."

Then I remembered. I had met them before we retreated to the forest. They were the ones who helped Mata understand that her dreams were a vision of the past. I wondered if their visit had anything to do with what had happened a few weeks earlier to that young woman and her mother.

As soon as Mata saw this thought enter my mind, she nodded and said, "I was only fulfilling the desire of many sages, especially the women. They all felt it was time to withdraw the power of the curse. Too often has it been abused. That day when I acted as I did, I had not realized I was fulfilling their desire. Sage Arundhati, who lost so many sons to a curse, Khyati Ma who saw her beloved Narayan be cursed, Sage Ahilya who herself was cursed, and how many others—this had to come about for them. Ram knew this and that is why he appeared that day. He understood that new laws would take the place of the sages' curses, and perhaps these laws would represent a more just system, not influenced by personal anger or hurt. That is our hope."

"Then there will be no more curses, Mata?"

"I am afraid it is not that simple. But over time the power of curses will diminish until they have no more effect. The power of speech is already declining. What happened that day was the result of the collective aspiration of many. In the future there will be few who have that command over sound, a command that has the power to manifest. But there will always be some sages hidden from human view who have this ability and this responsibility; that is necessary for the preservation and guidance of this material realm."

THE FULFILLMENT OF SITA'S WORK

L ife began to change for us after that. Word seeped out about the whereabouts and doings of Maharani Sita, and people began to come with various ailments and problems, first a few and then a steady stream. Mata would never turn anyone away, but I could see that it was beginning to wear on her physically. Shri Ram also began to notice, and on one of his visits he mentioned to her that perhaps it was time to return to the palace, where people would have greater access to her. He mentioned that it was also time to tell their sons who they truly were, something they had refrained from sharing with them so they could fully engage in the life of the forest and the hermitage.

Mata and I turned to each other and smiled, as we suspected they already knew. Many slips had escaped their lips over the last few years, and many times Mata had thought to reveal to them their secret, but she had held back, saying it was up to Ram to make the decision as to when to share their true identity.

After I had called them from their studies, Shri Ram seated the boys before him. He seemed to struggle for words, so Mata began, "You are both growing up and will soon need to assume your responsibilities in life." It was true. They now stood taller than both Mata and me. Rarely did they come for the evening story, as they were spending most of their time at the hermitage, sometimes even sleeping there. Shri Ram, who for the first time had arrived in his royal clothing, revealed that he was the same Ram who was the maharaja, and Sita was the same Sita who was the maharani, and the time was approaching for their family to be re-united. The boys glanced at each other and burst into laughter, with no look of surprise on their face.

"Why are you laughing?" asked Ram, now broadly smiling. He had naturally assumed they would be shocked by this news.

"Pitaji, we have known this for quite some time."

Shri Ram looked surprised, "And you haven't asked us any questions?"

"Pitaji, we would never question any action of our parents. We know that whatever decision either of you take would always be for some benefit," replied Luv.

Shri Ram gathered them into his arms and held them tight. Lovingly he said, "Your mother has taught you well. Had you been raised in the palace, your upbringing would have been very different, and you would not have had the benefit of her wisdom in quite the same way. I understand that now."

He sent the boys back to the hermitage and then turned to Mata. "Rishi Bhrigu and Sage Khyati will soon achieve their final freedom, and the curse will be released. Our family will soon be reunited. You must prepare to return to Ayodhya." He spoke with quiet joy, but Mata did not respond. She nodded, but by the expression on her face I sensed that something was amiss. After he had taken his leave to return to Ayodhya, I found Mata standing in the doorway, looking after him.

"Aren't you happy about returning to Ayodhya, Mata?"

"Even I wish it would be so, Soma. But it is not meant to be," she replied with a note of sadness. "There are consequences to every action."

"But why, Mata? What do you mean?"

She didn't answer. Casting the shadow of a smile at me, she went inside the cottage. That was Mata's way when she didn't want to answer a question. For many weeks after that, when the dark of night descended, Mata would sit outside gazing at the sky. I would bring her the evening drink and then retire, never knowing whether or not she went to bed. But one night when I brought her the evening drink, I sat beside her quietly and scanned the sky as she was doing. Suddenly she burst out, "Look, Soma, at the celebration!" Two great bursts of light appeared in the distant heavens, as if a star had just been awakened, turning on its fire.

"What does it signify, Mata?"

"Rishi Bhrigu and Sage Khyati have achieved union with Parabrahman. They are now free from all illusion and suffering. The stellar deities are celebrating. Can you not hear, can you not feel the joy permeating the celestial worlds?"

I smiled. I could not hear or feel anything. She often spoke as if I could see and hear what she did.

"I was waiting for this sign, an indication that our retreat is coming to an end."

"Then should we prepare to move to Ayodhya?" I asked.

"Not yet. Not quite yet. There is one desire left within me that must be fulfilled."

"What is that desire, Mata?" I could think of nothing that she could possibly want, as she never expressed the desire for anything.

She was quiet for some time. "It has long been my desire to set these human eyes on Mahadev in human form. I have had this desire since childhood. It stirred within me in Lanka when I conversed with Parvati Ma. During the great battle, I invoked him again and again and felt his presence, but I did not see his form the way I saw Parvati Ma. I have held this desire all these years, but my yearning for his presence has grown so much that I cannot take a step further until he appears before me. I am sure Parvati Ma knows this and will help me realize this last desire."

We sat quietly for a while. I didn't know why her words created such unease within me. Perhaps I was sensing that the fulfillment of this last desire was an indication that she would soon depart the human world, and this I could not accept.

Shri Ram did not return for many months. I put aside the issue of us returning soon to Ayodhya. When he did visit next, he seemed preoccupied with matters concerning the kingdom, and so he did not raise the matter of Mata's return.

Then one evening before Mata said goodnight to the children, she called them to come outside. The moon was absent and the sky was filled with countless stars. "Look up at the stars, Luv, Kush, and see how many worlds there are. And beyond them are so many universes, worlds we cannot see, physical worlds and celestial ones. When I am no longer here, I will be aiding those worlds, helping them to unfold their potential."

A look of concern came over Luv's face. "When you are no longer here?" His voice trailed off.

"I should not have said it that way," she hurried to correct herself. "For I will always be here. But there will come a time when I will be needed elsewhere, and I will be called there." She was quiet for a moment. "Look upon those star beings as friends. They emit a love that benefits all life. They help us fulfil our destiny, and even if they bring us challenges, it is for our own growth. It was Sage Bhrigu who brought to humanity the knowledge of how to read the language of the stars." She chuckled. "I was born as his daughter then, but only a partial knowledge was revealed, because humanity was not ready. There is much more to learn. In the future, when you are ruling the kingdom, look up at the stars and know that I will be smiling down at you, sending love from wherever I am."

"You will be beside us, Ma, when we rule the kingdom," Kush hurried to say.

Mata replied in a faint voice. "There are other universes not visible to the human eye. I exist there as well." Her voice trailed off. I could see Kush yawn and knew that neither of them was able to follow her words. Kush placed his head on her lap and, realizing the late hour, she saw them to their cottage for the night.

Not long after, the future became clear. Mata rose one morning and announced that we would be having special guests that evening; we had to prepare the most magnificent feast. I looked at her questioningly, waiting for instructions. We could prepare a delicious meal as we had so many times before, but a feast? Mata sent me to the forest to gather all the roots and edibles I could find, saying that she would gather the herbs. We spent the morning seeking out the food and picking the best from our garden. She seemed a bit anxious but also overjoyed. I could not imagine who would be coming. I thought surely Shri Ram must be bringing others from the palace. Perhaps they were coming to bring us back to Ayodhya.

Evening set in. Mata arranged a place outside amidst all the flowers, the place where she and Shri Ram often sat and where on occasion they ate their evening meal. "Bring the mats and cushions from my cottage, Soma; we will serve them here." This surprised me as we had never brought the cushions outside before. But she insisted on creating a comfortable and beautiful scene. When we were finished, we went inside to wait. The food was prepared. All we needed were the guests, but the hours went by and nobody arrived.

"It is getting late, Mata," I said. "Perhaps they will arrive tomorrow."

She shook her head, "No. They will come. I am sure of it. Soma, keep the food warm. They will arrive any time now." She began to wring her hands, and I could see that she was anxious.

"May I ask who we are expecting?"

She smiled and replied, "You will know in time."

Just as the stars were emerging, one by one, sprinkling their pointed lights across the sky, two beautiful young ascetics knocked at the door. I could hear Mata's heart beating as she went to open it. She stood there beaming, glowing in a way I had seen her glow only in the presence of Shri Ram. She bent to touch their feet. They tried to stop her, but Mata insisted. "Please Prahbu, Ma, this one time, allow me to serve you," she said in a quiet voice as she rose to look at them, her hands folded together in respect.

I wondered who these two ascetics were. The face of the woman was youthful and bearing an almost unearthly beauty, with pale skin like the mountain people and dark glowing almond-shaped eyes. The man similarly had fine features and also bore a mountain complexion, pale and soft, yet his features displayed great strength. I could not stop gazing at them. The woman spoke first, lovingly with a smile, "Sita, my dear," as if she knew Mata. Then the man spoke, "I have felt your yearning, Sita, and have come to fulfil this desire. I could not refuse any request of yours."

Mata showed them to the seating area. Just as they were getting settled, I saw Shri Ram walk up the pathway. He went immediately over to greet them. As they sat there, a soft light encased them. It was a dark night with only a sliver of moon to light the way, and yet they were embraced by a subtle light coming from no stellar orb. It seemed to be emitted from the bodies of the two ascetics. After sitting for some time, Mata rose to get the food. She insisted on serving the two ascetics and Shri Ram.

Once she had seated herself, I requested that she allow me to serve her. She nodded. They all ate in silence. After complimenting Mata on the food, the woman turned to Shri Ram and told him many things that had taken place during Mata's time in Lanka. When she finished, she gazed for a few minutes at Mata, then described Mata's battle with Yama Dev on the evening Lakshman had been struck with a poisonous arrow during the great war with Ravana.

"Lakshman would not have lasted the night had she not intervened," the woman said ever so quietly. Shri Ram turned to look at Mata, whose eyes were cast down. She had never shared these experiences with him. "But in exchange for Lakshman's life," continued the woman, "Sita had to give some years of her own. It was Yama Dev's demand." She fell silent.

As the words sank in, Shri Ram seemed to grasp the gravity of the situation. "But an extension can surely be given?"

The woman shook her head. "It was Sita's word," she replied quietly.

"Just as she gave years of her life, surely I can do the same?" he asked in a soft voice.

Again the woman shook her head. "The time is running out."

"How much time is left?" he asked.

The woman turned to face Mata. "You can choose the time of your departure, but it must be within the year."

"So soon!" exclaimed Shri Ram. She nodded.

Mata had been absorbing this information. At first she seemed startled, but she soon gained her composure. Turning to Shri Ram, she said. "I must honor my word. If I were to face the same situation again, I would gladly give my life for the sake of our beloved brother Lakshman, or any of our brothers. It would be my honor to do so."

"Then I will also prepare for my departure," he replied solemnly, as he grasped Mata's hand.

"That is not possible, Ram," interjected the man. "Your time has not come. You must remain here until your sons are ready to govern, the foundation for a new society is secure, and the laws of dharma are established, laws based on the universal love that pervades all. This was the reason for your birth, for the birth of both of you. With Sita's early departure, it is more urgent for you to remain and fulfill the task for which you have both come. Sita will aid you from your celestial home."

Mata then turned to the man and said, "My joy in seeing you counters any sadness I have in leaving my family and this world that I so love."

"That is why I have come," he replied with a loving smile. "Ram, Sita, I will show you both all that was, and all that will come to be, and who you truly are." With those words they closed their eyes and went into meditation.

I had been clearing the remains of the meal when this conversation took place, but as tears threatened to burst from my eyes, I quickly scooped up what was left of the meal and ran to the kitchen area. Once I reached my room, I collapsed on the floor. I cried and cried until there were no tears left in me, and then I drifted to sleep. I awoke some hours later. It was still dark outside. I glanced out of the widow and saw that the four of them were still in meditation, only the forms of the two ascetics had changed. Seated before Mata and Shri Ram were the forms of Parvati Ma and Mahadev. I thought to go to them, but my eyes were heavy and my feet would not move, so I sank back onto the floor and fell into a deep sleep. I awoke again just as the first morning rays were peering through the window. I found Mata sleeping alone on the cushions where the dinner had taken place. A subtle light clung to her body. There was no sign of the guests or of Shri Ram. I sighed in relief. Perhaps I had dreamed the whole scene. Perhaps the guests had never arrived, and Mata had fallen asleep waiting for them. I comforted myself with this thought and went to see about the children.

When I returned to the cottage, I found Mata in the kitchen area starting the fire for the morning meal.

"Mata, the guests never arrived last night, did they?"

She smiled broadly. "Don't you remember? You were there serving us."

"I . . . I was hoping that I had dreamed the whole thing . . . ." my voice trembled.

"Soma, do you not know who you were in the presence of?" I didn't respond as my mind was still confused. "Go, bring the cushions and mats back into the cottage and you will know."

As I lifted the mats, I discovered small jewels spread out in the area where the man and woman had sat. I grabbed a basket and began to gather them. I saw Mata smiling in the doorway. Looking up at her I realized that what I had seen was true. It was Mahadev and Parvati Ma. And then I remembered that I had awoken in the night and seen their forms. As this realization came to me, she nodded and said, "Please bring those gems to Gurudev and tell him that it is a gift from Shri Ram for taking care of his family for all these years."

Mata seemed undisturbed by the news of her early departure from this world. When I ventured to bring it up, she placed her finger over my lips and said, "Soma, do not think about tomorrow. We have to concern ourselves only with today. This world is ever uncertain, and nobody truly knows where they will be one day, one month, one year from now. Whatever will happen is as it should be, by our own design, and we must not question or bemoan the inevitable."

But I could not put it out of my mind. Every day when I awoke I ran to make sure she was still alive. One day she laughed and said, "I promise you, Soma, you will be the first to know when that day comes." In the evenings I would find her staring at the stars as if she were studying something.

One evening she said me, "Once I was born as the daughter of Rishi Bhrigu and I helped him bring to earth the knowledge of the stars, the understanding of their movements and their effects on human life. It was during the time when Narayan took on the curse. Had he not, the grief of Bhrigu over the death of his wife Usana was so great that he would have departed from this world. But Narayan knew his work was incomplete, and he needed to remain for a long time to come, until the end of the cycle. As a result, he is still with us, still bringing knowledge to human society."

"What are you watching for, Mata?" I ventured to ask, fearing that she was seeking an auspicious time to depart this world.

"The stars speak to me in the language of love. They are constantly emitting love and messages to us. And your thought is correct, Soma, they will tell me the right time to go."

"Mata," my voice trembled. Reading my thoughts, she answered, "No, Soma, you may not come with me. You are still needed here. Luv and Kush will take comfort in your presence. After all, they have not lived in the palace or with their father. You will be their connection to me for quite some time."

It seemed as if all of Ayodhya knew that Mata's time with us was limited, for they came, so many of them, sometimes just to catch a glimpse of her. It wore on her terribly, but she welcomed everyone. One morning she said to me, "How I wish I could see Ayodhya once more, to walk the streets and see how it is grown, how busy it has become."

"Mata, I will speak with Hanuman to arrange this," I replied. She nodded, but we both knew it was not possible. She was becoming frail and would not be able to withstand the long journey. But still we kept planning. Not long after this, Hanuman arrived. He knew her desires before she even expressed them. Often he would appear at our cottage with a basket of a particular fruit for which she had expressed a desire, or one that had appeared in her thoughts.

One time she said to him, "I don't want to trouble you, Putra Hanuman, so I will stop these small desires before they arise."

"I beg you, Mata, do not deprive me of the joy of satisfying the wishes that arise in your heart." And so she allowed him to continue. Now soon after she had expressed the desire to visit Ayodhya, he appeared and said, "Mata, come, I will take you to Ayodhya, but not by the normal route. Let us go in meditation." And so they went deep into the forest and remained there for several days. When they returned, Mata was elated.

"Hanuman took me to my beloved Ayodhya," she said with a broad smile. "I even bathed in the sacred Sarayu River and spoke with the devi. If you could see, Soma, how the city has grown, how many people live there now, so many foreigners and traders. It hardly resembles the city we left. With so many to govern, I wonder how Ram finds time to visit us."

"Mata, how could he possibly stay away? You are his guiding star, the foundation of his life," replied Hanuman. "I know how hard it is for him to be away from you at all."

"Through all our trials, our separations, through the assaults of time and the busyness of life, the love we share has not diminished in the slightest. Just the recitation or hearing of his name brings me such joy. That is what binds you and me, Hanuman, our love for him."

Tears came to Hanuman's eyes as she spoke these words. He said, "Mata, my love for him and my love for you are one and the same. I do not differentiate between you. As long as I walk this earth, I will proclaim the unity of Shri Ram and Mata Sita."

"And you will walk this earth for a long time," she replied with a slight smile.

"It is not my will but yours and that of Shri Ram. If that is your decree, so be it."

After Hanuman left, Mata told me that she found many souls from Mithila who had taken birth in Ayodhya, and she recognized some from our household. This gave her great joy— to know they were bringing the values and memories of Mithila to Ayodhya. When she shared this with me, I said, "It is their love for you that has drawn them to Ayodhya. They have followed you to this land."

Soma paused in her narrative. We waited eagerly for her to continue, but she seemed lost in thought. When she did finally pick up her narrative, she spoke from a faraway place, her voice filled with an otherworldly tone, as if it were not her speaking.

I came to know what they were doing in that last year, Mata and Shri Ram. They were planting thought forms in the human mind, in the collective, seeding ideas and concepts that would unfold centuries and even millennia into the future.

"This earth is in the descending arc of its cyclical movement," Mata explained to me one evening. "Humans are losing touch with the spiritual worlds, but gaining development of the rational faculty, which will increase man's mental capability. Some of these thought forms will not manifest until we enter the ascending arc in the realm where time operates. As the human spirit seeks to know itself in its full individuality, man's sense of himself will become much inflated and the thirst for power will grow, as will aggression. That is why structure and laws are necessary now, whereas they were not needed when there was a natural internal knowing of dharma. Eventually, when individuality reaches its peak, man will have to move beyond that and come to know himself again as part the whole; then he will be able to overcome these aggressive traits. That is a long way off. We cannot go against the cycles of time that have been established and that have their own rhythm and pulse. Much patience is needed when you abide in the realm of time.'"

Soma was quiet and then resumed speaking in her familiar voice.

After the visit from Parvati Ma and Mahadev, Mata seemed more inward and less accessible, except to her children. Whenever she was in their presence, she was fully attentive to every detail of their lives. But she was spending more and more time alone, and would often withdraw into silence for hours. She told me that Mahadev had given her a great blessing, enabling her to connect with him and Parvati Ma inwardly while performing all her outer activities. I suspect they told her many other things that Mata never shared with me. Inwardly Mata seemed to have gained new strength, but I could also see that on the physical plane her life force was weakening.

Mata had a way of erasing from your mind any negative thoughts, and so I gradually lost the fear of her departure. Honestly, I didn't think of it much in the next few months, but I did observe certain changes. I watched as she wandered into the forest and stood before a tree, or an animal, or a plant, and gazed at it with such tender care. Sometimes she would run her hands along the bark of a tree or rest her back against the trunk and close her eyes. A smile would burst across her face, and I knew she was sending and receiving love from that tree. Once, at such a time, she said, "I see him in every ray of sun, in every leaf and plant. Here, there, everywhere I see my beloved Narayan. Where is he not?"

Shri Ram tried to come as frequently as he could that last year. I remember one visit, when they were enjoying themselves as a family, as they had done so often when Luv and Kush were young. But now that they were older, I rarely saw them play in this way. Mata was laughing with them, seated on the ground, trying to pull them both onto her lap, even though they were quite a bit taller than her now. As they laughingly pulled away she would draw them close again, trying to coddle them as if they were still small children. Shri Ram was watching their play with great amusement.

I was quietly observing the scene when suddenly a feeling of sadness came over me as I noticed the few strands of silver hair that now peered out around her face, and the shallow lines that like small footprints had crept around her eyes, and the thinning of her cheeks that were once so perfectly formed. She was still beautiful no doubt, but I could see the threat of age waiting to ripen. "I cannot bear to see you age, Mata," I thought to myself. Shri Ram caught this thought and went over to the three of them. The boys had finally extricated themselves from Mata's grip, and they were all still laughing. "Sita," he said in such a loving voice, "you are even more beautiful now than when I first met you." Tenderly he stroked her hair as he spoke these words.

She paused and looked at him and then quietly said only, "Ram."

"It is the truth, for the love and joy that now pour out of you are such . . . I have no words to describe your beauty."

I realized then that he was quietly reminding me to see not just the external but the internal reality, and that he wanted their children to experience this love between them so they would remember it always.

"Thank you, Prahbu," I silently whispered. "You never fail to catch and correct my thoughts." This was the way he helped steer me to the true reality. Rarely did he openly correct me, but how often he discretely brought me back when my thinking had gone off track.

When I look back upon that last year, I think Mata was saying goodbye to all the things she loved on earth. She was filling that last year with such love, the love had always been there, but somehow it seemed even more intense. It was the same with the children. In addition to her occasional fondling of them, she now engaged them in serious conversations; she took advantage of every moment to see to their mental and emotional development, and to remind them of things she felt were important. No moment was wasted or lost.

And so the months passed. Her joy was as palpable as ever, and I dared not think anything could disturb this happiness we all felt. When Shri Ram came, they often wandered alone into the forest. For the first time, I saw her holding onto his arm when they walked. The thought crossed my mind that her physical form was weakening, but I chased away that thought and said no, it was affection that made her cling to him.

The year was coming to a close, the year since that extraordinary event with Parvati Ma and Mahadev, and still there was no indication of any change in our situation. Then one night I was bringing Mata her evening drink when I heard her speaking with someone in her cottage. I hesitated at the door, wondering if I should interrupt. I had not seen anyone arrive and so could not imagine with whom she was speaking in such quiet tones. I could make out a man's voice and could tell it was not Shri Ram. She never retired without first taking the drink that she had taught me to prepare, and so after waiting for several minutes I decide to knock.

"Come, Soma." I pushed open the door and to my shock I saw Janak Baba standing before her. Overcome with emotion, I let the drink slip from my hand and it crashed to the floor, spilling the contents everywhere. At first I was paralyzed, unable to move, but then my feet carried me to him and I fell to the floor. Placing my forehead on his blessed feet, I could not prevent my tears from washing over him. All of my longing for him and for Mithila these many years suddenly came to the fore. "Baba," I cried.

He placed his hand on my head in blessing. Then lifting me, he said, "I am indebted to you, Soma, for taking such care of Sita all of these years. Never did your devotion waver."

Raising my head and drying my eyes, I shook my head. "Baba, you gave me the great honor to be able to serve her." Then realizing the mess I had caused, I took my shawl and started to clean the floor.

"Leave it, Soma," said Mata. "But let us prepare some food for Pitaji before he leaves." I left them together and went to the kitchen area to begin the food preparation.

Soon after, Mata joined me and I asked, "Mata, why has he come in this manner to visit us?"

She looked off into the distance. "Do you remember when I was young in the forest and went so deep in meditation that I almost didn't return to this physical body?"

I nodded. "I will never forget that day, Mata. It was Shri Ram who brought you back, although you hadn't met him yet. It was then that you saw your future with him."

Mata smiled. "Yes, and I also made a promise to Pitaji that I would not leave this body without his permission. Do you remember?" Again I nodded. "He has come to help me fulfil that vow," she said simply. "Pitaji sees into the past and the future. Nothing escapes his view." As if to return to the present moment, she took up the cooking utensils and said, "Now let us quickly prepare a wonderful meal. He told me that he has missed my cooking all these years."

I didn't comprehend Mata's words or the meaning of his visit until later. So many hints she dropped for me, but I didn't catch them. I didn't want to see what was right in front of me, staring me in the face. I think she sheltered me from realizing too much. The rest of that evening passed with much affection displayed between Mata and her father. I asked if I should prepare a place for him to sleep, but Janak Baba shook his head and said he would soon leave. I retired and don't know what took place after that, but I assume that he departed in the same mysterious way as he had arrived, because he was gone when I awoke the next morning.

A few weeks later an extraordinary event took place. It was just as the sun was setting. The light had already grown dim, but a beautiful pink hue filled the sky with a softness and quietude that was deeply nourishing. Mata and I stepped out of the cottage to take in the scene.

"How beautiful!" I exclaimed. Mata nodded. Her face was beaming with joy. Just then we saw two ascetics emerging from the forest, a woman and man.

As they came closer, Mata exclaimed, "Anasuya and Atri!" She hurried down the path to greet them, and ushered them into the garden area. After they had been settled, two more figures emerged. It was Arundhati and Vasishtha. Shortly after Khyati and Bhrigu arrived, and then Lopamudra and Agastya, and so on until many great sages were seated in our garden area.

I wondered what we should do. Should I begin to prepare food? By the expression on her face, I saw that she was as baffled as I, and there was no time to discuss preparing a meal as more people kept arriving. After so many of the rishis and sages were seated, I saw a group of what appeared to be celestial beings arrive. They came ten, twelve at a time. I recognized some, but many I did not. Mata seemed to know them all. Each one pranammed to her. Mata was standing on the path to her cottage in amazement as she received all the beings who were emerging from the forest and walking down the pathway that led to our cottage. Our garden could not accommodate everyone, and so they found places wherever they could, some at the edge of the forest, some on all sides of the cottage. They seemed to be waiting for someone. Finally, after the arrival of so many, I saw a most beautiful pair walk down the path. I recognized them at once as Parvati Ma and Mahadev. They approached Mata, and she pranammed to them. Then she whispered to Parvati Ma, "What is this? Why has everyone come?"

"It is your wedding day, dear. Shri Ram has called us all."

Mata looked shocked. "My wedding? But I am soon to leave this earth."

"Your celestial wedding. Shri Ram wanted everyone to witness your reunion in the celestial world."

Mata still looked confused. I saw her look down at her clothing, but before our very eyes, Parvati Ma transformed Mata's simple ascetic dress into a celestial garment of magnificent beauty. With a smile, she and Mahadev went to sit right in front of the dais that had magically been erected. As Mata looked around at the scene in wonderment, we saw Shri Ram emerge from the forest and walk down the pathway to where we were standing. He also was clothed in wondrous celestial garments. He stopped in front of her and smiled. He had done all of this for her. I realized later that he wanted her to depart this world in a scene of great joy and celebration.

Taking her hand, Ram led Mata to the dais. A canopy of light enfolded them as they sat there together. A hush fell over the crowd as Shri Ram acknowledged each one who had come with a nod of his head. He didn't speak for some time, but all of us could feel the great wave of love that swept over us.

Finally he spoke. "I have asked you to come to be with us, to witness the love that Sita has awakened in this creation, the love that was embedded in the universe, waiting to be roused. It is her love that will sustain her mother Vasundhara Ma during her difficult times, her love that will guide humanity forward. It is her love, my love, there is no distinction." Sita didn't take her eyes off Shri Ram as he spoke. He looked around at the gathering and then said quietly, "And for the love you have displayed and for your service to this creation, we are most grateful."

To the sages he said, "To you who have sacrificed your lives and left your places in the celestial spheres to serve this world, we are most grateful." He addressed the devas and devis: "To you who maintain the balance of the worlds, without whom the natural order would be in disarray, we are most grateful." Then turning to Mahadev and Parvati Ma, and to Saraswati Ma and Brahmadev, who had quietly arrived and were now seated near them, he expressed his love: "Without you, there would be no worlds, no life. It is you who give rise to all that is and maintain the constant movement of time, transforming one life into another for the progression of the seen and unseen universes."

A great light emanated from Shri Ram. Turning to Mata, he fell silent. When he spoke he said, "I have no words to describe the one who is my guiding star, the sustainer of so many universes, the one without whom I am not." Mata continued to gaze at him with fixed eyes and an expression of great peace and joy. After he spoke these words, he fell silent.

Mata said, "The love you describe, the love that sustains creation, is a love that only you can awaken. I may express it and spread it through the universe, but it is you who have awakened it in me."

Shri Ram added, "When Sita returns to our celestial home, she will take with her a part of me. There can be no separation."

At that moment a beautiful chant arose. It seemed to come from all directions. *Shri Ram, Jai Ram, Jai Sita Ram . . .*

It was not until we were well into the night that the thought of food came to me. How was I to prepare a meal for all these guests? Just as this thought arose, I saw a large group of celestial attendants emerge from the forest with baskets and trays of food. They waved to me to come, as if they knew me, and so I joined them. Handing me one of the trays, they indicated that I was to lead the way. I began to approach Mata with the tray but, from a glance of her eye, I understood that the others were to be served first. I set the food before Mahadev and Parvati Ma, then Brahma Dev and Saraswati Ma. In this way all the guests were served a wonderful feast of many food items. After the meal was finished, the attendants took the trays and baskets and disappeared into the forest. Everyone went into meditation, but the chanting continued through the night. I seated myself in the doorway of Mata's cottage and closed my eyes as I listened to the chanting. Never had I heard such a beautiful choir.

Eventually I drifted to sleep and awoke only when I heard the birds stir. Everyone was gone, except Mata and Shri Ram, dressed in their ascetic clothing. They were seated in the garden. He was in meditation, and she was resting beside him with her head upon his lap. There was no sign of anyone else, no sign of what had taken place the night before. I wondered if it had been a dream, a most beautiful dream, but a short time later when Mata awoke she told me that she was glad I had witnessed the event of the previous night.

"Last night was a great blessing for all of earth's creatures and for Vasundhara Ma, to have so many great ones gathered together in one place is most rare. It was Ram's gift to the world," she said.

"It was an expression of his love for you," I added.

"Is there any distinction between me and the world?" she asked with a smile.

I didn't understand her comment but responded, "Of course not, Mata."

Mata hardly spoke that morning. Her consciousness was interiorized, inward looking. She asked to spend some time with the children alone in her cottage, so I brought them to her. An hour passed, and they remained inside. Shri Ram emerged from meditation and asked after her. I told him she was with the children inside her cottage. He entered and remained there for some time. Finally, Shri Ram and Mata emerged and said they were going into the forest for meditation. Before leaving she looked over at Hanuman and me; we were standing just outside the cottage. Suddenly she drew me to her and held me tight. I thought I heard a sigh. When she released me, she placed her hand on Hanuman's hand and gave it a slight squeeze, and then she and Shri Ram began to walk down the path, his arm around her. I thought to follow them with a pitcher of water and a basket of fruits as I usually did.

"Stay with Luv and Kush," Mata instructed as she turned to face me. "They will need you." Then she continued walking.

When Hanuman heard these words, he emitted a cry, "Mata!" It was then that I realized what was happening. In near panic my mind cried out, "You are leaving this world, aren't you, Mata?"

As this thought entered my mind, she paused. With such a loving look, she turned around and replied, "How can I leave this world, Soma, when I am the world? You of all people should know that." She clung to Shri Ram's arm as the two of them continued down the path that led into the forest. Hanuman started to follow them.

Mata again turned around and said to him quietly, "You must stay, Putra. Look after Soma and the children." Tears were rolling down his cheeks.

I heard him whisper, "Mata." She approached him and wiped his tears, and gazed at him lovingly until she saw a smile cross his face. She said in a gentle voice, "This is a time for joy, not for tears." Then grasping Shri Ram's arm once more, she disappeared into the forest.

The hours passed. The children had gone to the hermitage for their classes. I tried to busy myself with various chores in the kitchen, but finally I could stand it no longer. I had to go to her. Under the pretext of bringing them nourishment, I filled a jug with water and a basket with fruit and headed into the forest. Hanuman was seated by the gate waiting for both or one of them to return. I knew where they would be as there was a spot on a large boulder in a clearing where they liked to meditate.

Soma stopped and gave a small chuckle. "That spot is right here outside, where I had them build my hut. This is where they always came for meditation, Shri Ram and Mata." She continued:

So I went with the food and water. I found them meditating. One of Shri Ram's hands was resting on top of hers. That was how close they sat. As I laid down the basket and jug, Mata briefly opened her eyes. "Thank you, Soma," she said with such kindness. "Thank you for everything you have done." Then she closed her eyes again. I couldn't say a word and simply retreated back onto the forest path. But something made me turn back. I felt a great pull coming from her, so I swung around just in time to witness Mata's absorption into the world.

First I saw a great light emanate from her body. It encompassed Shri Ram and then spread out from the two of them. This emanation divided into many points of light, spreading out in every direction, like a rain of light filling the sky, pouring into the earth, blanketing the forest. Everywhere I looked these points of light streamed over the earth and sky. It was a beautiful sight, and stayed for quite a while. Rivers of light poured from the spot where her body had been. As I followed the streams of light, I saw it break into a multitude of colors, a rainbow of light. When the light finally cleared, I saw that her form was no longer there. It had become one with the earth, the sky, with everything.

I had been fixed to the spot, witnessing this amazing occurrence, but when the light cleared and I saw that her body was no more, I was filled with despair and ran back to the cottage. I told Hanuman and Lakshman, who had also come the night before, what had happened. Hanuman tried to calm me down, but Lakshman ran to where Shri Ram was seated.

Shri Ram and Lakshman didn't return until the next morning. When I finally saw the two of them emerge from the forest, I ran to them. At first I thought Shri Ram was Mata, as he seemed to wear her appearance, or so my mind thought. But as I got closer and saw that it was him, and Mata was nowhere in sight, I fell at his feet and began to cry. "Mata is gone. She is gone from us."

Shri Ram lifted me and looked deep into my eyes with such calmness, with that steadiness for which he is known. He replied so sweetly,

"She is only gone if you think her gone, Soma. Do not let your mind deceive you. If she were gone, this world would cease to be."

The next few days passed like a dream. Shri Ram prepared Luv and Kush for the reality of their mother's transformation, and it was decided the boys would divide their time between the hermitage and the palace until their studies were over. That way they could gradually become accustomed to life in Ayodhya, a world with which they were totally unfamiliar. And so I continued to care for the boys. Hanuman came and went. He took on a new role of caring for me, bringing me food, as if Mata were acting through him, as if the roles had been reversed and Mata was now caring for me. That was something I was unaccustomed to, but it gave me much comfort. When it was time for Luv and Kush to shift to the palace full time, Shri Ram pleaded with me to come, but I couldn't leave this place.

The years passed, and a time came when I began to miss Mata terribly. All the years during the exile, I never felt her absence, but this was different. One day the sorrow became overwhelming and I fell onto the ground calling out to Vasundhara Ma. "Why have you taken my Mata?" I cried. "Why could I not follow her?"

Just then I heard footsteps, and I felt two arms gently lifting me from the ground. I heard his voice, that sweet and caring voice. "Why these tears, Soma?" I looked up and into the calm and steady eyes of Shri Ram.

"Prabhu, the only purpose of my life was to serve her. Now that she is gone . . . ."

"Gone?" he exclaimed. "Have you forgotten her words to you that day?"

"But why, Prabhu, can I not see her, feel her presence if she is here?"

"Sometimes we humans cannot see what is right in front of us. Look, Soma, and see her step out of the sunlight. See her beautiful form rise from the earth. Look, Soma, open your eyes." He gently tapped me on the forehead and, indeed, I saw her smiling at me, stepping out from between the streams of sunlight, emerging from the earth and swaying in the gentle breezes. She was everywhere.

Shri Ram stayed with me for several hours and allowed me to fix him a meal. Then he left, but his blessing has stayed with me until today. Everywhere I look, I see Mata, so I continue to abide with her here. Since our two cottages belonged to the hermitage, I had them build me a small hut near Mata's meditation spot in the forest. That is how I came to live here. Shri Ram would bring the boys every year on the anniversary of Mata's transformation, and I have held their daughters, Mata's granddaughters, just as I promised her. But since Shri Ram left this world, I have rarely seen Luv and Kush.

Soma smiled. "I learned from Hanuman about the time when Shri Ram left his body."

It was early one morning, well before dawn, when Shri Ram arose and went down to the river for meditation. He found a quiet spot where he could be undisturbed. Hanuman was away from Ayodhya at the time but suddenly felt a call from Shri Ram, and so with great speed he made his way to Ayodhya and found Shri Ram meditating by the river. Dawn had broken and many of the residents were gathering to see their Maharaja, but he sat undisturbed. Suddenly, Hanuman saw Mata approach. No one else seemed to see her. But as she approached Shri Ram, Hanuman asked her sadly, "Mata, you have come to take my lord?" She nodded. "Then take me as well. I have no more purpose here."

She shook her head. "Hanuman putra, you must stay here until this cycle of time finds completion. You must feed the world on our behalf." Hanuman said he couldn't tell if it was Mata or Shri Ram who was speaking. It was as if their voices had become one.

Mata sat down beside Shri Ram. For a moment Shri Ram opened his eyes and looked at Hanuman. "Hanuman, you are our eyes and ears, our feet and hands, feeding and serving the world, and our hearts sending love continually to everyone and everything. That is why you have come into this world, so that our love will carry the world forward through this cycle of time."

After speaking these words, he closed his eyes. Mata placed her hand upon his, and Shri Ram's body dissolved into a million points of light, falling on the river, the trees, and filling the sky, blanketing the earth. In the same way that Mata had left her physical form, so did he. When the light cleared, neither form was present. In this way, they returned to their celestial home.

Soma's eyes were closed and she fell silent, her narrative over. For what seemed like a long time there was complete silence in the darkened room. The evening had slipped into the depths of night, without us noticing. Suddenly small lights were lit. I opened my eyes and looked around and saw that the room was filled to capacity with hermits, some seated, some standing, some outside the widow. They had all come to hear Soma once again recite the story of Shri Ram and Mata Sita.

Soma suddenly opened her eyes and exclaimed in surprise and joy, "So you have come after such a long time!" I turned to see who she was addressing. An ascetic stood in the doorway, bending so that his tall frame could fit through the door. His appearance was unusual, different from the rest, but there was not enough light to catch a good glimpse of him. He seemed to be someone with whom she was very familiar.

"Forgive me, Soma. I have been far away. I heard the names of Shri Ram and Mata Sita and so I have come, and I have brought food for your guests." The other ascetics in the room made way for him to approach Soma, and as they did, one by one they touched his feet in great reverence. He laid the basket before Soma. She made an effort to get up, but he said, "Don't rise. I have come to give you these."

She shifted onto her knees and laid her head at his feet, saying, "It is enough for me to catch sight of you." He smiled, and as quickly as he had arrived, he left the room and disappeared into the night.

A great joy emanated from Soma now. Whoever the ascetic was, he had a great effect on her. She distributed the food and then one by one the ascetics all took their leave. Only my mother and I remained.

Thanking Soma profusely for her hospitality and for sharing her stories with us, my mother said, "We will never be the same after hearing your stories of Maharani Sita and Shri Ram. I feel now as if I know them personally, as if they are near and dear." My mother's voice became tearful.

"They are near and dear. And they care for each one of us as if we were their child, because in fact we are. I have come to know Mata and Shri Ram much better since their departure from this physical world. Departure is not accurate, it is not the correct term, for they never left. But our language is so limited. Mata once told me that words will never replace the way we used to converse, through images, through thought. Now we are reduced to language. They are as active today as ever. When Mata was before me in the physical form, that is what I saw, that is what I knew, that was who she was to me. Now I see the reality of what she is, of what both of them are. And I see their hand in everything that transpires in this world." There was a twinkle in Soma's eyes as she concluded, "And sometimes, sometimes, I see her form walking through the forest, a flicker of her form, and I know she has come to remind me that she is not gone."

My mother said, "I will try to remember that. I don't know how we can leave you, Soma, but I am afraid that we must depart tomorrow at the first rays of dawn. We have a long journey home and Anasuya's father is waiting for us."

At those words, I could not contain myself. "Please, Ma, a few more days."

"I'm afraid that is not possible."

"But I am not ready." Tears welled up in my eyes.

My mother took my hand and said, "I am as reluctant to leave as you are, but we must return to our life. We have stayed away many days, and your father would not approve of any further delay." I began to cry.

Soma turned to my mother and said, "Let your daughter remain with me through the night. I assure you she will be ready to leave in the morning when you come for her."

A student from the hermitage had come to guide my mother back to our cottage, and so she departed with him leaving me alone with Soma. As soon as my mother left, Soma got up to prepare me a warm drink. "This is the drink I used to prepare for Mata before she retired for the night. It will help you, my dear."

"Soma," I began in a pleading voice. "Please help me convince my mother to let me stay with you. I want nothing more than to serve you, to live here with you. I don't want to leave. I cannot . . . ." My chest began to heave in pain.

She seemed moved by my request. "But you must, child," she said gently. "I am nearing the end of this life, and you are beginning yours. You must let go of the past and look toward the future."

Covering my face with my hands, I cried, "But I can't see the future, and I don't know the past. All I know is that I feel a peace inside of me when I am with you."

Taking my hands in hers, she looked into my eyes and replied, "That is Mata's peace, her presence. I have enabled you to feel her again. That is why you have come. Hold on to that feeling. She will guide your life."

My tears ceased. "What do you mean?" Soma didn't answer. She led me around to the kitchen area where she lit a fire and began preparing an herbal drink. After we went back inside and she handed me the drink, she spoke again.

"Drink this, and then you will sleep. Listen carefully to me. You may not understand what I say, but inside you will know it is true. Your past birth was in Mithila, as a servant in the Janak household. We both served there together. You were very devoted to Mata. We came together to Ayodhya, but you did not live to see Mata's return." She looked off into the distance as she continued, "There was a young man in Janak Baba's household who wanted to marry you, but your father wouldn't have it. He forbid you to marry and so you never did. That is the cause of your resistance. Somewhere, deep inside, you remember your father's insistence that you not marry. He was afraid something terrible would happen to you if you married. This young man was a good man, and Mata was very fond of him. He took care of the animals and had so much love for them. Mata once said nobody loved the animals as he did, and she was grateful for this. He has taken birth in Ayodhya, and he is the one your father has chosen for you. Accept him, my dear. He has great love for Mata.

"This is Mata's design. When Mata retuned with Hanuman from her last visit to Ayodhya, she told me that many people from Mithila had taken birth in Ayodhya and were now children there. She recognized them. She would not say it, but I knew that it was their love for her that drew them to Ayodhya after their death. She said that those who came from Mithila would bring the values instilled in us by Janak Baba to this kingdom, which is gaining great importance and power. It is for the future, and it is all by her design. We may not understand the larger picture, but we can trust it is for the greater good."

I looked at her blankly. I had no memory of any of this.

"Do not worry if you do not remember. There is a reason for that. It is better not to dwell on the past, but to see what this life has to offer. You will find many surprises ahead. Just cling to Mata as best you can.

"I will tell you one more story before you leave that was told to me by Hanuman, and this is a story for the future, a future that you and so many others will help create. When Hanuman found Shri

Ram seated by the river, with Mata by his side in her light body and not visible to the physical eye, many of the citizens of Ayodhya had gathered as word had spread that Shri Ram was in deep meditation. Shri Ram had been waiting for Hanuman's arrival before leaving his physical form. After he spoke his last words to Hanuman and his physical form dissolved, Hanuman heard words coming from the invisible realms, as if from the combined voice of both Mata and Shri Ram. It said, 'The love that permeates the celestial worlds now also permeates the earth and all her creatures. But it is the human being who has the potential and power to awaken this love. You are the perfect expression of this love, Hanuman, and you must seek to awaken this potential in all.'

"This is their lasting message to us, to awaken our own potential for love," said Soma as she closed her eyes. I could feel that she had entered another state of awareness. A few minutes later, she opened her eyes and added, "That love cannot be a mere concept in our mind, but must become real; it can only become real by loving others. Show your husband the same love I have spoken about these last days. Let the love between Mata and Shri Ram shine in your life with your husband. That is what we must do. Now you must take some rest as your mother will be here before long to fetch you."

The thought of returning to Ayodhya no longer was painful. There was something soothing in Soma's words. I realized how weary my body was, so I lay down on her bed and drifted into a sound sleep.

It was sometime between night and day, in the unlit place where the light is internally generated, between the inner and outer world, somewhere between it all, it was there that I saw a brilliant light of a totally different quality from sunlight. The thought came to me that this is the light Soma spoke of when she described the dissolution of Mata and Shri Ram's bodies. But instead of dissolution, there was a formation. The light formed into the body of Shri Ram. A great love emanated from the form, and out of his form rose the body of Mata Sita. She stepped out of the light and looked at me with such love.

She spoke these words: "Forget what has passed. A new life has begun for you. Will you help us create the world that is yet to be born?"

"I will, Mata. I will," I replied, feeling the immense joy of her presence. She smiled, and then her form disappeared. Even the light disappeared. My eyes slowly opened, and I became aware of the external world.

Soma was seated beside me, looking at me intently. Neither of us spoke for some time. I didn't say anything about what I had seen and heard. She didn't ask, but I suspect she knew. Finally she said in a quiet voice, "Never think that she is gone. She resides right here now, helping every moment to awaken the world to the love she embodied. She is even more active now that her physical limitations are gone."

I simply gazed at Soma, too stunned to speak. I had seen her. Nothing could be more miraculous than that.

Soma continued, "Your mother will be here soon. I will fix some food for you." I nodded, not moving from my position on the bed. My mind was still engrossed in the vision I had seen. After some time I rose and Soma showed me where I could wash. Then she served me the morning food. When I was done, she said, "You received what you needed last night." I nodded. "Are you ready now to return?" she asked.

"Yes, Soma, I am."

She smiled and placed her hand on my head in blessing. I pranammed before her, too moved and grateful to utter a word.

SOMA'S DEPARTURE

After we had been on the road for several hours, my mother and I stopped for rest and refreshment. I stepped down from the chariot and walked over to a nearby tree and sat beneath it. Drawing my knees up, I wrapped my arms around them and rested my head on my knees. My mother and I had hardly spoken since we had started on the journey. My mother came and sat beside me and offered me water and fruit. I shook my head, indicating that I was not hungry.

My mind drifted off. As we had ridden further from the hermitage, a memory had returned to me, a memory of standing before Shri Ram when I was a young child. I remembered staring up into his face. I remembered his smile and his kind eyes returning my look, his eyes of such stillness and depth—eyes that had been with me since childhood, providing me comfort in the night and in times of distress. I tried to remember more, but I couldn't. All I could recall were the eyes and the smile. After meeting Soma and hearing her stories, suddenly this memory had become very personal. I had seen Shri Ram. He had held my young face between his hands and stared into my eyes. He had spoken to me. A bond had been formed, a bond that would be eternal. I had this memory to hold on to. Suddenly I lifted my head and turned to my mother. "Do you remember that day when I was a child and Maharaja Ram came to our home?"

"Of course," she smiled. "How could I forget that day?"

"He spoke some words about me, didn't he?" She nodded. "I remember his smile, his face, his incredible eyes, but I don't remember his words. What did he say, Ma?" I asked innocently.

She looked away. I asked again, but still she didn't respond. "Ma, why are you silent?"

She turned to look at me, "It is better, Anasuya, that you ask this question of your father."

"But why?" She didn't answer. "Don't I have a right to know what our Maharaja said about me?" I looked inquiringly at her, not understanding her silence.

After several more minutes, she replied quietly, "You do. And I will tell you everything." She turned her face away and closed her eyes as she spoke, as if to recapture that day. "I was standing in the doorway while our Maharaja was discussing some administrative matter with your father. It was the first time he had come to our home, and it was a great honor. It was his custom to visit the homes of the citizens so that he could hear their concerns personally, but the Maharaja was getting on in age and such visits had become less frequent. I could not restrain myself from trying to come close to our Maharaja, whom we so loved and revered, and thus I stood in the doorway, hoping your father would not mind. You were curious, peering into the room, holding on to my leg, half hiding your face within the folds of my clothing. Suddenly our Maharaja noticed you, and in such a sweet voice invited us to come forward.

"My heart pounded at the thought that I could approach him. Your father introduced us. He inquired about you, and your father said that you were our youngest child and only daughter. He asked you to come closer. Shyly you inched forward until you stood before him. Your father explained how whenever we passed the palace when you were very young, you would point to the palace and call out 'Mata.' One time you even escaped his arms and ran to the palace, saying you wanted to see Mata. When he caught and restrained you, you wept. Maharaja Ram smiled. Then holding your face between his hands, he looked deeply into your eyes. His smile broadened, and he said quietly, almost to himself, 'She was one of the servants who came with Sita from Mithila. She didn't live to see our return.' He was quiet for a few minutes and then added in the most gentle voice, 'She loved Sita very much.' After that he turned to your father and said, 'You must send her to the gurukulum now established for young girls. Sita would want that.' Then turning again to you, he said, 'I will give you a blessing, child.' Placing his hand upon your head, he closed his eyes and said, 'There will always be someone to bring you back, to remind you of where you came from, in all of your future lives.' This is what took place that day."

"Why did you not tell me this before?" I asked in a voice filled with emotion, thinking there were so many questions I could have asked Soma had I known this earlier.

"Your father did not want you to know that you had been a servant. He did not want you to think of yourself in this way. He saw that you had a tendency toward this."

"Is there anything nobler than serving our Maharani or Maharaja?" I exclaimed in disbelief. "Nothing could make me happier than to know our Maharani had once been my Mata, just as she was Soma's. Had I known this, I could have asked Soma about my past. I could have asked so many questions." My voice trailed off. I recognized that I had never stopped thinking of myself as a servant. I remembered how in childhood I had loved to serve my parents and was happiest when I was invisible, unseen, performing the simplest task in the household.

My mother shook her head. "I am ashamed to say what I just told you, but it is how your father felt and still feels. We will go back to visit Soma, I promise you."

My mother took my hand and said, "Let us not share this conversation with your father." I nodded. My mind was racing as I now recalled Soma's last words to me. She had told me as much, but now what she had spoken was confirmed by Shri Ram himself. I had no memory of the past, or of the exchange between Shri Ram and my father. My only memory was his eyes, eyes that would never leave me.

I could not forgive my father for having kept from me Maharaja Ram's great blessing and his revelations about my past, yet in order to honor my mother's request I could not discuss it with him, and so a distance developed between us. He was pleased that I agreed to the marriage and did not take note of my silence in his presence. My mind was far away, and I mentally reviewed again and again the stories we had heard from Soma in the hopes of not forgetting a single word. I continued with my household duties, physically engaged but mentally absent. When one day my father told me I was soon to be meet my future husband, I nodded, not thinking much of it.

A few days later, after finishing my chores, one of the household servants accompanied me on my walk down to my favorite spot at the river. I sat there watching the rushing water, thinking back to the stories Soma had told us. Lost in thought, I suddenly became aware of another presence. Turning, I found a young man standing not far away, looking at me. Seeing that I had noticed him, he introduced himself.

"I am Ajit," he said in a nervous voice. "And I assume you are Anasuya? I went to call upon you at your home but was told you were here by the river." I nodded, turning my face away. My heart was pounding. I had never been in such a situation before, alone in the presence of a young man who was not my relative. This was the young man I was destined to marry!

"May I join you?" he asked. I nodded, still not daring to turn my face to him. "You have found my favorite spot," he said. "This is where I often come to reflect, to sit with the river." I didn't answer. He continued to make conversation. I could hear the tremble in his voice and began to feel badly for him, but I was tongue-tied and could not respond. After speaking for some minutes, he fell silent. I gathered the courage to turn toward him. His eyes were on the river, so I could examine him without him noticing. He was a good-looking young man, nothing extraordinary but fine featured, and he had a kindly expression on his face that caught my attention. The afternoon sun was pouring down, but we were spared its heat by the shade of some trees. Suddenly I noticed that he was staring at a furry animal who seemed to be struggling by the side of the river.

"That animal might be hurt. I must go to it," he murmured. I watched him as he went over to the animal who was too injured to run away. He returned and placed the animal on his lap and began to rub its leg. "A large bird may have attacked his leg, but I think he will be all right," he said caringly. Then removing a silver pendant that hung around his neck, he placed it on the animal's leg and closed his eyes for a few minutes, whispering, "Mata's love will heal you." Opening his eyes, he smiled as he saw the animal squirm in an attempt to free itself. Releasing the animal, he said, "There now, you may go on your way." He watched as the animal limped off. I continued to stare at the pendant, which he had again placed around his neck.

"That pendant you are wearing, where did you get it?" I asked in a shy voice for the first time venturing to speak.

"My grandmother gave it to me before she died. I believe it has healing power."

"How did your grandmother come by the pendant?" I asked with new interest in him.

"There is a long story behind this pendant."

"I would like to hear it."

"Well, you might not believe this, but it was given to her by the Maharani herself when she returned from the exile. She said that her mother had given it to her when she left Mithila."

My mouth dropped open at these words. "That was Mata Sita's pendant!"

"You call her Mata as well?" he asked with a slight laugh. "That is what my grandmother called our Maharani. She had so much love for her."

I didn't know why I called Maharani Sita "Mata" at that moment. I had never done so before, but the word slipped from my mouth, and from that moment forward that was the only word I used when referring to her.

"As I said, it is a long story. You see, when Rajah Ram and Rajakumari Sita first rode into Ayodhya after their marriage, the whole city came out to see them. My grandmother was among that crowd. But what she saw was different from what the others saw. She didn't see a rani, she saw a great devi, with a great light emanating from her. She saw Rajakumari Sita for who she truly is. And so when they were forced into exile some months later, she realized that there was a far greater purpose to the exile, and it was not as people thought. She often said to me that the exile would not have happened unless Rajah Ram and Rajakumari Sita deemed it necessary for their work. She also realized the dangers they would encounter, and so she began going down to the river before dawn to offer prayers and chants for them, especially for Rajakumari Sita's safety and well-being, and for the success of their mission."

"That was your grandmother!" I exclaimed, interrupting him. Now I was piecing together the story, remembering what Soma had told us.

He nodded. "You know about her?" He asked in a surprised tone.

I nodded in amazement. "Please continue," I said.

"Throughout the fourteen years, she didn't miss a morning. Through rain and thunder, sickness and whatever difficulties she was facing, she went to the river to offer her prayers. I often wonder what motivated her so. She was a relatively poor woman, with not much knowledge of the world, but she was a pure soul, the essence of goodness. She would never turn away a person in need. She always extended herself to help, never considering her own needs. That is how I remember her. Her husband had died not long after their marriage and she was raising her son alone, her only child, my father. She struggled, but still she went down to the river every day before dawn, before the day's work began. Soon other women joined her, and by the end there were many who came, the women of Ayodhya." He fell silent after saying these words about his grandmother. I was now looking directly at him and saw clouds of emotion settle on his face. My heart went out to him.

"You must have loved her very much, your grandmother."

He nodded. His voice displayed a slight tremble when he began speaking again. "She had a great influence on me, and even though she died when I was quite young, I remember her well. I remember her by her deeds, not her words, as she spoke little. But her life was an example to me."

"Can you tell me how your grandmother came by this pendant?"

"After the return from the exile, my grandmother took quite ill. My father was seeking some medicines for her when Rajakumari Sita happened to be passing in her chariot. When she saw my father she quickly got down from the chariot and took him to where the plant medicines could be found along the riverside. She then asked that my grandmother come to see her when she was well enough. After her recovery, my grandmother tried several times to see Rajakumari Sita, but the guards wouldn't let her through.

"One day Rajakumari Sita and her attendant visited my grandmother in disguise. It was then that Rajakumari Sita told my grandmother how she knew of her prayers and the prayers of the women of Ayodhya and how these prayers had protected her during her captivity in Lanka. Then to show her appreciation, she took off this pendant and placed it around my grandmother's neck. It was the most precious thing she owned, but she said there was no way to express gratitude for the service my grandmother had rendered. You can imagine what this meant to my grandmother, who never wanted any recognition or acknowledgement for what she had done. Then Rajakumari Sita told her that we don't know the effects of our prayers. They can have far greater impact that we imagine. This is something my grandmother repeated to me again and again."

"So that was your grandmother," I murmured in disbelief.

He nodded. "My mother died when I was young and so my grandmother cared for me during my early years. Up until that time my father had been struggling, but after that visit of the Maharani, success came to him in everything he did. He became quite wealthy, but this never mattered to my grandmother. She never changed her way of life. My father eventually married again and we moved into a much larger home, but she refused to shift. She said she always wanted to live as our Rani did."

I could not believe what I was hearing. We were quiet for some time. I felt quite comfortable with him now, as if we were old friends, and so the silence was not an awkward one. I was even enjoying the space between words, the quiet that had now come between us. I was reflecting on Soma's last words to me and asked, "You like animals, don't you?"

His whole face beamed as he exclaimed, "That is an understatement. If I could, I would spend all my time with them, caring for them, but my father has other intentions for me," he sighed.

Soma's voice rang within me, informing me that the man I was to marry had looked after the animals in Maharaja Janaka's household, and that he had wanted to marry me, but my father would not permit it. Now my father in this life was arranging it. How strange, I thought, that what couldn't be in that life was coming to be in this.

"What is it that your father wants for you?"

"To go into administration. That is what they have planned, our fathers. It is not what I want, but it is what I will do."

It was then that Mata's words in the vision came back to me about building a new society. "Perhaps it will be for the better. We must be open to that," I replied with a smile. Then added, "I am sure there are other stories you have to tell me from your grandmother, stories about Mata."

He laughed. "I have many stories. You will hear them in good time." Facing me, he said, "I feel that you also have love for Mata. My grandmother would be so happy about that. But you also must have stories."

"Many," I replied. "And you will hear them in good time."

The sun was quickly descending, and it was time for us to head back, but I didn't want to leave. By now I was hanging on to his every word. "One more story before we head back?" I asked meekly.

"All right," he smiled. "I will tell you a story that my father shared with me. He once told me that, unlike what people say, Maharani Sita never really left Ayodhya, even after she retreated to the hermitage. Her presence was still felt here, and every now and then people would catch sight of her. A number of years after the birth of Rajahs Luv and Kush, Maharaja Ram's ministers and a handful of sages had gathered to talk about the new gurukulum that was being established for the training of young boys. Everyone was seated, but there was an empty chair beside Shri Ram. My father was present, although he was still quite young. Because of his success he was able financially to assist one of the hermitages. Shri Ram sat listening to everyone and then he spoke. Everyone was surprised at his message, which was the need to set up a gurukulum for girls. One by one, they shook their heads, unconvinced. Rarely did they raise objection to anything the Maharaja said or did, but about this matter they were firm. They said it would bring disharmony to our society as it had not been the tradition.

"Suddenly Shri Ram paused in the middle of the discussion and asked everyone to wait patiently before taking up the topic again. They waited and waited, but Shri Ram seemed in no hurry. My father guessed that Shri Ram was expecting another person, but he had no idea who it could be. All the required people were in attendance. An hour passed and a few of those present began to stir, but Shri Ram hushed them and gently asked for patience. Suddenly into their midst walked several of the rishis with Maharani Sita by their side, fully arrayed in her royal garments. She smiled at all the people in attendance and then took her seat beside Shri Ram, who then said he had asked her and the rishis to join them in person to explain why a gurukulum for girls was needed.

"She first asked the rishis to speak. Rishi Vasishtha said that had his wife not been fully educated in the sacred texts, she would not have received the gift of Kamandhenu, who fed so many in times of need. Had his daughters not been educated, they could not have created the beautiful world they formed for their mother when she was in despair at the loss of her sons. Then Sage Atri spoke and told them that had his wife not been educated in the sacred texts, she could never have gained entrance to the celestial world and seen the Mandakini River, which she later brought to the earth to nourish the drought-stricken region. Then sage Agastya concurred and explained that had his wife not been educated in the sacred texts, she could not have held at bay the rakshasas who ruled the forests in the south, threatening every hermitage. Then Shri Ram spoke. He said had his wife not been educated in the sacred texts, perhaps she would not have been able to withstand the torment of Ravana during her time in Lanka.

"The sages were all quiet, but Shri Ram knew what was on their minds. He said, 'There are some traditions that should be maintained because they link us to the past and carry a universal truth. Such is the recitation of the Vedas and the sacred mantras. But other traditions must adapt as society and the human mind develop. Traditions that are no longer useful are like empty vessels. Clinging to them holds back the progress of society. You sages must have the discrimination to know the difference between what is essential and what can be discarded because it has outgrown its use.' His words had an impact, and there was a visible change on the faces of many who were seated in that august hall.

"Then the Maharani spoke about the women sages who had taught her in Mithila and the many women sages who came to her aid in Lanka. She said, 'The wives of these great rishis offered me the fruit of their tapasya, tapasya that was as intense as any male sage could perform. And this is what sustained me, this and the women of Ayodhya, the mothers who are the strength of the society. Our future mothers must receive an education for the sake of the whole community.' She then said that Ayodhya was growing rapidly and unless the women could keep up with the changes, the kingdom would not be able to advance. When she was done, not one voice opposed her. Although it took many years to establish the gurukulum, there is now one for girls. Without Rajakumari Sita's intervention, this would not have been possible."

"Yes, I went to that gurukulum as a child." I reminisced. I didn't share that I had left the training early because of my outbursts when the teachers told the story of Maharani Sita.

"My grandmother said that Maharaja Ram could not have married an ordinary woman, and that no ordinary woman could have survived the long years in exile and captivity in Lanka. And when Mata retired to the hermitage for the birth of her children, my grandmother understood that there were reasons for this, reasons we couldn't understand. She trusted her implicitly, but she also told me that her presence never left Ayodhya. She was there for every *yajna*, every ritual sacrifice, and for every grand occasion." There was such reverence in his voice as he spoke that I almost felt as I did when I was in the presence of Soma.

We were quiet for a few minutes. "I am so grateful that you shared with me these stories. I almost feel as if I knew your grandmother."

"There will be much time for stories in the future, but now I am afraid we must head back or your father will come looking for us."

"You are right. But I also have stories that you will later hear," I said with a smile. "A few months back my mother and I visited Mata's attendant Soma, who is very old but still living near the hermitage where Mata spent her last years. She told many, many stories of Mata and Maharaja Ram."

His eyes opened wide. "She is still alive?" I nodded. "I must go see her."

"I will take you. Let us speak with my father about it."

My face must have been glowing when I reached home, because my father took one look at me and said, "Can I assume that you like

Ajit and are happy with the arrangement?" I was greatly embarrassed that my face revealed what was in my heart. In that moment all my anger toward my father melted away. It didn't matter any more that he had withheld from me details of my meeting with Shri Ram. I had come to know what was said, and so there was no loss.

"There is something that you should know about his family," my father said.

"About his grandmother." My father nodded. "He told me. I know about how she used to pray by the river."

"It is not just that. She was a woman greatly esteemed in the community. Her father was well established. Her husband died early and left her alone to raise their son, Ajit's father. But after the Maharaja and Maharani left for exile, she took off her beautiful clothing and ornaments and adopted a very simple dress. She moved from the family's large home to a simple abode and began giving everything she had away. She said she wanted to live as simply as the Maharaja and Maharani. She tried to mirror the life they had in exile."

"Ajit implied that they were poor, and that she was a simple woman."

My father laughed. "That was his perception. A very humble woman would be a more accurate description. She became poor through her own choice, and that is how he remembers her. He doesn't know about her past, the life she gave up. Many women followed her and would join her by the river to pray for Rajakumari Sita. Your grandmother, my mother, was one of them. That is how I came to know the family.

"While the Maharani was abstaining from food during her time in Lanka, Ajit's grandmother was feeding many people in Ayodhya. She said that by feeding them, she was providing sustenance for the Maharani, but she herself took very little food that year, only what was necessary to keep her alive. The love she displayed helped to protect not only the Maharaja and Maharani, it also helped to protect Ayodhya because it enabled the people to stay connected to them.

There were many times when our kingdom was threatened during the fourteen years, and of course it was the Maharaja's brothers and the army who protected us, but I know it was also the prayers of these quiet women, who were doing their sadhana unnoticed by the rest of us, humble, unseen, not wanting to be known." He paused as I took this all in. Ajit had described his grandmother to me as a very simple woman, but obviously she was much more.

"So is that why you thought to arrange a marriage between our two families?" I asked.

He nodded, but then added, "Actually it was our Maharaja who put the thought in my mind, when you were very young before we could even conceive of a marriage for you."

"Shri Ram did that?"

"Yes, when he came to visit our home one day toward the end of his life. You might not remember, but he blessed you at that time. Before taking his leave, he causally remarked that I might consider the youngest son of Sudama as a suitable husband for you. He said it so casually. He never instructed people, he just offered suggestions. This was the way he taught us. He wanted us to come to our own conclusions, but he would insert a thought in our minds. I thanked him for this counsel and forgot about it. But some years later, his words returned to me and I spoke with Sudama, who was by then working with me in the administration." My father laughed. "As soon as I mentioned this to Sudama, he told me that our Maharaja had suggested the very idea to him many years ago. And so that is how your marriage came to be."

I was astounded to hear these words. In his last years, Shri Ram was fulfilling what Mata's intention had been. "Did he do this with other people?" I asked.

"Oh yes," my father responded. "He took an interest in the lives of so many, even as Ayodhya grew. People said that he learned this from Maharaja Janak. He put into effect on a large scale what Maharaja Janak had started in the smaller kingdom of Videha." My father continued, "Your mother has told me something of your meeting with Soma. I also would like to go meet her. Shall we plan another trip?"

I was bursting with joy at the thought. "Can we take Ajit?" I asked. "I would like her to meet him."

"Of course. We will plan for the very near future."

A few days later my father came to tell me that he had set the date for our visit for the following week, but that got delayed. He set another date, and that also got delayed. I began to be impatient and suggested to my mother that we go without my father, but he was insistent about joining us. Finally he set another date and this time there was no delay. We embarked on the journey with three chariots.

It was late the next day when we arrived. My father insisted on going first to pay his respects to the teachers of the hermitage, but I was impatient to see Soma, and so Ajit, my mother, and I headed in the direction of her hut. As we entered the forest path that led to her hut, we encountered an ascetic walking from the opposite direction, leaving the area where Soma lived. He stopped us. "Are you looking for Soma?" he asked. My mother nodded. "You won't find her there," he said.

"Where is she?" my mother asked. He smiled. My mother pressed him again.

"She has gone home." he replied softly.

"Home?" My mother asked. "Back to Mithila, at her age?"

"No, lady. Her true home." Seeing the perplexed look on our faces, he continued. "It was a few days back when I heard Mata's voice calling me to hurry to Soma. I was far away from here but came as fast as I could. As I entered the forest, I saw two beautiful women approaching me. They were lavishly dressed, and I though it odd to find two women dressed that way in the forest, but I was in such a hurry to meet Soma that I didn't take note of it. They stopped when they reached me and the woman who was leading the other one, smiled and said, 'Putra, you won't find Soma there. I have already taken her.'

"I pranammed to the women. Not realizing what I had just heard, I continued to hurry toward Soma's hut in great haste. I had not gone far at all when suddenly it hit me. That was Mata who had spoken to me. It was Mata and Soma I had seen. I turned and ran back to where they had been, but there was no sign of them. In their place I found Soma's aged body lying on the ground, with no life in it." Tears came into his eyes as he spoke, but he continued, "I did not recognize our Mata." But then his face brightened and he added, "She did not want me to recognize her, for I would have fallen at her feet and begged her to take me as well. But it is the will of Shri Ram and Mata that I remain to remind the world of the love that is their very being, and to serve all in their name." With those words and with a pranam, he hurried off into the forest.

My mother froze, unable to say anything. I burst into tears at the realization that Soma had died. When my mother could speak, she turned to Ajit and said in a hurried voice, "Go after that ascetic. Find him if you can. Quickly." With these words, she sank to the ground.

"What is it, Ma?" I asked between tears.

"Do you realize the great blessing we just had?" I shook my head. All I could think of was the loss of Soma. "Let's see if Ajit can find him." But it was no use. The ascetic had disappeared. Ajit soon returned with the news that he was nowhere in sight.

"He was the one who came that last night to Soma's and brought fruit for all of us. Do you remember him?" my mother asked me.

I nodded. "But that ascetic was so tall. He could barely fit in the doorway. This one was small. I don't think he was the same one, Ma," I replied in a controlled voice.

"He was the same. His size changes. I saw it that night and again today. I recognize him by the glow that emanates from his body. Most unusual. That glow lit up the room that night and today it outshone even the brilliance of Surya Dev. Do you know who he was?" Both Ajit and I shook our heads.

"I believe that was Hanuman. It is said that he comes in many forms, always changing so that people will recognize him only by the love he spreads, not by any one body. Did you feel the wave of love that spread over us as he hurried away? That is the sign of his presence." My mother wiped the tears that were still staining my checks and took hold of my hands. "Shri Ram and Mata Sita gave you a great gift today, my dear. It was Soma's time to go, and we should rejoice with her. Whatever questions you had for her were meant to go unanswered. Instead of seeing Soma, they gave you darshan of Hanuman, they gave this to you both, perhaps as a wedding gift. Take the love that he has spread over us and let it grow in your hearts."

Ajit was deeply touched by what he heard, but I was still suffering from the news of Soma's departure. "I must go to her hut," I mumbled as I hurried down the path, leaving the two of them to reflect on the blessing we had all received. Once inside the hut, I sank down on the cushion that Soma used for her meditation. "I only just found you, and now you are gone," I murmured in a choked voice. "I was hoping you could help me remember, to remember just one moment when I was with her." A short time later, Ajit entered and found me seated. Feeling the pain in my heart, he sat quietly beside me and asked in a gentle voice, "She meant a lot to you, didn't she?"

"I can't explain my feelings," I replied quietly, and then added, "She told me something about my past and I wanted to learn more."

An awkward silence followed and he asked, "Did I tell you the story about when Maharaja Ram came to our home and blessed me?" I looked up at him, surprised by his words.

"He blessed you?"

Ajit nodded and started the story. "Toward the end of his stay on earth, our Maharaja was visiting many of the homes, meeting the children. I suspect he was seeing to the future of Ayodhya. He came to see my father and asked to meet his children. We were three boys. My father presented us, and as he looked at us, he took me aside and looked at me for what seemed like a long time. Then he said to my father, 'This child of yours must go into the administration. He will look after the forests. He has great love for the animals, and I trust that he will care for their welfare.' He added, 'Sita would be happy about that.'

"I don't remember those words, but my father has recounted this story to me many times, as if he wanted to etch it into my memory forever." He was quiet. After a few minutes, he began again in a reflective voice. "I don't remember much about our Maharaja, as this was my only meeting with him, but I do remember his eyes. They were unlike any eyes I have ever seen. He blessed all of us that day, and then he said to me, 'The animals will always befriend you. Never have any fear of them.' Turning to my father he told him that when he and Rajakumari Sita were traveling through the forest during their exile, Rajakumari Sita had no fear of any animal, and the animals often guided them to where they needed to go. After this my father used to take me frequently into the forests so that I would gain a love for all the life there. But I already had this love. I think I was born with it."

As I listened intently to him, his words soothed my sorrow. As I was later to learn, this was Ajit's way of chasing away any sadness that would come over me. All he had to do was turn the conversation to Mata or Shri Ram, and a subtle joy would enter my heart. "I think I was not meant to meet Soma again," I said. "Perhaps she told me everything I needed to know, and perhaps it is better not to return to the past."

"The past has given us the present," replied Ajit with a smile. "Whatever knowledge we gained in the past is somewhere locked in our memory. We should only look ahead of us, Anasuya. I believe that is what Shri Ram was doing when he visited our homes. He was sowing seeds for the future. What is to come will be his creation, his and Mata Sita's."

"I never want to forget that," I replied quietly.

"We must pledge not to let each other forget. This will be our vow to one another."

I lived many happy years with my husband in Ayodhya. We had four daughters and no sons, and with the birth of each daughter, we brought her to the sacred Sarayu River and held her at the river bank, exclaiming, "Sarayu Devi, see Sita's daughter, bless this child that she may serve her Mata."

We watched the kingdom grow and flourish under the guidance of Maharajas Luv and Kush. Ajit spent much of his time traveling the forests of the kingdom making sure the expansion of human settlements was not encroaching on the territories of the animal kingdoms. For the most part, there was peace between humans and animals.

One day years later, as we found some time alone to walk by the river, I had the impulse to share with him what Soma had revealed. By now, we were both in our middle years. "Do you remember after we first met we went to try to see Soma, the aged attendant of Mata?" I asked him.

"How could I forget that day? A certain bond formed between us as we were seated in Soma's hut. Do you remember that?" he replied with a smile.

I nodded. "The last words Soma spoke to me were about our past."

"Our past?" he inquired.

Again I nodded. "She told me that I had been a servant in the household of Maharaja Janak and came with Mata from Mithila after her marriage. She told me that you had also served in the household, caring for the animals, and that Mata was very fond of you because of your love for all the creatures." I saw the look of surprise on his face as I continued. "Then she told me that when we were young, serving in that household, you had wanted to marry me but that my father had forbid it. He insisted I never marry, and so I never did. Because of that, I was able to follow Mata to Ayodhya. Then she told me that you and I should marry because it was Mata's desire."

"You are telling me this now, after so many years!" he exclaimed.

I don't know why I had never shared this before, but for some unknown reason I had thought to keep this knowledge locked in my heart. Perhaps it was only for my ears, I had reasoned. "Did you not tell me that day that we should look to the future, and not to the past?" I asked him with a reassuring smile. "And that is what I have done, Ajit. I am so very grateful that Mata and Shri Ram brought us together in this life. I think they arrange so much more than we know."

His shock turned to joy and he said, "Thank you, Anasuya, for sharing this now. It gives me great happiness and peace to know that I served in Mithila and was known to Mata. But aren't we all known to her, every being on earth? I think we cannot even imagine all that they have done and are doing . . . ."

"Someone once told me that Mata and Shri Ram would be even more active, more effective once they released their physical forms, that they would be able to do more . . . I heard that from someone, perhaps it was Soma, I just can't remember . . . ."

The years passed. My daughters were well married and Ajit had left his physical form. I was quite old when, for the last time, I made my way down to the sacred Sarayu River, which was more crowded these days. Markets had sprung up, boatmen, salesmen, and women shoppers lined the shores. I found a quiet spot and sat down. Leaning back against a tree, I watched the river for a few moments and then closed my eyes and let my mind wander. The words that Mata Sita had spoken to me that night I slept in Soma's hut returned. She had asked if I wanted to help create the new society.

"But what have I done, Mata?" I silently asked her. "I have only loved you. I have done nothing more."

I felt myself drifting off. The darkness melted and a scene appeared before me: a woman struggled in the river, fighting for life as the river engulfed her and washed her further and further from the shore. I felt the water pulling, as if it were I who was gasping for breath. As I was about to go under, I saw a very stately and dignified man staring out at me from the river's edge; he seemed to be commanding the waves to release me, and they obeyed. The waves drew me closer to the shore until a final wave deposited me onto the sandy bank. He lifted my drenched and shaking body and as I looked up at him, I felt such care and love emanate from him.

The scene shifted. The woman and a few other women servants were standing by the side of a chariot. Their expressions were sad, as they were preparing to leave the only home they had ever known. The same man who had rescued the woman from drowning now called them over and embraced them, saying, "You, too, are my daughters."

Then *she* appeared, Rajakumari Sita, youthful and ever so beautiful, dressed in her royal garments. Such joy flowed from her, and her beaming smile chased away any sadness the women felt.

I awoke with a start. "That was me," I murmured. "That was me, the woman drowning, the woman servant taking her leave. That was me." Wanting to return to the scene, to see that life once again, I closed my eyes, but nothing more revealed itself before my inner sight. A realization came to me that Mata had fulfilled my last desire, to recall a memory of Mithila. "Thank you, Mata," I whispered. "I will remember this always."

My mind drifted. "How have I helped to build your society, Mata? I have done nothing but love my husband, love my children, try to help those in need. . . ."

I heard a response, "All I have ever asked of you is to love. That is how we create the new society, one based on love, his love, my love."

These words slowly faded into the background, and I began to hear the quiet movement of my breath, in and out. I heard the gentle lapping of the waves, rising up and sinking down. My breath seemed to synchronize with the water as I listened to the gentle sounds coming from within and without, like a humming, ever so slight, until I could no longer distinguish between the rise of my breath and the rise of the waves. Was I my breath or was I the waves? Or were we one?

The sound became ever more distant, ever fainter, but I continued to listen—in and out came my breath, in and out came the waves, smaller and less discernable, and less frequent, until there was no more sound . . . and no more breath.

One more life falls away but all that was learned, all that was loved continues, helping to frame and guide the new life that is to emerge. I look behind and see a long, long trail of lives, stretching back to beyond what the mind can conceive. I look ahead and see how many more imprints need to fulfill themselves, flickers of light on the great ocean of being.

COMMENTARY

In this day and age, when the earth is trembling on the brink of environmental devastation, I was led backwards to a much earlier time when the people of earth were going through another period of upheaval and transformation. The more time I spent with Mata Sita and Shri Ram in Mithila and Ayodhya, and during their forest exile, the more important their message seemed to be for those of us on the planet today. The following is the story of how I became so involved in their lives . . . .

When I began meditating in the 1970s under the guidance of my gurudev Paramahansa Yogananda, my understanding was that meditation was meant to bring about deeper awareness of one's true nature and the purpose of life. Back then, meditation was considered an esoteric practice, little understood or appreciated. Over the years, meditation has gained acceptance and popularity in the west, so that today it is regarded as a mainstream practice, which has also led to its growing secularization and commercialization. I could see that meditation was helping many people deal with the anxieties of our fast-moving modern life, but I wondered how we could help steer it away from a focus on the self—meditation for stress reduction and a bit more personal peace— to a focus on dharma, living in harmony with the universal laws of life so that all may benefit.

To bring these concerns into public discussion, the Global Peace Initiative of Women (GPIW), the non-profit organization

I founded, organized a conference in 2015 on the theme of "How to Uphold Dharma in the World Today." Our aim was to see how to imbue the growing meditation/spiritual movement with the concept of dharma.

After the gathering, I wanted to visit Rishikesh to sit by the Ganga (Ganges River) for a day or so. Ganga had long been one of my most precious and sacred destinations in India, and I try to meet Her every year when possible. On the way I decided to make a brief stop in Ayodhya, the birthplace of Shri Ram, just a short train ride from Varanasi.

My desire to visit Ayodhya was in part related to the peace work of GPIW. Ayodhya is a place of contention, perhaps equal to Kashmir as a cause of great strain in Indian society. In the past, when the Islamic invaders moved into India from the North, the only way they could conquer the stronghold of Ayodhya was by destroying the temple, which the Hindus regarded as their protector and source of strength, and building a mosque in its place. Centuries later, when India gained its freedom from British rule, a movement began to rebuild the Hindu temple in Ayodhya but was derailed when Pakistan was sliced out of India. In the late 1980s, some Hindus tore down the mosque, and riots ensued between Hindus and Muslims. The issue of building a new temple to Shri Ram went to the supreme court of India, where it remains today.

But I had a more personal reason to visit Ayodhya. I held a deep love and reverence for Shri Ram, and so the visit was the fulfillment of a desire I had had as a young woman first coming upon the spiritual path. I decided to visit the ancient city, accompanied by a few friends who were journeying with me to Rishikesh.

Often in India it is not uncommon to enter into another state of consciousness when visiting an ancient holy place, despite what it may look like today. It may be nothing but a pile of rocks, and yet the vibration of the meditations of past sages stretches across the ocean of time and lifts you into another reality, opening doors long held shut. People know this, which is why so many undertake pilgrimages.

Some go to receive a specific blessing or healing or to fulfill a desire, but for others these sacred places function as portals to the spiritual world where one can see and hear what took place long ago.

Over the years I have traveled numerous times into the high reaches of the Himalayas to visit sacred places; I always felt as if I had entered another realm as only a thin veil separated me from the celestial worlds in these upper atmospheres. But Ayodhya was in the plains, and I had never been affected that way other than in the Himalayas. Would I be able to feel ancient presences in Ayodhya, especially since it was the modern-day scene of so much conflict, so much division, pain, and death? Would I be able to bring the past to life? Would I be able to feel the presence of Shri Ram and Devi Sita? I didn't know and had no expectations at all.

As soon as I stepped off the train, I felt a subtle shift in my awareness. It was as if the present city is but an entry point to the past, at least for those who visit for the purpose of accessing that ancient time. The Ayodhya of today is a small, quiet town. It doesn't seem like a place of conflict. The streets are lined with outdoor markets and many temples, and people going about their daily affairs. We walked from the train station to the major sites: the place considered to be the old palace, the special quarters where Sita lived, and the nearby temple to Hanuman. The stone walkways have been trod over by many hundreds of millions of people, and yet one could feel the presence there.

As I walked with my companions through the ancient streets, only half conscious of what was taking place in the here and now, every structure seemed to awaken the imprint of a memory of an earlier time, and yet I couldn't quite capture the picture. Feelings were emerging that I couldn't fully access. They remained hidden in the murky subconscious mind, but I felt an agitation, a bubbling up, so to speak. I wanted to cry. I wanted to laugh. I wanted to give thanks, to express gratitude for having the blessing of walking those streets once again.

Finally we approached the place marked as the spot where Shri Ram was said to have been born some 5,000-7,000 year ago, where once stood a temple, and then a mosque, and now nothing but barbed wire and armed guards. No place to worship, to prostrate. No place to pour out one's heart in an appropriate fashion.

We had to pass through checkpoint after checkpoint. There was more security than at the entry to Shrinigar in Kashmir, which spoke volumes. When we approached the spot of the birth and were able to stand for a moment behind the barbed wire, I felt such an overpowering urge to touch my head to the ground, but of course I could not stay long at that spot for security reasons. My sorrow was too great for tears. I desperately wanted to experience Ayodhya as it was, not as it is now; sadness engulfed me. I wanted to see beyond the soldiers and checkpoints and decaying temples. I didn't want to see remnants. I wanted to recapture the reality of what it once was.

My friends and I walked down to the Sarayu River, mostly in silence, and looked for a place to sit for a few minutes to process what we had experienced. There I felt the presence of Shri Ram and Devi Sita most strongly. I asked a boatman to take us to the middle of the river where we could feel its life more intimately. As I sat in the small boat glancing out at the water, sullied and stilled like so many of our rivers today, a quiet flicker of love stirred within me. She must have been a beautiful river once. I began to imagine what she was like when she ran freely, full of life and energy, when flowers bloomed around her and fragrances sweetened the air, and the branches of trees swept over her. She is sister to my Ganga Ma. In fact, she is an offspring of the Ganga, flowing out as one of her many branches. How much history has she silently observed? What could she tell us?

We returned to the shore, and my friends were ready to leave. I took one last long glance at the river. I knew you once, and I am grateful to be able to pay my respects again, I whispered internally as I pranammed. I don't know who you were to me, but I know I held you dear. As we walked back to the town, I purchased some orange cotton cloth at a stall. It did not occur to me then that this would have been the type of cloth that Shri Ram and Rajakumari Sita would have worn as they went into exile, but unconsciously this may have motivated my desire for orange cloth from Ayodhya.

Two planes and a short taxi ride later, we arrived in Rishikesh, where I could renew myself in the spiritual currents of my beloved Ganga Ma. As I rested by her side, the feelings that Ayodhya had stirred began to foment and coagulate, breaking through the mist, first as the faintest recollections and then as clear visions. I was surprised by the memories that emerged while sitting by the feet of my Mother Ganga, which led eventually to this book.

MEMORIES

Memories secrete themselves in the fabric of creation, in the etheric film that separates the material from the non-material worlds. Both individual and collective memories are stored there. The memories of the human race have not evaporated; like a very fine but enveloping mist, they are ever-present, available to those who know how to access them. No deed, word, or thought ever disappears. Rather, all is preserved in this etheric database, helping to shape and guide present and future events.

On an individual level, our past deeds and thoughts retreat to a part of our being of which we are not conscious on a daily basis, but which has guided us to our present condition. It would be overwhelming if we were to live in total recall of our extensive past. These memories are silently present, helping to shape who we are today and all of our current experiences. Every now and then, the curtain separating the conscious from the unconscious mind slips open just a bit and a memory slides through. But due to its fleeting nature, we may not even acknowledge it.

Over the course of my life, I have recalled events from numerous past births, but those births have been relatively near in time, going back a mere few hundred years. I have recorded these experiences in *My Journey through Time: A Spiritual Memoir of Life, Death and Rebirth*. I have not pressed to see what came before, although I have known there was a before . . . a much before. The time periods I recalled seemed like relatively recent events, and it is said that our journeys extend over many, many millennia, not just centuries.

I have often wondered what life was like in those earlier times, curious about our collective history during a more enlightened period, if you will.

According to Eastern thought, many millennia before the common era (BCE) was a time of great spiritual awareness, but it was also a time of declining spiritual knowledge. Spiritual perceptions were receding, and thus the seers sought to contain and preserve this knowledge for the future, when it would once again predominate. In India, this knowledge was gathered in the Vedas, although it is said that only a fraction of that knowledge remains today. It was during this time that Shri Ram and Mata Sita took birth on earth to sow the seeds for what was to become modern civilization.

What was life like during this time? For several years I held this curious thought to myself. One day on a pilgrimage, the curtains slipped open and I found myself in that time period.

PILGRIMAGE IN KASHMIR AND VAISHNO DEVI

It was May of 2016, and the Global Peace Initiative of Women had been called back to Kashmir, where for many years we had been holding dialogues with spiritual leaders and young people. It is one of the main stress points in modern-day India, and if it breaks apart, all of India and indeed the world will be affected. So we kept going back, trying to bring the various groups—the Buddhists, Hindus, and Muslims—together in dialogue. The work of GPIW has long been to try to raise the spiritual consciousness in places of conflict as a way to help untie the karmic knots that prevent such disturbances from reaching a resolution.

We organized a Unity *Yatra* (pilgrimage) composed of Hindu yogis, Buddhists, and Sufis. The Indian state of Kashmir & Jammu is divided into three parts: bordering Tibet is Ladakh, a traditionally Buddhist area; Kashmir proper is now mostly Muslim; and Jammu, in the foothills of the Himalayas, is mostly Hindu. In all my visits to Kashmir, this was the first time we included all three regions of the state.

Fifteen of us pilgrims began in Ladakh as guests of Venerable Sangasena, a Ladakhi Buddhist monk of the Theravadan tradition, at his beautiful retreat center, 12-13,000 feet above sea level. As I am a lover of the sacred rivers of India, I had long wanted to see the Indus, which has its origin in this region. We paid homage to the river as our feet entered her icy waters, although it was too cold to immerse ourselves totally.

Venerable Sangasene had arranged for a Buddhist-Muslim Dialogue at one of his centers in Ladakh, and we were sorry to see that some of the fundamentalist tension gripping Kashmir was now seeping into this holy region, although historically there had been good relations between Buddhists and Muslims there. During our visits to the mostly empty monasteries, I was conscious of the fact that the last war between Pakistan and India took place not far from where we were, and now there were reportedly 30,000 Chinese soldiers guarding the India-Pakistan border. Violence could erupt at any time. We offered many prayers that this rooftop region of India remain peaceful and protected.

We went on to Shrinigar, a lush counterpart to the starkness of Ladakh, during the season of flowering gardens and rushing rivers. There we held a dialogue with young professionals —teachers, journalists, agriculturalists, and business people—on how to tap into their inner spiritual resources. We felt the possibility of integrating the Sufi, Hindu, and Buddhist energies. Kashmir had once been a great center of learning and spiritual training, where the great mystical traditions came together in love and appreciation for each other. On our last night in Shrinigar, we got lost on narrow roads and felt the simmering discontent among the people, and saw darkening shadows of radicalization and anger that made us uneasy. Violence would break out a few weeks after we left, and has continued to this day.

Our last stop was Jammu, where we met with a group of young Kashmiri Pandits, as the Kashmiri Hindus are called, whose families were forced to flee their homes in Shrinigar in 1989. They had spent their childhoods in refugee camps. The Pandits are of mixed mind: troubled by and fearful of the radicalization and yet, on a deeper level, longing for their ancestral home. We were moved by their plight and determined to bring together the young Muslims of Shrinigar and Hindu Pandits of Jammu for our next dialogue.

I also had a more personal reason for wanting to visit Jammu. Not far from Jammu City in the Trikuta Mountains is Vaishno Devi, a million-year-old cave tucked into the Himalayan foothills and one of the most revered shrines to the Devi. One story tells that long ago the three shaktis—Parvati, Lakshmi, and Saraswati— joined their energies together in this cave so they could defeat a fiercesome asura (demon).

Each time I have gone on one of these holy pilgrimages, I have mistakenly envisioned myself quietly meditating and absorbing the energy of a sacred site. And each time I have been rudely awakened to the fact that one gets but a few seconds in the space before being pressed forward by the ever-moving, hard-charging crowd. Many millions of devotees come to this shrine each year; we visited in peak season (early June) and were inundated with people pressing and pushing everywhere. Despite the heat, the crowds, the odor of many different street foods, and sheer exhaustion from the long walk, there were powerful blessings to be had there.

By some miracle, we were taken by our guide ahead of all the people on the narrow path to the cave and were allowed to stand in the sacred interior space in front of the shrine for a few minutes of prayer. I was too overwhelmed by the crowds to be able to feel much at the shrine, but mentally offered my heart's love to the three Devis, in particular to Mahalakshmi, whom I have long regarded as my mother. I cannot say that I felt anything at the time. Over the years I have come to recognize a time delay between prayer and response. The effects are experienced mostly in one's deep interior, and this can take days, weeks, months, or years to be revealed fully.

In this case the response came rather quickly.

The next day, the last day of our yatra, we visited two Shiva temples in Jammu City and then were taken to the Raghunath Temple, dedicated to Shri Ram. Although Kashmir is Shaivite land, it had been ruled by the Dogras, who came into the area long ago from Punjab, the state to the south. The Dogras claim their ancestral line stems from Shri Ram and Mata Sita's twin sons, Luv and Kush. The Raghunath Temple is one of the great temples to Lord Ram in all of India, but it does not seem to be much visited because our small group found ourselves pretty much alone in the temple that day, allowing us ample time and space for prayer and meditation. Although I was eager to see it, I was not expecting anything special, as my mind was still on all the Shiva energy of Kashmir.

I was with a few swami friends. After we entered the Temple, we stood silently before some of the images and my mind became interiorized. When I went to bow before the central images of Shri Ram and Mata Sita, I was immediately withdrawn from this world and taken back into the ancient past.

As so many times before in such experiences, it was as if I were being sucked back through a hole in time. I saw myself as a young child, no more than about five years old. I was leaning against my mother's leg, watching my father speak to one I knew immediately to be Shri Ram himself. The Maharaja noticed me and my father introduced me as his youngest child. Then my father explained somewhat modestly that from the time I was very young, each time we passed the palace I would call out "Mata" and try to escape his arms to run to the palace gates.

"Come here, child," Shri Ram beckoned to me. My mother gently pushed me forward and I timidly approached him. He took my face between his hands and looked into my eyes. I gazed back at him, completely unafraid. All my shyness vanished as I stared into that beautiful and calming face, aged by the passage of time but with a chiseled beauty and dignity. Finally, he said very softly, "She was one of the servants who came with Sita from Mithila. She loved Sita very much. She did not live to see our return. I am glad she has come into a good birth."

Letting go of my face and turning to my father, Shri Ram said, "Make sure she has an education. There is now a gurukula for girls. Send her there. Sita would want that." He placed his hand on my head and said very gently, "I will give you a blessing." He closed his eyes, muttered some words, then said to me, "There will always be someone in every life to bring you back, to point you in the direction of your true home." With those words he rose and my father saw him to the door.

That is my memory of Shri Ram.

I don't know how long I was on the floor of the temple pranamming before Shri Ram and Mata Sita. It seemed like years, but perhaps it was only minutes. As I came back to the present, I rose and left with the others, unable to speak. Part of me was still very far away.

As I sat in the hotel room that night, I realized that this vision had been a blessing from the Devis, from my visit to Vaishno Devi the previous day. Deeply embedded in my subconscious mind was the memory of standing before Shri Ram as a young child. Those few moments in his presence were to guide my future. I knew it was Sita Ma who enabled this to occur, who granted the blessing of Shri Ram's darshan. I could hardly speak for the next few days. Fortunately our journey was over and work on this trip was done.

The memories or narrative of the Sita story unfolded over a period of seven months after I returned to New York, drawing me back into a past and to a region for which I felt great love and deep attachment.

344

Although the Ramayana had been a foundational story for me since early adulthood, and I had long felt a love for Shri Ram, I had felt only an impersonal love for Sita and had no special feeling for Mithila. But suddenly a deep love and longing for Mithila burst forth, along with a very personal connection to Janak Baba and Mata Sita.

Over the years I have experienced many memories of past lives and never questioned them. There were signs that always accompanied these memories that indicated to me their verity, but this time I had doubts. Had I in fact been the servant I was now seeing in my visions, or was I channeling the spirit of the Mithila servant? After dwelling on this matter for some time, I realized the question was irrelevant. The experience of recalling the life of the servant Meenakshi was transformational for me, as I experienced Janak Baba and Mata Sita as living beings in a very intimate way. They became part of my world, part of my consciousness; they were no longer mythological or historical figures, or abstractions, but real-life incarnations of divine beings who are still working for the well-being of the universe.

Most importantly, the teaching for me, the whole purpose of the memory recall, was that these beings could still be accessed today. From that point on, my connection to the Divine Mother took the form of a personal relationship with Sita Ma, which was far more intimate and real than a relationship to the abstract form of the Mother.

I spent months processing this story and found a part of myself in the servant Meenakshi. Being a servant was once a dignified role; it was an honor to serve a noble and righteous being. The role of servant not only teaches humility, but also dedication and selflessness, lessons of critical importance for the upward spiritual journey, a lesson we all too easily forget as we move into new roles and positions.

Recalling this narrative also gave me the tiniest peek into life during the last Treta Yuga, something I had long sought to understand.

THE MOVEMENT OF TIME

The modern Western view of time emerged from Europe, and sees only the linear development of history, the physical evolution that propels life on earth forward toward increasing complexity. According to this version of history, humankind emerged from caves around 11,000 BCE when the last Ice Age ended and the glaciers retreated, oceans rose some 400 feet, forests began to flourish as the oceans now began to produce abundant rains. Over the next few millennia humanity moved from a hunter-gather society to an agricultural one gathered in settlements. This was seen as progress, as an evolutionary advance. During this time, mental development moved toward greater individuation and a separation from nature, which led to the belief that mankind was meant to control the natural world. The sense of the collective weakened as individual ego development became more prominent. Of course, this took many millennia to unfold.

The ancient Eastern mind saw the nature of time differently, as cyclical rather than linear.

In India, time was viewed in terms of long cycles known as yugas, which correlated to the movement of our solar system within our galaxy, divided into four discrete time periods that make up a cycle of around 24,000 years: a 12,000-year time period when our solar system is moving away from the galaxy's center of magnetism, called the descending arc, and an ascending cycle of 12,000 years when our solar system slowly returns to the point closest to the center. Such is the cyclical movement of time as understood by the ancient rishis—the master mathematicians and astrophysicists who long ago calculated the movement of our solar system through the galaxy based on the position of certain stars.

The *Satya Yuga* (*satya* meaning truth) is the longest of the time periods in terms of years. It happens when our solar system rotates closest to the galaxy's center, which is the source of magnetism holding the galaxy together; this magnetic energy impacts humanity and allows for direct perception of spiritual truths. Whether humankind is living in caves or cities is irrelevant. The main attribute of the satya yuga is heightened spiritual awareness: the deities and divine energies that animate the rivers, mountains, solar bodies, etc., can be seen behind the created or manifest world, and the thin etheric veil that separates the material from the nonmaterial worlds is easily penetrated.

All religious traditions retain the memory of a time when humanity lived in harmony with the natural world and there was abundance beyond description. Such is the Garden of Eden story in the Abrahamic traditions. The animal kingdoms communicated through the exchange of mental images. Plants communicated their qualities, such as the imbalances they could heal and how they could nourish the body. While many discard these stories as myth or symbolic narratives, they clearly contain a remnant of a collective memory when there was ample bounty on this planet and a balanced relationship with the whole of nature.

The next time period is the *Treta Yuga*, a descending movement away from the center of magnetism. It is said that during the Treta Yuga, humankind can still perceive the nature of magnetism and of time and can view the past as well as the future, but spiritual perceptions are not as clear as during the Satya Yuga, and the perception of the deities that animate the natural world begins to fade.

Then comes *Dwarpara Yuga*, in which the perceptions decrease further but humankind still is able to perceive the nature of electrical energies. During this era, humankind focuses on conquering the outer dimension of space.

During the last descending age, the *Kali Yuga*, which is fortunately the shortest, only the material world is perceived, not any of the finer energies. Humanity in general, with the exception of a few advanced souls, is not able to perceive anything beyond the physical universe.

And then we enter the ascending part of the cycle, going from the Kali yuga to the Dwapara and on to the Treta and Satya.

Yes, the Satya Yuga will come again, but it is far in the future. Yet there will always be those who live in that consciousness no matter what the position of our solar system, and there will always be those who have not yet evolved to the level of the collective. There is continually a wide spectrum of consciousness manifesting in the human species as people are at different stages of spiritual evolution.

Where in the cycle are we now?

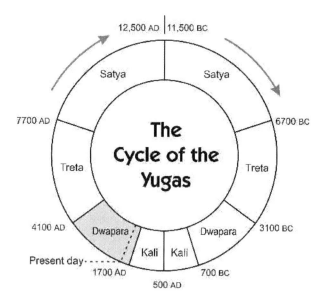

There is not full agreement on this matter, in part because the recent Kali Yuga has clouded so much of our spiritual perception and there are not currently many who can perform the complex astronomical calculations. My own guru's guru (*paramguru*), the revered Swami Shri Yukteswar, was a master astronomer and mathematician; in his book, *The Holy Science*, he concluded that we entered the ascending Dwarpara Yuga not long ago (around 1700 AD) and are now finally emerging from the effects of the Kali Yuga, which darkened humanity's knowledge over the last 2,400 years (1200 years in the descending arc and 1200 years in the ascending arc). This would explain why so many of our society's structures and institutions that were created with a Kali Yuga mentality are failing. Eventually they will be replaced with institutions and structures that reflect a higher awareness.

Others, however, insist that we are still in the Kali Yuga and that the cycle of the Kali Yuga is far longer. Since I am not an expert in this field and have little knowledge of such advanced mathematical formulations, I'll abide by my paramaguru's calculations, especially when seen in the light of the rapid development of science in the last few centuries and the current spiritual awakening that seems to be taking place on the planet. Surely, there is still much ignorance because we are only in the very early years of the 2,400-year ascending Dwarpara Yuga. One must think in terms of centuries and millennia, not decades!

Just as the western mind places 11,500 BCE as the time when the glaciers began to retreat and humanity entered a new era of development, according to Shri Yukteswar's calculations, that was the beginning of the descending Satya Yuga, when the spiritual perceptions were entering a time of decline. It was during the Satya Yuga that the Vedas, the direct perception of universal truths, were compiled and organized, but only a small portion of that knowledge was retained as it was not written down until much later. There was no need for writing during the higher ages; the power of mental communication and the power of memory were much greater than what we have today.

Many people are feeling intuitively that we are today in a transition period from one state of collective consciousness to another. Thus, the Ramayana narrative is of great significance, as it also took place during a time of transition—some time during the last descending Treta Yuga when the Dwarpara Age was approaching, a time of further loss of spiritual knowledge and of direct communion with the natural world. Hermitages, the first educational institutions, were established to preserve the knowledge that the great rishis had brought to the human community during the Satya Yuga. New forms of government and institutions for administering justice had to be established as the intuitive knowledge of right and wrong, of dharma, no longer governed human behavior. Individuality was asserting itself in new ways, a sense of a separate self apart from and above nature. For the first time, man saw that he could control the natural world, and this influenced his ego development and sense of power. With this growing power emerged the desire for more acquisitions, for grandeur, which led to an enhancement of greed.

Gender relationships changed. Women rishis had participated in the articulation of sacred knowledge. They had helped to address the needs of mankind—causing rivers to flow where there were none, seeding forest foods, keeping negative forces at bay. The plentitude of life had been maintained through *mantras*, the sacred use of speech. The sages' blessings and curses were the means for keeping righteous order. But in the transition from one yuga to another, from the declining Treta Yuga to the descending Dwapara Yuga, new norms had to be set and laws established and grounded in dharma, universal truth, if humankind was to progress. The focus was shifting from the inner realms to the development of the material, physical world.

SHRI RAM AND MATA SITA IN THE TRETA YUGA

During every stage in human evolution there have been realized beings who have manifested great love, but as humanity evolved at the end of the last descending Treta Yuga, when the spiritual vision of humanity was weakening, this love needed to be made more visible by establishing dharma as the foundation of human society. It was at this time that Shri Ram and Mata Sita appeared on earth for the purpose of manifesting a complete and perfectly balanced human love. They demonstrated the possibility for humanity to realize on earth the rarified quality of a higher, divine love, which is based neither on emotion nor self-interest, not on desire or possessiveness, but on the well-being of the whole.

When the earth or humanity needs to take an evolutionary leap, it is said that the aspect of divine consciousness that preserves and advances the cosmos incarnates in physical form to aid with this process. This preservative aspect of the divine consciousness is known as Narayan or Vishnu, and its feminine form is Narayani or Mahalakshmi. The tradition states that Shri Ram and Mata Sita were incarnations of this aspect of divine consciousness and appeared on earth to guide the evolutionary transition and establish the roots of a new civilization that would see humanity and the earth community through its journey away from the galactic center of magnetism.

During the months I was enmeshed in what I called "Sitaland" or "Sitaloka," I saw that during Shri Ram and Mata Sita's time on earth, the natural world was relatively undisturbed and the human communities lived fairly harmoniously with the other creatures of this earth. But I also saw that this was changing as the human population grew and expanded its territory, leading to the loss of wild foods and the need for Janak Baba to pioneer agriculture. I developed a great appreciation for Janak Baba, and felt his contributions have not been sufficiently recognized. He set in motion some of the patterns that gave rise to our civilization, patterns that Shri Ram then developed further.

What began in Mithila was advanced in Ayodhya. Shri Ram's acknowledgment and respect for Janak Baba moved me greatly. The deeper meaning of the marriage between Ayodhya and Mithila became clear: for civilization to advance, the power and might of Ayodhya had to unite with the wisdom and knowledge of Mithila in order to establish a society based on dharma. Mata Sita's contribution cannot be overstated, as she had absorbed the knowledge of Mithila and could guide the development of Ayodhya.

In the West we are taught that the seeds of democracy were sown in ancient Greece, but this western-centric view ignores what took place in other parts of the world at earlier times. The seeds of democracy were sown in ancient Mithila millennia before Greece was even conceived. That is why modern India has become such a vibrant democracy today, the largest in the world. Janak Baba saw that, with the decline of spiritual wisdom, the maharajas of the future could be seduced by power, as was Ravana during Shri Ram's era. He understood the need to develop self-governance by and for the people, so he set up village councils as the way to implement the concept. It is these thought patterns that guide human evolution. One of the roles of the avatars and great masters is to establish beneficial thought patterns that can be adopted by the collective, leading to more evolved forms of life.

During that stage of history, I also saw that the rational faculty was developing as the intuitive faculty declined. As humanity focused more on the external, the connection to the internal worlds weakened. The devas and devis were no longer seen, except by the few who could still partially view or feel them between the strands of sunlight, in the shadows of the moon, and as mist emerging from water. Increasingly, they were becoming abstractions, or human projections subject to superstition. The real understanding of their essence and function retreated to the hermitages, which had been tasked with retaining the knowledge of the higher ages and the connection to the higher worlds. That is why the establishment and survival of these educational institutions was of such importance.

What took place so long ago in the lives of Shri Ram and Mata Sita must be understood according to the sensibilities of each era. The stories must be retold not in a form frozen in time, but in a living form that speaks to changing human conditions. We must understand not only the outer narrative but also the inner one and perceive what took place on the invisible planes that drove the external action, for this is the deeper teaching. Many versions of this historical narrative focus on the outer achievements of Shri Ram, but the true work of Shri Ram and Mata Sita was and continues to be guiding the evolution of the human mind and heart. As avatars of Narayan and Narayani, their main responsibility is to preserve that which has been created by aiding the unfolding of the outer and inner worlds, preventing them from self-destructing, in concert with the divine forces of creation (Brahma and Brahmani) and of transformation (Shiva and Parvati). Their presence, therefore, is a continuing one, whether or not in human form.

MATA'S MESSAGE

The narrative of Shri Ram and Mata assumes special importance now as we also are in a time of transition from one era to another. They appeared on earth to help preserve the knowledge of dharma when humanity was losing awareness of and access to the inner worlds, when humanity was beginning to become consumed with externality and the development of the material world. These days in our contemporary world, having plundered and developed our physical environment to the point of near destruction, we now must reconnect to the inner field; we must bridge the inner and outer worlds to correct this imbalance.

One of Mata Sita's most urgent messages is that of love for the earth and all her creatures. Through this love we honor the divine forces that have set in motion the laws that enable the functioning of our world, not just earth, but throughout the universe. We speak buzz words of *interconnection* and *interdependence* casually today. But does the true meaning of those universal laws really inform our consciousness and behavior? Interconnection applies not only to the earth and her ecosystems, but also to all the planetary and stellar bodies, no matter how distant, and to the higher planes of existence, the worlds unseen by the human eye. Every part of creation is connected to and influences every other part. This is the knowledge that the sages of Mata's time tried to preserve for humanity. When it is fully regained, we will far better understand our place in the universe.

Shri Ram and Mata lived before the patriarchal worldview fully manifested and shaped society according to its narrow vision. Yet the traditional accounting of their lives does not reflect this pre-patriarchal view. Rather, their lives are seen through the prism of patriarchy, which most likely developed many centuries later; this is why so little of Sita's life has been preserved in the traditional telling. Her story can only be captured by diving deep into the collective memory bank. Now is the time for that effort as the recall of the feminine energy is of supreme importance.

During Sita's life there were numerous great women sages, who were as active in shaping human society as their male counterparts. These women sages of the past had total freedom of movement during the Satya and Treta Yugas, but this was to change shortly after Sita's departure from the world. These sages were at the end of a long lineage of women rishis. I say "end" because they retreated and become less visible with the passage of time, until their muted voices were all but gone. This was as true in the East as in the West.

The development of human society in the declining Dwarpara Yuga and to an even greater extent in the Kali Yuga brought with it a repression of the feminine psyche and female role, and thus the traditionally accepted Ramayana narrative is told in the context of these attitudes, which conveyed the teachings that patriarchal leaders sought to imbue in the human mind and in society. Part of my deep joy in experiencing the story of Sita, and one of her messages to us today, is the memory of these higher ages. This is important for all of us—east and west, north and south, male and female—as we struggle to free ourselves from the many subtle ways in which this Kali Yuga world view has molded our thinking and penetrated deep into the recesses of our unconscious minds.

When we look at the patriarchal narratives that have shaped western society, we also see a succession of women being victimized, or depicted as the cause of sorrow, beginning with Adam and Eve, where Eve is blamed for causing the expulsion from paradise. In fact, that story most likely refers to the ending of the last Satya Yuga, when the pull of materialism, felt equally by both genders, led to the loss of spiritual knowledge and the sense of oneness, when greater individuation and ego consciousness began to create the illusion of separation.

Then there is the story of Abraham, the founder of the Abrahamic religions, and his wife Sarah, whose maid—and the child she bears with Abraham—was banished to the desert so that Sarah's son could be Abraham's successor. We can surmise that there was much more to the story than a jealous wife. Sarah, after all, was said to be a woman of great spiritual stature, and yet she is portrayed in this unflattering light. These narratives developed long after the time of Shri Ram and Sita, when the Treta Yuga had passed and the patriarchal worldview fully shaped the collective mind.

CONCLUSION

We are in a new era now, tiptoeing into the ascending Dwapara Yuga, and the repressive attitudes of the Kali Yuga have no place in the emerging consciousness. Women are stepping out from the shadows, and thus a retelling of Sita's story is essential. We must erase from our collective consciousness the imposed view of Sita as victim, or even as having a secondary, supportive role, and see her as an equal partner to Ram in shaping the narrative that unfolded. We must erase the outdated view that duty can be divorced from love. We must throw off the mental shackles of the Kali Yuga if we are to know who Mata Sita and Shri Ram are in reality.

Sita was far more than only the chaste and obedient wife of Shri Ram. To see her in this light is an injustice to both women and men. To think of Sita as only a devoted wife is to deny the reality of Shri Ram, who was the embodiment of dharma and of love. His message was that dharma is based on love, both then and now. This is why he incarnated with Narayani, the feminine form, to manifest this love in the human body and to show the necessity of gender balance for human advancement.

They realized that the future of humankind depended on the development of the human mind and heart—on a cultivation of discernment and a sense of justice, on the assuming of personal responsibility. Shri Ram is known for having established a civilization based on dharma, universal law. What is at the heart of this dharma? Love. Love is what keeps the universal laws in motion. Love is the container of the magnetic and gravitational fields. It is the force of love that is the cause of all manifestation, keeps it all in motion, and will eventually transform it all back into unmanifest ultimate reality. It is this love that Shri Ram and Mata Sita displayed for each other, for all the people of their kingdom, for the life of the forest, for Mother Earth herself, and even for the stars that shine at such a distance.

Without love there is no dharma. Without love, there is no justice. Love is the very fabric of creation, of all that is, and the purpose of Shri Ram and Mata Sita's lives was to bring that love to earth, to awaken it, to manifest this divine quality on the physical plane so it could serve as a model for all and the foundation for the future, which we have yet to achieve. Love was and is the basis of their lives, and it directed all of their actions. And this is their message to us today.

There is another important reason for all people, those of the West as well as the East, to delve into the story of Shri Ram and Mata Sita. They are not just historical figures, appearing at a particular time in human history, or figures of symbolic and mythic importance, archetypes, if you will. They are living realities who continue to guide the human race. They continue to appear to people, to give messages, to bless and uplift, to flood the earth with love. I have felt this love and have known their blessing.

My hope in sharing the stories in this book is that you, too, will experience this very special quality of love that is brought to earth through Shri Ram and Mata Sita, and that you, too, will help manifest it on earth.

Jai Sita Ram. Jai Ma.

ACKNOWLEDGEMENTS

I want to express gratitude to my editor, Parvati Markus, who has helped bring this book to fruition; to my dear friend Sraddhalu Ranade, who has accompanied me on so many pilgrimages, including Ayodhya, Vaishnodevi, Rameshwaram, Chitrakoot and Badrinath; to Marianne Marstrand for her untiring work on behalf of the sacred feminine; and to the many friends who share this deep love for Shri Ram and Mata Sita and bring this love into the world.

Appendix I

SHORT SUMMARY OF RAMAYANA

The Ramayana, written in the 4th century by the sage Valmiki, is made up of seven *kandas*, or books, covering Ram's boyhood and youth; the events leading to Ram and Sita's exile; their life in the forest and Sita's abduction by Ravana; the quest to find Sita; Hanuman's exploits; the war and defeat of Ravana by Ram and the return to Ayodhya; and the last book, the authenticity of which has been questioned, detailing Sita's "banishment," the birth of the twins, and the deaths of Sita and Ram.

SUMMARY

Dasaratha, the King of Kosala, lives in the capital Ayodhya, and has three wives: Kaushalya is the mother of Ram, the eldest son; Kaikeyi is the mother of Bharat; and Sumithra is the mother of twins, Lakshman and Shatrughna. Their family priest, the rishi Vishwamitra, takes the teenaged Ram and Lakshman into the Dandaka forest to battle a rakshasi (a female demon) named Taraka, and teaches Ram sacred mantras that can call up divine weapons in the fight against evil. Taraka is killed, and then Vishwamitra takes the brothers to the neighboring city of Mithila to attend a fire sacrifice, and to meet King Janaka's daughter.

In Mithila, the capital of King Janaka's kingdom of Videha, Sita, who was born from the earth, is of marriageable age. A *swayamvara* ceremony is being held in which potential suitors are asked to string Shiva's giant bow. No one but Ram can even lift the bow, while he breaks it in two. They marry and their love is a model for both kingdoms. Lakshman marries Sita's sister Urmila, and Bharat and Shatrughna marry Sita's cousins.

Dasaratha plans to retire and wants to give up his throne to Ram, and everyone is pleased but Queen Kaikeyi, who has been influenced by her maid Manthara. The night before the coronation, she calls on an old promise the king had made to her and demands her son Bharata should rule and that Ram should be banished for 14 years. Ram, Sita, and Lakshman set out for the forest.

In despair, Dasaratha dies. Bharat finds Ram and implores him to return. Ram sends his sandals back with Bharat, who places the sandals on the throne and rules the kingdom in Ram's name.

The three are happy in the forest. Ram and Lakshman destroy the rakshasas that have been disturbing the sages in their meditations. As the last year of their exile begins, Surpanakha, the sister of Ravana, who is the ruler of Lanka, tries to seduce Ram and is wounded by Lakshman when she tries to kill Sita. She wants retaliation, and tells her brother about the beautiful Sita.

Ravana sends a golden deer and the brothers go off to get it for Sita, telling her not to step outside the magic circle of protection they draw around her. Ravana appears to her as a holy man and Sita steps outside the circle to give him food. He grabs her and carries her off in his aerial chariot. On the way, Jatayu, the king of the vultures, tries to stop him and is mortally wounded. They land in Lanka, where Sita sits in a grove and will not even look at Ravana, who alternately tries to sweet talk or threaten her into marrying him.

Ram and Lakshman meet up with a band of *vanaras* (monkey-men demigods), who search everywhere for Sita. Hanuman, one of the vanaras, takes a great leap across the ocean from the tip of India to Lanka and finds Sita under the Ashoka tree in the grove. He tells her Ram will soon come to rescue her. He then allows himself to be captured by Ravana's men. Ravana orders his tail to be wrapped in oily rags and set on fire, but then Hanuman escapes his captors and jumps from house to house, setting all of Lanka on fire. Then he flies back to Ram with the information about Sita and Lanka.

Ram, Lakshman, and an army of monkeys and bears build a causeway from India to Lanka and a mighty war takes place. Lakshman is gravely injured during the battle, and Hanuman flies to retrieve the herb needed to save him. Ram kills Ravana and Sita is free. She is made to go through a blazing fire to prove her purity after spending most of a year in Lanka.

The exile is now over and they return to Ayodhya, where Ram is crowned king.

In the last questionable book, Sita is banished to the forest, where she gives birth to twin sons, Luv and Kush, and later is taken back into the earth.

Appendix II

CAST OF CHARACTERS

THE GODS & DEMI-GODS

Agni – the god of fire, considered the "mouth of the gods" who relays the offerings to them, with the power to consume, transform and convey.

Hanuman – the monkey god who is a great devotee of Ram and Sita. He plays a big part in the search for Sita and afterwards.

Hiranyakashipu - king of the asuras, Ravana's previous incarnation

Indra – the king of the gods.

Jatayu – the king of the vultures; he tries to stop Ravana from abducting Sita, Ravana cuts off his wings and Ram performs his funeral rites.

Jaya – the gatekeeper (with his brother Vijaya) at Vaikuntha

Kamadhenu – a divine cow-goddess, the mother of all cows and a miraculous "cow of plenty." Cows are worshipped in Hinduism as the embodiments of Kamadhenu.

Mahadev – the supreme Lord Shiva, the destroyer and transformer of the universe, and the destroyer of ignorance.

Narasimha – the fourth avatar of Lord Vishnu as part lion/part man who comes to destroy evil and kill a great demon. Known as the "Great Protector," he defends his devotees from evil, like his devotee Prahlad.

Narayana – a cosmic emanation of Lord Vishnu, the supreme deity who sustains, maintains, and preserves the universe. His heavenly abode is Vaikuntha, a realm of bliss and happiness.

Narayani – the female counterpart of Narayana. She is the supreme goddess, Adiparashakti or simply Shakti, and as Sita she is the goddess of the material world and its preservation.

Parashurama – the sixth avatar of Vishnu (Ram is the seventh), who comes to correct the cosmic equilibrium by destroying the Kshatriya warriors who have turned evil.

Parvati – Shiva's female counterpart, the gentle and nurturing aspect of Shakti, the goddess of love and devotion, divine strength and power.

Prahlad - son of the asura king Hiranyakshipu and devotee of Maha Vishnu, his father's enemy.

Surya – the god of the Sun, and one of the nine heavenly "planets" in Hindu astrology.

Taraka – a Yaksha princess who turned into a demoness (*rakshasa*) that destroys the rituals of the rishis with rains of flesh and blood, especially Sage Vishwamitra, who asks Dasaratha's help. He sends the teenaged Ram and Lakshman to kill the demoness.

Vasundara Ma – Mother Earth

Vayu – the lord of the winds, father of Hanuman.

Yama – the god of death and the underworld and the guardian of the south direction.

THE SAGES

Agastya – sage; noted recluse and scholar, married to Lopamudra, with whom he wrote hymns in the Rigveda; hermitage on the banks of the river Godavari in the Dandaka forest. He gives Ram a divine bow and arrow and describes Ravana's nature to him. He is regarded as the founder of an ancient science of healing.

Ahalya – sage; the wife of sage Gautama; created by Brahma as the most beautiful of all women, seduced by Indra and then cursed by Gautama and turned to stone, eventually released from curse by Ram; her son, Satananda, is the family priest of King Janak.

Anasuya – sage; daughter of Sage Kardama and Devahuti; wife of Rishi Atri, living in small hermitage in a forest near Chitrakut; attained miraculous powers through practice of devotion and austerities. During a time of severe drought, she brought the Mandakini River down to earth to remove the suffering of the sages and animals. Brahma, Vishnu, and Shiva were born to Anasuya and Atri as Chandra, Dattatreya, and Durvasa.

Arundhati – sage; wife of Vashistha; eighth of the nine daughters of Sage Kardama and Devahuti; identified with the morning star; rivalry between her husband and Vishvamitra leads to the death of her hundred sons.

Atri – one of the seven great Vedic sages, married to Anasuya. Ram and Sita visited their hermitage during their exile.

Bhrigu – one of the seven great Vedic sages; married to sage Khyati, parents of Bhargavi (incarnation of Narayani). Usana, second wife of Bhrigu, mother of Shukracharya, guru to the asuras.

Devahuti – a great woman sage, daughter of King Manu, wife of sage Kardama, mother of nine daughters (Kala, Anasuya, Sraddha, Havirbhu, Gita, Kriya, Khyati, Arundhati, and Shanti) and a son, Maharishi Kapila (a manifestation of Narayan).

Gargi – daughter of Sage Vachaknu, invited by King Janak to the world's first conference on philosophy, where she challenged Yajnavalkya in public debate on the nature of Brahman; considered the world's first woman philosopher.

Gautama – author of many hymns in the Vedas, husband of Lady Ahalya.

Kardama Muni – great sage, manifested from the shadow of Brahma; husband of Devahuti.

Lopamudra – a princess in the kingdom of Vidharbha, accepted the austere Agastya as her husband; a philosopher and a rishi in her own right.

Manu – the first man, a mystical kshatriya ruler of earth; married Devahuti, his middle daughter, to the sage Kardama.

Rishishringa – sage, son of Rishi Vibhandak; born with a deer horn on his forehead; married to Shanta, Dasaratha's daughter; conducted the ashwamedha yajna.

The Four Kumaras – the first mind-born creations of Brahma, named Sanaka (ancient), Sanatana (eternal), Sanandana (joyful), and Sanatkumara (ever young).

Vasishtha – most revered Vedic rishi; first sage of the Vedanta school of philosophy; married to Arundhati.

Vishwamitra – Ram's preceptor who teaches Ram and Lakshman the knowledge of celestial weaponry, trains them in religion, and guides them in the killing of powerful demons. He leads Ram to the swayamvara for Sita. Author of the Gayatri mantra, his name means "friend of the world." A former king, he renounced his kingdom and went into a thousand years of tapasya so he could become a greater rishi than Vashista, who had destroyed Vishvamitra's entire army and his divine weaponry by breathing the Om syllable.

THE ROYAL FAMILIES

The Kingdom of Kosala (Ayodhya)

Maharaja **Dasaratha**
Rani **Kausalya**, mother of Shri **Ram**
Rani **Sumitra**, mother of **Shatrughna** and **Lakshman**
Rani **Keikeyi**, mother of **Bharat**
Luv and **Kush**, twin sons of Sita and Ram
Shanta, Ram's older sister, wife of Rishi Shringa

The Kingdom of the Videhas (Mithila)

Maharaja (Seeradhwaja) **Janak**
Maharani **Sunaina**
Sita
Irmila

The Mithila Servants

Aditi
Meenakshi
Pitaji Dushyanta
Usha
Rohana
Soma – Sita's personal attendant
Kiran – in charge of the animals

Ravana's Kingdom

Ravana – the Rakshasa King of Lanka; name means "roaring;" devotee of Shiva; great scholar.
Keikesi – Ravana's mother
Sage Vishrava – Ravana's father
Rani Mandodari – his wife
Surpanakha – his sister
Trijata kindly guard of Sita in Ravana's garden

OTHERS

Anasuya – reincarnation of Meenakshi, Sita's servant

Ajit – reincarnation of Kiran, future husband of Anasuya

Abhitha – woman who led chanting and prayers down by the river for Sita during exile; Ajit's grandmother

Chandrika – wife of young sage seduced by Surpanakha

RIVERS

Sarayu – flows beside Ayodhya

Godavari – India's second longest river, called the Ganges of the South; Sage Gautama and Ahalya hermitage located by river. Gautama led the Ganges to flow through Central India as the Godavari.

Ganges (Ganga) – the most sacred river to Hindus. When the Ganga descended from heaven to earth, Shiva received the waters in the coils of his hair to break her fall; she is also the vehicle of ascent from earth to heaven. She is not only a mother goddess, but is consort in various forms to Brahma, Vishnu, and Shiva.

Mandakini – means "she who flows calmly." There are two Mandakini Rivers: the most known is the river that is one of the headwaters of the Ganges; the other is a river in Chitrakoot that was brought to earth by Sage Anasuya.

Appendix III

GLOSSARY

Aarti – ritual part of puja, in which light from wicks soaked in ghee (purified butter) or camphor is offered to one or more deities.

Amrita – literally means "immortality," synonyms for *soma*, the drink of the devas, which grants them immortality.

Asura – a class of divine beings or power-seeking deities, always battling with the devas.

Avatar – incarnation of a Hindu deity on earth.

Ayodhya – the capitol city of the Kosala kingdom.

Baba – refers to a father, grandfather, or wise old man. "Babaji" means "revered father."

Brahman - see Parabrahman

Brahmin – priestly caste.

Dadi – paternal grandmother.

Devi – goddess, masculine is *deva.*

Dharma – universal law, a key concept in Indian religions; behavior in accord with the "right way of living;" cosmic law and order.

Guru – literally, the dispeller of darkness; spiritual teacher, guide, or master who helps spiritual evolution of devotees or students.

Gurukula – residential system of education in ancient India; primary education system before British rule.

Jnani – one who seeks liberation through the path of knowledge (jnana yoga); the other two paths are karma yoga (path of action) and bhakti yoga (path of loving devotion to a person god).

Kanda – book. There are seven kandas in the Valmiki version of the Ramayana.

Kshatriya – one of the four social orders of Hindu society (brahmin, kshatriya, vaishya, and shudra), traditionally the ruling and military class, fighting in wartime and governing in peacetime.

Kosala – an ancient Indian kingdom ruled by Ram from the capital of Ayodhya.

Mahadev – Lord Shiva

Maharaja (or Maharajah) – great king, a ruler of one of the native states of India.

Maharani –great queen, wife of the Maharaja

Maharishi – great sage

Mata – Mother

Mithila – see Videha.

Maya – illusion, the world we experience is a modification, projection, or manifestation of Prakriti. It is an illusion even though it exists, because it is not what it appears to be.

Murti – an image, statue, or idol of a deity that is considered an embodiment of the divine.

Narayana – another name for Lord Vishnu, the supreme god, the Para Brahman (Supreme Lord) who sustains, maintains, and preserves the universe.

Narayani – a form of Lakshmi and the consort of Narayana. Narayani means the "exposer of consciousness," or "she who provides the basis for all living things."

Nay – no.

Om – a sacred sound that contains the essence of ultimate reality or consciousness; the most important spiritual symbol in Hinduism, referring to *atman*, the soul, and Brahman, ultimate reality.

Parabrahman – formless spirit pervading the universe and beyond.

Pitaji – father, dad.

Prakriti – nature, source. The eternal and indestructible material energy of which all matter is composed; the primordial state of anything that is found in the entire creation.

Pranam – literally, "complete salutation." Hands are held palms together in front of your heart. It's a salutation meaning "The light within me perceives and adores the light within you."

Puja – prayer ritual in devotional worship to a deity, to honor a guest, or to celebrate an event; means reverence, honor, homage, and worship; involves the offering of light, flowers, water or food to the divine, the essential ritual of Hindus.

Putra – son

Rakshasas – a race of both good and evil creatures that make up Ravana's army; powerful warriors, magicians able to create life-like illusions.

Rajah – king
Ram (Rama, Ramachandra) – the seventh avatar of Lord Vishnu, born to Kaushalya and Dasaratha in Ayodhya, the ruler of the Kingdom of Kosala, and the central figure of the Ramayana.

Rani – queen.

Rishi – seers or sages who do intense *tapasya* to realize the supreme truth and eternal knowledge.

Sadhana –any spiritual practice, like meditation, that aims at progressing the seekers in consciousness; anything that leads the seeker from attachment and bondage to liberation

Sanjivani – the herb of immortality.

Shakti – the formless (adiparashakti) that takes different forms to do different tasks.

Shri (or Sri) – polite form of address.

Sita – an avatar of Sri Lakshmi (Narayani), central character in the Ramayana; the daughter of the earth goddess, adopted by King Janaka of Videha and Queen Sunaina; known for dedication, self-sacrifice, courage, and purity

Swayamvara – in ancient India a way a girl of marriageable age chooses a husband; as part of Sita's swayamvara, the suitors had to lift and string Shiva's bow.

Tapasya – literally, "to heat;"certain spiritual practices requiring self-discipline, meditation, and inner self-purification.

Treta Yuga – the second out of the four yugas, the ages of mankind, with this one lasting 1,296 human years; there were three avatars of Vishnu during the last treta yuga, including Ram.

Videha (also known as Mithila) – the kingdom ruled by the philosopher-king Seeradhwaja Janaka, the father of Sita, in the 8th or 7th century BCE. It was a region located east of the Gandaki River, west of Mahananda River, north of the Ganges river and south of the Himalayas, and is now divided between the Indian state of Bihar and the Terai region in Nepal.

Vimana – aircraft; Ravana's vimana was called *Pushpaka*.

Yajna – any ritual done in front of a sacred fire, often using mantras.

ABOUT THE AUTHOR

**Founder and Convener of the Global Peace Initiative of Women
Founding Member, the Contemplative Alliance**

DENA MERRIAM is the Founder and Convener of the Global Peace Initiative of Women (GPIW), bringing spiritual resources to address critical global challenges, such as conflict, social justice, and ecological scarring of the earth. Over the years she has worked to bring greater gender balance and balance between the Abrahamic and Dharma-based religious traditions for a more inclusive interfaith movement.

Merriam served as Vice Chair of the Millennium World Peace Summit of Religious and Spiritual Leaders, held at the United Nation in New York in the year 2000. She subsequently convened a meeting of women religious and spiritual leaders at the Palais des Nations in Geneva, and from that gathering founded the Global Peace Initiative of Women in 2002. Among GPIW's many programs is the organization of a session on the inner dimensions of climate change at the annual UN Climate Summits. In 2008, Merriam was one of the founding members of the Contemplative Alliance, which later became a program of GPIW, to explore how meditation and contemplative practices are reshaping the spiritual landscape of our societies.

For over 40 years, Dena Merriam has been a devotee of Paramahansa Yogananda, a practitioner of Kriya Yoga meditation, and a student of the great texts of the Vedic tradition. Merriam received her Master's Degree from Columbia University in Sacred Literature. She has served on the boards of the Harvard Center for the Study of World Religions, the Interfaith Center of New York, The International Center for Religion and Diplomacy, Manitou Foundation, All India Movement for Seva (AIM for Seva), The Gross National Happiness Center in Bhutan and as an advisor to the board of Dharma Drum Mountain Buddhist Association. In 2014 she received the Niwano Peace Prize for her interfaith peace efforts.

She is the author of *My Journey Through Time: A Spiritual Memoir of Life, Death and Rebirth.*

Made in the USA
Columbia, SC
25 October 2020